Growing Up Girl

Growing Up Girl

An Anthology of Voices from Marginalized Spaces

Edited by Michelle Sewell

GirlChild Press • Washington, DC

Growing Up Girl:
An Anthology of Voices from Marginalized Spaces

Compilation and Introduction copyright © 2006 by Michelle Sewell

Individual selections copyright © by their respective author(s)

Published by

GirlChild Press
PO Box 93
Hyattsville, MD 20781

First edition, third printing

Book cover and layout by Kendra Kuliga
Cover Photograph by Megan M. Walsh
Model – Jailen James

Permissions acknowledgements appear on page 324
Printed in the United States of America

ISBN 0-9779372-0-8 $19.95/$23.00 (Canada)

To my mother Vertentis James
who prayed ceaselessly
that her girls would always find favor.
Mommy, we have.

Acknowledgements

First and foremost, I would like to thank all the girls and women whose work appears here. Without your stories this anthology would not exist. Thank you for trusting me with your vision and taking the time to craft these well-told tales of growing up girl.

Thanks to all my cheerleaders who never doubted I could pull this off: My sisters Debyann James and Amanda James who told me everyday that I was talented and they loved me; my niece, Jailen James, who braved 22 degree weather to be my cover girl; my niece, Tabitha "PJ" James whose very existence reminds me that life does go on; my sistercircle (Faye Williams, Lois A. Wiley, and Lisa Joyner) who let me talk about this project every week!; my best friend and photographer, Megan Walsh, who was the first to tell me that I was fearless; and Carmen Shorter who validated me and this idea many years ago.

Much appreciation and respect to Lisa C. Moore (Redbone Press) who generously shared her knowledge and resources; Del Hornbuckle whose immeasurable generosity and support made these very pages possible; Kendra Kuliga who swooped in and rescued this project and quelled my anxiety about meeting the deadline; the Prince George's Arts Council that provided the seed monies; and the various social workers, teachers, coaches, pastors, mentors, and community activists who saw fit to usher many of these submissions to my mailbox.

A special thank you to Sisterspace and Books. There is where I learned to listen and really understand the needs of women and girls.

And finally to Patricia Corbett who endured my many late night writing sessions, early morning whining sessions, indecisions, and fears, and still found the compassion to hold my hand through the birth of this project. Thank you for being my midwife.

Introduction

... I find myself obsessing
about the complexities
of being a girl child.
Mingled with the pink and lace
are the heart stopping moments that make it unclear
if we'll make it to the other side.

As I sit at my desk
my pen poised
I fantasize about creating a practical guide.
Tucked away for special emergencies
that can only be deciphered by girlchild eyes.

The above stanzas are from my prose poem, GirlChild, and in many ways it is the precursor to this larger project, Growing Up Girl: An Anthology of Voices from Marginalized Spaces. I wrote the poem after reading a newspaper article that confirmed that there are still places in the world where being born a girl is a liability, and that for too many girls, death sometimes quickly follows birth. The poem ultimately looks at not only how "Third-World" countries treat their girls, but how "First-World" places are also complicit in our destruction.

The impetus for this anthology lies in my conviction that by focusing on the marginalized voices of girls and women, we have the opportunity to learn more about our humanity. More than a few people have asked me why I thought this anthology was necessary. Weren't there enough books about the life of girls? I believe that anthologies like these create a place for girls and women to tell their individual stories and in turn, speak for many. The sheer number of submissions I received informs me of the dire need for a collection like this, one that could foster more understanding and that would fill in the gaps in society's knowledge of our existence.

I am honored to be in the position to weave these stories and poems together revealing a compelling and complex tapestry. Here you will find poetry, first-person accounts of struggles both internal and external, and provocative fiction on what it means to grow up girl.

One of the most exciting aspects of editing this anthology is that so many new and emerging writers have the opportunity to be printed alongside more established and seasoned writers. The ages range from 14 to fifty-something and all the experiences in between. The contributors, much like the writings, span the spectrum of diversity and an array of writing styles and voices are represented here.

The contributors are passionate and their stories are unflinching in ways that might make the reader uncomfortable. Some of the pieces are but small swallows of experience, while other pieces demand that you digest them over a period of time. I was humbled to have a glimpse into some of these complicated spaces. Read it in chunks if you must, but read. Absorb. Connect.

In the end, it is my hope that Growing Up Girl creates bridges to isolated places and nurtures a sense of survival and defiance in those who need it.

Enjoy!

Michelle Sewell
February 25, 2006

Table of Contents

Table of Contents

The Back Door
Elisabeth Robinson

My life
takes place
inside
a house
where things
with no purpose
happens
like the girl
who's there
just because
she knows
she should be

I try to find
my way out
of this place
that makes me hurt

the back door
lies
open
wide open
and I venture
to leave
but
something
like an
apparition
wont let
me
so I
stay
in my pain

I stay

Actually, I
Joy Lee

There are six Asian students in my sociology class. Me. Jon. Adiba.
Amy. And Bo. But from the sounds of these discussions, you'd never
know. You'd think there was only Adiba. That's Arabic for cultured.
Refined. Advanced. Adiba, the Diva. Our one requisite, politically
correct, enraged at the system Asian.

She fills our classroom discussion dialogues, with Asian oppression
monologues. Her indignation at the debates, never abates, it's always,
"actually, I find it customary in Asian cultures,"
"actually, I recall the Japanese internments,"
"actually, I believe sweatshops stand for slavery,"

In our talks of Black and White, she inserts the lacking, primary yellow,
and its cousin, brown,
always bringing the talk around,
for Adiba- there's no reservations in tingeing these social relations
conversations with yellow coloration narrations

but corruptions of rage threatens emerging eruption from me at each
new interruption from her and I want to say, "Stop it!" I want to say,
"Stop. Actually, in Asia they mock my accent for being American and
my politics too liberal, in Asia"

I want to tell her because I'm afraid for Adiba, our Asian diva.
if she keeps interjecting you'll only hear the Asian view she's
projecting, and soon you'll start rejecting- glossing over her slender
arms, and dark brown eyes, and caramel skin,
and only see her as Asian,
you will not see her as student, female, full body of beauty,
and that's my biggest fear for her,
or
perhaps for me.

Yes, I fear that I will forever be the Asian student writing angry Asian

2

poetry, don't let this label me, don't let this consume my writing, I am a full body.

But nothing deters Adiba, the little Asian that could,
and her arms keep shooting into the sky and she keeps shouting,
shouting, "Actually, I!"

because of a deeper fear running in her, that same unrealized fear in all of us, that same dread that once led me to tread as the dreaded PC voice, until I was blinded by uncomfortable stares-

So she's saying, don't let us just fall away, a slow death of silent decay.
No, you must heed our call because you can't ignore us all-
in the United States-
that's 12 million Asian faces, and Asian wounds, and Asian prides.
There's no way you can ignore the 3.7 billion Asians in the worldwide.
Yes, that's a big number, we are so good with numbers and we are so relevant, and every time I stand silent in the classroom the number shrinks to three billion six hundred ninety nine million nine hundred ninety nine thousand nine hundred ninety nine
and when Amy is silent the number drops to ninety eight.

ninety seven.

ninety six.

And soon we are a race people assume as muted
submissive and
docile.
Does that sound at all familiar?
And it takes Adiba, and that long, slender, brown arm of hers to keep raising, and raising up the generations of ancestral dead to say, "actually, actually, I!"
Actually I have a voice, and I demand your attention because I have a place in this country, because this land is mine.

And so we strap on thousands of years of history for countries we've
never set foot in, claim customs we don't practice, speak for forefathers
whose tongues are foreign,
because as Asians, we have to stick together,
blending the borders of nationality to embolden the colors of our
humanity,
so that yellow and brown will not stand for fading, withered voices,
and stains in the earth,
so that our characters are not jaundiced, weak, and diseased,
but it will stand for us-
all six students in the class, all 12 million of us in this, our country,
and all 3.7 billion of us worldwide,
raising our arms to say, "actually, I!"

*it's the fear of irrelevance of being glossed over in the classrooms, and history
books, and current events, that in blending in, the 4.2% of us are dwindling
down to zero. pointing the Asian disad-vantage point*

One Melting Rose

Stephanie Croft

She sits in desolation. Knees clutched into her body, trying to block out the darkness. No success. The feeling of bittersweet iciness continues to flood her confused mind: numbs her sense of logic and forces her into her frozen shell. She wants to break the ice. She wants to break out. She struggles; mind and soul fight a battle. Viscous. The battle leads to further self destruction. No one can help her because nobody knows. She's alone.

Outside, the icicles gather in clusters among the creeping branches. They signal the turning of the seasons: autumn to winter; cold to freezing; grey to black. Her tears fall. Drip. Like the icicles that freeze and melt, depending on the harshness of the frost. The white snow sits pure and innocent, elegant and stunning. She reflects this image; pretty and delicate. Different on the inside. Her blackened, miserable mind contrasts with the white snow, yet both are crystallised and confused. She may appear happy, but, slowly, her frozen mask of beauty melts away. Falling off her face in droplets, chunks, large, sickening pieces. The smiling lips and wondering eyes disintegrate revealing her torn, pained inside of depression.

• • •

Sixteen years ago a baby was born. The mother suffered throughout the birth; deep, burning pains tugged at her abdomen with strength, draining her motivation and power. White, sterile bed sheets were soaked with deep, crimson blood; a horrifically beautiful sight. She released one last scream, piercing, painful; leading to a baby of perfection. The crucial moment that mother held infant, a cord was broken and a new bond was created. A bond that was to grow into the deepest love.

A child of such beauty was worthy of one name: Rose. Her new-born scent, comforting to the mother, sweeter than a rose's perfume. Her delicate hands, clutching onto her mother's finger, more fragile than a rose's petals. Her piercing eyes, fixated on her mother's, sharper than a rose's thorns. Exquisite.

5

• • •

She walks outside. The freezing temperature has no effect; she feels nothing. No senses, no emotion. The cold air settles quickly on her body. She's learnt to ignore the persistent, continuous, icy haze. Goosebumps rise on her bare, golden arms giving her the appearance of old age. She will never be old. Her steps are careful, timid and slow. She slips once, twice, on the fragile sheet of silver ice; the weakness and clumsiness of an elderly lady. She regains her balance and continues her journey to nowhere. A journey of the mind. Her sharp eyes stare; weary now; still innocent, yet enclosed by deep, painful contours and harsh, grey skin. One white rose lies withered and weak among the weeds. Once beautiful, now dying and empty. Pure and pallid.

A snowflake falls gradually from the absence that is sky. So tiny. So gentle. It strokes her cheek gracefully as it drops and settles. Hypnotising her into a state of tranquillity. The freezing touch on her face is a blessed relief; removing all emotion and light. A tear drips from her grey and cloudy eyes; it freezes into sharp spears, like the icicles she often stares at. Her face glows golden under the light of a street lamp; a contrast to the shadowy surroundings. She resembles an angel wearing a gown of purity. She would play the role so well. This sweet, pretty Rose is about to collapse and break. No one sees her because no one looks.

• • •

Rose woke from her childhood dream when she was 15. It was a happy dream; she lay in complete comfort and serenity; body unconscious but smiling nonetheless. A smile of many compliments. Lips rounded and pink, framed by a defined and delicate cupid's bow. Innocent; yet to touch another's lips. Her eyes peeled open with effort, slowly, slowly, like the moment she entered that sterile room from the comfort and warmth of her mother's womb. She perceived a different sight. Unnatural. Dark, grey, cloudy. She lay still, wrapped tightly in thin, white sheets; her mind had been dissected, extracted and soaked in darkness before being replaced.

Young and innocent; she had become a victim to something deadly; the depression was crueller than cancer. Her life would be short. The simplest of tasks became challenges. Each day a marathon draining her energy and eliminating the sparkling wonder from her eyes. She couldn't see the beautiful image that her mother knew and loved. She stared absently into the honest, reflective mirror. Painful. Two faces stared back at her, motionless; one screamed; one cried. Frustrated. Traumatized. The trapped demons beat her as she forced her powerfully gentle fist against the glass. The mirror shattered; like the ice that would follow in winter.

• • •

She's home again now; safe but not comfortable. The warmth is too positive for her gloomy mind. Her mother gazes into her eyes and sees, for the first time, something she hasn't seen in her perfect child: pain. She's shocked, afraid for her daughter, yet still unaware of the darkness oppressing her. Naive. Not a word is spoken. Silence. Once more mother takes baby in arms, embraces her tightly, desperate for her darling to feel protected and secure. A goodbye hug. Rose pushes her mother away with aggression; pushes her away from her secret. To admit her depression would worry her mother. Love and affection cannot win their battle against misery.

In her bedroom once again. Safe in the capsule space. The snow continues to fall; heavier now; more powerful. Too cold. She watches a flake with fascination as it weaves around the wind, wondering where it will land. Her tears, icy, drop in synchronisation with the snow flakes. She knows what to do. She's planned this scenario in her head for too long but only now has she built up enough courage to go through with it. Rose picks up the heavy rope with her delicate hands; blessed with softness. It's rough and tightly bound. She removes the hammock seat that she's spent hours curled up in, uses the hook on the ceiling to attach the rope, forms a deadly noose. She climbs onto a stool; wobbles; nervous; confused. She reminisces on the times she used to play on the swings. Sweet. Happy. Innocent. The rope that hangs will end what the cord of love gave birth to.

• • •

There she swings. Back and forth. Eyes still wide and tearful; face drained of colour; body hanging limply; lifeless. Her mask of ice has melted completely and her inside is revealed at last. Her mother enters the bedroom to ask if Rose is alright. She sees her baby girl staring at her blankly. Eyes wide open.

It's too late.

AMSTERDAM IT!
Cherien Dabis

My mother smiled only in the summertime. It had nothing to do with warm weather, extra hours of daylight or the smell of freshly-cut grass. It had even less to do with the beaches my family never enjoyed at the resorts we never visited. It certainly wasn't because we were out of school. My mother smiled only in the summertime for one simple reason: she got to go home. Home wasn't small-town Celina, Ohio, where we happened to exist. Home was the land of her memory, a memory that clung to the limestone cliffs of Amman, Jordan. Not the Amman of the present, but the Amman of 1975; the year before my parents migrated west. This was the land that never left her consciousness, the country that kept her homesick for nine months of the year, the city that we returned to every June. My mother existed in this time bubble. And each summer she enlisted her husband and children in taking a trip back in time.

It started the same way every year. We went back to school, and my mother fell into a deep depression that took her months to climb out of. By the holidays, she was in stable condition, spending half of her time staring out into space, crying, and occasionally shouting delusional phrases: As long as you live under this roof, you live in Jordan.

After-Christmas sales inspired shopping sprees, buying presents for relatives I never knew I had. Walkie-talkies for distant cousins, size sixteen dresses for full-figured aunts, Frosted Flakes for my uncle, Oil of Olay anti-aging cream, Cover Girl Long Lash mascara and Stayfree maxi pads - superior American products from superior American relatives. With the New Year came preparation, working hard to lose the fifteen pounds she looked forward to putting back on over the summer. By the time the snow melted, my mother was budding with hope as she began her search for the best airline bargain. It didn't matter which airline we flew; the cheapest deal inevitably meant a long layover in the city I'd never have the pleasure of visiting-Amsterdam.

As we landed, I looked down upon the city's canals, weaving their way through the green pastures. It was my eleventh visit to the

Schiphol International Airport. In all those years, I'd never stepped foot outside the terminal. I had heard that Amsterdam was the city of free thinkers, where people sat in cafes smoking every drug imaginable. It was legal; encouraged even. It's not that I wanted to do drugs. I just wanted to watch other people do them. Maybe this year will be different, I thought. Maybe I'll convince them to leave the airport.

Inside the terminal I was swept up by the mob. I always made it a point to look at each face that passed before me, my eyes darting in all directions until the faces were nothing but a blur. I didn't want to miss anyone. Who were these people? I wondered. What language did they speak? What were their lives like? Did I want to go where they were going? Did I want to be them? I was fascinated by the natural wonder of people in transit. Then, we'd arrive at our connecting gate, and I'd make the mistake of looking at the clock.

"Why can't we leave the airport?" I whined.

"With three babies you want me to go on a tour of the city? Are you going to help me take care of them? Will you carry them? What happens if we miss our flight? Or if one of you gets lost? Or run over by a bus? Or kidnapped?" My parents were naturally suspicious of anyone who wasn't a family member. Big cities, carnivals, even Walmart inspired fear. And with all the time they spent worrying about the terrible afflictions that could cause our untimely deaths — beer, rock and roll, premarital sex, poisoned Halloween candy — there was little time left to take us places we might've enjoyed visiting. People age 18 or younger - commonly known as children - weren't fully human yet anyway. They didn't have the ability to experience real pain. "What do you have to be sad about?" my father often asked upon seeing the long face I was accustomed to wearing. It wasn't worth trying to convince him otherwise. My parents didn't believe in psychology just as I didn't believe in the tooth fairy.

We hunkered down in a corner of the gate and spread out our baggage, as if warning others not to come too close. We were setting up house across the rows of seats, preparing for the twelve-hour layover.

"Amsterdam it," I muttered as I settled into a cold, hard seat. It was a phrase my older sister Amira and I coined during one of our layovers. We had giggled for hours over how clever we were.

"What did you say?" my mother asked.

"Nothing. I just said I want to see AmsterDAM! God. It's not just an airport. It's a city too, you know." Amira chuckled, the way you do when someone is pathetic but not worth the energy of a hearty laugh. Her eyes were only half open signifying she only half cared about the world. I'm a tortured teenager, they said. No one understands my pain. When Amira was angry, I was her punching bag. Only instead of her fists she used her words. I preferred fists, hands, legs, even baseball bats.

"Amsterdam it? You are OUT. I mean, you are so OUT," Amira spat. This was news to me. Last I heard I was in. Who knew that you could so easily be thrown back out? I was never good at this game.

"We made it up together," I argued.

"Last year!" Amira inspired in me a restlessness that couldn't be ignored. Somehow I knew she was superior. How could I compete with those squinty eyes?

"If I'm out then you're way out."

"Nope. You're definitely the only one who's out."

"YOU'RE the one who's out," I said inching closer to her in a threatening manner. As I was taller than my sister and most other twelve year-olds, I often used my physical strength to bolster my social status. In short, when people didn't like me, I beat them up until they did.

"You're so far out you're on the North Pole."

"You're so far out you're on Jupiter."

"Why don't you get OUT?"

"You get OUT."

"Get OUT of my face."

"Get OUT of my life."

"Get OUT of my sight!"

"Enough!" My mother was on the edge of her seat. At any moment she could spring forward and kill us. Fearing for our lives, we kept our mouths shut, but our faces continued bickering back and forth.

I stood on my seat and began walking along the empty rows.

"You're going to make a scene. Sit down," my father scolded.

It was exactly what I wanted. A scene. If I couldn't outwit Amira, I would compete by acting out. Maybe one of the gate employees would yell at me and send me to the airport equivalent of the principal's office. I wouldn't care. No one scared me. Not even my dad. A little bald man, he was scrawny on the ends and thickest in the middle. He liked to grit his teeth and tell us to sit still. In fact, we couldn't do much more than breathe in his presence. Everything else we did was on the brink of embarrassing him, as if he was a sought after celebrity who had to worry about his public image. I made a face back at him, trying to be his mirror reflection. He apparently didn't think he looked attractive, because he immediately lost the face. My father usually ended up being the one to make the scene. When he'd try to get us to stop whatever harmless form of trivial entertainment we pursued, he'd swat at us, yell and make sickly faces until people started to stare. Then he'd blame us for calling attention to ourselves. *We are such a pain in the you-know-what family*, he always said. *Wherever we go, we cause trouble.* I was proud of that fact. I wanted to leave my mark. I wanted to be remembered. I wanted to be trouble.

My mother was nursing my little sister Alia, while Rana lay asleep in her lap. Selwa sat in her stroller, wailing. My mother looked at Amira and I as if we were supposed to do something.

"Don't look at us," we both said. "It's not our fault you had five kids." I'm sure my mother wanted to say that it wasn't her fault either. She glanced at my father who pretended to be invisible, then turned away, as if wishing someone would rescue her. My parents' attempts to have a boy left them with five girls. I think I was supposed to feel sorry for them. Instead I thought they were pathetic.

"Can I go to the bathroom?" I asked. My mother looked at me, trying to assess whether or not my bladder was full then gave a slight nod. She preferred not to speak when she didn't have to. Instead she'd developed a series of twitches that we learned to interpret. Come right back, she said with the flair of her nostrils, the tilt of her head and the raise of an eyebrow. I walked away, a huge smile on my face, an extra sway in my stride that spelled freedom. As I passed the bathroom and made my way toward the duty-free shops, I couldn't think of anyone who had it better than me.

The truth was, I didn't belong to my family. I always knew it. I was too good for them. God had made some sort of mistake placing me in their care. I was sure these kinds of errors occurred frequently, what with the enormous volume of people God had to sculpt and families he had to create. A mismatch was bound to happen now and again. Not even God can be perfect with that kind of workload.

As I zigzagged my way through the swarms of people, I imagined the life I was meant to live. I certainly wouldn't be traveling to Jordan with the clan I was forced to follow around. I would be alone. Traveling to Paris to meet my lover, a man who worshipped me more than life itself. I would never marry him. I would just keep him there, locked up in an apartment overlooking the Seine, anxiously awaiting my visits.

As I approach the apartment door wearing a ruffled, red and white polka dotted dress, he senses my impending arrival and bounds to the door like a grateful pup. We embrace like the lost lovers we are, and after twirling me around, he tells me how beautiful and skinny *I am. I know, my darling. I know,* I say, because I'm confident. I am superior. I kiss him passionately then give him a gift, a little something I picked up for him in the duty-free shops.

The record scratched before I could get to the good part. I couldn't decide what to buy him. What do you give to someone you've imprisoned and forced to worship you? I perused the selection of perfumes, cosmetics, fashions, electronics and chocolates at the duty-free shop. How was I to know what he liked? I barely knew what I liked. As it stood I usually liked what others liked. But how was I to know what others liked when I was alone? That was the trouble with traveling solo. I parked myself in front of the liquor and stared at all the different kinds, wondering if each one offered a different drunk — vodka, scotch, whiskey. Was there a difference in the way they made you feel? If vodka made you belligerent, did scotch make you black out? I knew I'd find out one day. I'd make it an experiment. Maybe I'd write a scientific article on it. I wouldn't care to let the world know I was a swaggering drunk. Seemed as good a way to live my life as any other. It was better than getting out of bed each morning and drudging to work come rain, snow, tornado or apocalypse. It was better than changing dirty diapers and sweeping crumb covered linoleum floors for the rest of my life.

I stumbled out of the shop, pretending to be drunk, trying it on for size and noticing a few adults believing me. I was already making a good drunk.

"Easy there." I had run into a fat man wearing nylon track pants and a striped Polo shirt. "You okay?" I stared at him like I didn't understand. He had a big ball nose and the kind of skin that's red and raw, as if worn inside out. He looked at me the way Americans do when they think someone's not privileged enough to understand English.

"Where are you going?" I asked in perfect English. He looked relieved. He no longer had to feel sorry for me.

"Minneapolis". His voice seemed to come out of his nose. He spoke like a lazy American, barely pronouncing the end of his words. They weren't worth the effort.

"I'm going to Paris," I said. He raised his uni-brow.

"You traveling alone?

"Yeah."

"Where's your luggage?"

"Over there." I made a random motion suggesting my luggage was somewhere on the ceiling.

"How old are you," he asked, eyeing my flat chest. He kept his hands on the tops of his thighs, where he could not-so-accidentally brush up against his excitable parts. I tried to gauge whether or not he found me exciting. Did men find me exciting? I felt as though I would never find out. I wondered why I even cared.

"How old do you think I am?" Don't get the wrong idea. I asked everyone this question. It gave me pleasure to know people thought I was more mature than my age. The man cocked his head to the side as if it aided his thought process. I imagined the blood flowing to the lowered half of his head. If his skin gave any indication of what his insides looked like, I figured he was gruesomely bloody, like a pound of fatty pink ground beef. Just as he was about to answer, a perturbed woman with buck teeth yanked him away. Poor ground beef and his homely wife. They didn't look happy. Then again, no one I knew looked happy. As far as I was concerned happiness was make-believe. Or maybe it was what you felt after consuming too much alcohol but before throwing up.

I ended up at the newsstand next door, its walls lined with

newspapers and magazines from around the world. I loved the news. It was dark, tragic and strangely familiar. The large print, the words, other people's pain, it all made me feel alive. Like for a moment, the world could be condensed into a paragraph for me to experience. I loved learning, though I couldn't let anyone know, lest I ruin my reputation for being stupid. Smart wasn't cool in junior high. Everyone knew that.

I browsed the magazines, the hundreds of them covered with the faces of the most beautiful women in the world. Which one did I want to look like? The brunette with big breasts, a mirror-smooth face and a waist the size of my twelve-year-old calf? Or the All-American Tommy Hilfiger dirty blonde with tanned skin, tousled hair and freckles dabbling her button nose. I knew I'd never be the All-American. Despite my pleas and prayers to wake up blonde-haired and blue-eyed, God never answered. In fact, I was beginning to question whether this God everyone spoke so highly of actually existed. I imagined myself on the cover of one of those magazines one day. I wasn't sure if I'd be smiling seductively, half nude, my breasts popping out of a two-sizes-too-small bathing suit, or if I'd be accepting an Academy Award in a sleek black evening gown. Most likely I'd be looking away in attempt to avoid the camera while several cops handcuffed me and read me the riot act before throwing me in the slammer for perverse public thoughts. My mother and father would decide to keep me in jail where I wouldn't be able to punch any more holes in the wall. They would want me to learn my lesson. But they'd visit me, and my mother would tell me that she liked having one less kid to watch after. *It's like free babysitting,* she'd say, kissing the prison guard once on each cheek for looking after me. She'd bring me Arabic food in a Tupperware and arrange for the prison to feed me her cooking. Even in jail I'd be forced to eat her food. Prison would toughen me up so that when I got out I could punch holes in the wall, and it wouldn't be surprising. I wouldn't even cry afterward. People would know not to mess with me. *She did time back in '93. You don't want to get on her bad side.* Did I, in fact, have a bad side? If not, it was about time I got me one.

When I reached the back of the aisle, a big, burly leather-clad bald man dropped the periodical he had been engrossed in and rushed away. I looked over at him, sensing my arrival had somehow scared him off. Maybe he thought I was pretty. I sucked my gut in for good measure and stood tall, pretending to be ten years older. Then another man bumped into me and nervously fled. I looked down at the magazine he threw back onto the rack, its cover cheaper and thinner yet more colorful than the others; it's large print flashier. The women on the cover were blonde, and their breasts bulged like balloons out from under their skin, threatening to tear through their flesh. I inched my way over to the magazine, sensing that no one was supposed to see, as if when the men fled they transferred their anxiety to me. My heart was already pounding. It was the thrill I'd been waiting for. The coast clear, I squatted down and slowly lifted the cover.

There are certain things we see for the first time in our lives that we never forget. Perhaps for some, it's a beautiful sunset somewhere like North Dakota, where there are no buildings or mountains to obstruct one's view of the majestic sky when sun meets horizon. From that moment on, every sunset seems to evoke nostalgia. Remember the time we drove cross-country? For me, there are few things I remember as vividly as when I lifted the cover of that magazine.

From a strictly educational perspective, I wondered why I'd never seen this before. Why were parts of the body exposed and others kept so hidden? As I stared at the woman, standing there, bent over, naked and wide open, I felt a rush between my legs. I turned the page and saw more naked women, some of them touching themselves, others touching one another. But all posed so that I could examine them. I am like a doctor, I told myself. Like my father. Just looking. Making sure it all looks healthy. Could there be shame in looking? Or did the shame come when you couldn't look away? I wanted to stand there and stare at them forever, but I sensed a presence, a breath on my neck. Someone was standing behind me.

I turned around and there he stood. My father. I don't know how long he'd been there. But the look on his face said it all. He'd seen what I'd seen. I dropped the magazine and pretended not to know what it was. It never happened, I told myself. I was in bed, asleep. It was all just a bad dream.

My father stared at me, too shocked to say a word. Surely he couldn't see the pounding of my heart, the ache between my legs. Could he? When we returned to the gate, Amira looked pissed off. "Where the hell were you, stupid?"

"Nowhere," I answered without looking at her. Could she see it? Maybe they all could see it, even the people passing by. They were all laughing at me. I felt naked, exposed like the women in the magazines. I sat in my seat and vowed not to speak or move. I would sit there until no one could see me, until I disappeared. I was done being me. From now on I would be someone else. Someone my parents weren't embarrassed by. I looked at the clock and decided that for the next nine hours, I would be the raw man from Minneapolis who loved his homely wife.

My mother took one look at my downcast face and sensed that something was wrong. Her eyes narrowed as she studied me carefully, wondering why I was sitting so nicely in my chair. Quiet. Subdued. She looked me over, ready to question, then looked away. Her hands were too full. It didn't surprise me, of course. My mother didn't care about anything, so long as she was going home.

Rant!

Marie Cornejo

So his excuse was:

I don't know what to do with my life and you do. I want to travel and live my dream. I'm afraid that being with you will not allow me to do that. You're already unhappy as it is.

Live your dream MOTHERFUCKER??? So you leave me and do whatever the FUCK you want to do 'cause you want to live your fucking dream?? What the FUCK? What about me? What about my dream? I guess that doesn't matter to you. My dream was to have a family with the man who fathered my child. The man who I have loved since high school. My dream was to travel too, but you know what you bastard? I can't really do that 'cause I have to take care of my priorities as a parent.

I did everything for you.
I was there through EVERYTHING! Who was the one that was there making sure shit got done when your father died? Who was the one who was there when you felt like you wouldn't amount to shit 'cause you have a job that pays you shit? Who was there when shit went down at home with your family? Who was there to help you through your pain? Who took you back and loved you even more, even after you cheated on me back in college, and called me a bitch in front of your co-workers and friends last week at your office holiday party??????? Yes, that was me MOTHERFUCKER! I was there through it all. Through all the drunken nights where I had to drive your drunk ass home. Through all the tears. Through all the laughs. Now tell me what woman would do that? What woman would go through all the shit with you and still love you like there was no tomorrow? What woman at the age of 23 with a fulltime job and going to school fulltime would get up in the morning to feed her son breakfast, get him dressed for school, feed him dinner, and put him to bed EVERYDAY - knowing that his father is a full-blown bastard? That EVERYDAY she looks into her son's face she can see his father in him? I am that woman or had been that woman.

18

The only thing good that came out of this relationship was a wonderful baby boy. Other than that, it was a waste of 6 years...yes I said it... A WASTE OF 6 YEARS! I wasted my time thinking about our future together. I wasted my time loving you. I wasted my time giving you my heart and my soul. It was all a waste of time.

Now you can go do whatever lost 23 year old boys do. Find themselves and travel. Forget that I ever loved you and that you ever loved me. All that shit was fake. All you have done to me for the past 3 years was step on my heart. YOU ARE YOUR OWN WORST ENEMY even if you don't want to admit it. I have done nothing to deserve this shit from you because all I have done is love you and support you through all your shit.

Guess this is what I get for taking you back the first time.

Dear Diary
(based on true events)
Teri Ellen Cross

5/96
he always be over after everybody go to work
when first period bell would be ringin'
if we wuz in school
i like him best outta all the boys
when he asks
i let him put it in me
i figure 'dat make him my boyfriend now

8/96
it's Friday
grandma's fryin' fish
i dreamt about eatin some
so i just can't get enough
grandma is lookin' at me funny
but mom is laughin'
callin' me her new garbage disposal
but i must be sick or somethin'
cuz i keep throwin' everythang back up

10/96
i'm getttin' fat
jus a little cuz i can't fit
my favorite pair of jeans
my boyfriend be like oh, it's all good
since he like his women thick
me-i'm his woman
i can't wait to see what he got me for my 13th birthday

1/97
mom's trippin'
keep askin' me if i'm pregnant
cus i'm all fat and stuff
dat bitch just jealous
cuz i got a man
and she ain't been able to keep one
since we moved in with grandma last year

3/97
my stomach is killin' me
i think i got gallstones or somethin'
i'm scared to say anythin' dough
but this shit feels like i'm gon' die or somethin'

turns out i was pregnant
i got a son now
i'm gonna name him LaShae

6/97
my baby daddy live with us now
he ain't goin' to school no more
besides, that teacher that got him arrested was trippin' anyway
he slangin' so we got fly clothes and everythang
and he can ball
he keep sayin' he goin' to the NBA
'dat would be 'da shit
i hope it happens

8/97
LaShae was actin' funny
crying all night
i told my man to get him
cuz shit i ain't gotta do everythang
he hit me and was like get the fuck up
i was like nigguh bunk dat i'm tired
'da baby just probably fell of 'da couch or somethin'
he be alright
mommy say i gotta let him cry
that i be spoilin' him anyway
holdin' him all the time

whatevah

11/97
mom ain't goin' watch 'da baby tonight
damn she be trippin'
and grandma at church
so i gotta take 'em wid' me

just came back from my girl's
we smoked a philly and chilled out
they all think LaShae is the cutest baby
he had on his Baby Gap outfit
i know i'm lucky to have a man like mine
it sucks sometimes but i'm happy we live together

1/98
9th grade is hard
LaShae don't cry as much at night
so 'least i can sleep

3/98
yesterday i picked up LaShae
his chest felt all soft and squishy
my cousin called 911
ain't nobody know what happened to him
why he wuz like 'dat
they just said he probably fell off 'da couch or somethin'

by the time we got to 'da hospital
my son was dead
he was only 11 months old
now he gone

4/98
the police arrested LaShae's daddy today
told me he kill't the baby
that he beat him up and kill't him
my brother said if they put him in jail
he can get one of his boys to shank him

what am i goin' tell everybody at school?

Not a Little Bite
Liza Monroy

My mother's job in the Foreign Service meant we had to move to a different country every few years. I was just getting used to life in Italy when she announced we were moving to Mexico. A few months later, the movers had already come to take our furniture, but we were still sleeping on mattresses with blankets in our apartment. I noticed the sound of my voice echoing when I was on the phone. It was an empty sound, like the house, like the feeling within me. It was the sound of something ending.

I started high school that fall in a city of twenty-five million people, where I only knew one: my mother.

That first night, she stood in the small yellow-tiled kitchen making dinner, smashing avocadoes into a bowl, alternating squirts from a lime and stirring in diced onions and tomatoes. She loved to blend in with the locals wherever we moved, whether in the cuisine department, or dating native men.

She put dinner on the table but I couldn't eat. I moved shredded chicken taco filling around on my plate with a fork. There was a loneliness in the room, with its beat-up old furniture, dingy off-white walls and lighting like a cheap motel. There was loneliness and there was a silence, a lack so deep it ached in my chest cavity.

"What's wrong?" asked my mother.

"I wish I knew even one person in this city." I said, a single tear rolling down my cheek and falling straight into the bowl of guacamole.

"You're going to meet Sisley tomorrow," she said.

Sisley and I had been exchanging letters for months. Her father worked in the Consular Section in the area my mother was joining, Citizen Services. She was a sophomore who had lived in Mexico City since the seventh grade, and always said in her letters what an amazing place it was, that people our age had so much more freedom, and I was going to love it. I hoped that she would turn out to be right. So far, I was terrified of the overwhelming, enormous and loud urban spread. I went to bed that night grateful that I had one friend, someone to introduce me to people and show me the ropes. She was picking me up the next morning to take me to ISM's new student orientation. She was the one who convinced me to go to ISM, with her letters about how much fun it was, how much she loved the people. That night, I tried to fall asleep but couldn't shake the first-day jitters.

I got a ride from Sisley in the morning. She was a sophomore and fifteen, so she already had her license. It was an especially smoggy day and the air was thick with haze and morning dew. We'd ridden pretty much in silence until Sisley rounded the corner of a tall gated complex.

"Well, here we are," she said. "Good old ISM."

"This is it? It looks like a prison," I said.

The school was like a fortress. High, peach-painted concrete walls provided a pastel illusion of pleasantry, a distraction from the fact they were topped with barbed wire. Even the run-down houses within a few blocks had their own version of protection from the neighborhood outside. Amber and green glass from broken beer bottles were implanted atop high concrete walls, protruding like jagged teeth from cement gums.

Sisley parked outside and we entered through a guarded gate, where we had to show picture ID and sign a form for the guard.

"You can't leave campus during the day," Sisley told me. "Unless, of course," she nudged her shoulder in the direction of the guard, "you give him a mordida."

Mordida? I searched my limited Spanish vocabulary. Didn't that mean-

"You bite him?" I asked, recalling the word's translation. Sisley rolled her eyes like I had a lot to learn.

"Well literally it means 'little bite' in Spanish. You don't, like, physically sink your teeth in. It's more of a metaphor, see, you pay him. Money is, like, magic here. You'll learn soon enough."

In the hall between third and fourth period, a girl said something to me in Spanish. I was too shy to try out the language in response.

"I'm sorry," I said. "I don't speak Spanish. Yet."

This was a big mistake, much bigger than I knew.

The girl shrugged, turned and walked away. It was my first encounter with the icy treatment of the "outsider" kids by the jet-setting, Prada-clad, fifteen year old socialites.

I ran into Sisley in the hall after the bell rang for lunch.

"How's it going?" she asked, looking around for her friends.

"This girl talked to me in Spanish, and when I didn't speak it back she totally snubbed me."

"Was she a Fresa?"

"A what?"

Sisley explained that these kids were called "Fresas" - literally, strawberries — kind of like preppy, only far more chic.

"Basically they're the Mexican elite," she said. "There's even a 'most Fresa' category in the yearbook. Except the yearbook's in English so they call it 'Best Strawberry' — how retarded is that."

They wore designer clothes and leather shoes with, for the girls, very high heels. As I went from class to class I noticed them in the halls, standing in their cliques, gossiping and looking perfect. (Amanda, a girl in my grade, went on vacation with a big nose and came back with a button. She subsequently won the best-looking category in the yearbook.) It surprised me that as an American coming to Mexico, I turned out to be one of the "underprivileged" in my school.

The other memorable thing that happened that first week was Dave moved in to the Embassy apartment building.

He was tall and well-built, with floppy blond hair and blue eyes, his head perpetually covered by a navy blue Dallas Cowboys baseball hat. There was something almost shy about him, in spite of his homecoming king looks. He was sitting in the back of our Colegio Internacional #11 bus, listening to his Walkman on the way home. He walked up and stood in the front a few minutes before my stop, as if scanning the street for something familiar. He got off at my stop, half a block from the apartment building. As I walked a few feet behind him, I prayed he would open the door to the temporary Embassy apartments and my heart skipped a beat when he did.

"Hi," I said when I got in the elevator behind him, pressing 2 while noticing the already-lit 6. "I'm Liza," I smiled and made eye contact like I'd read about in a Seventeen article on how to flirt correctly.

"My name's Dave," he offered.

"Did you just move here?"

"Yeah, yesterday."

"I didn't think I saw you at orientation," I said. "Where are you from?"

"My parents just got transferred here from Manila, in the Philippines. I grew up in Dallas, mostly," he said, pointing at the hat.

"I was in Rome before," I said. "I sort of hate it here."

"It'll get better. Remember living in this shithole is only temporary."

"I think it's mostly that I haven't met anyone yet."

"You've met me," he said.

We saw each other every day after that, getting take-out food and sitting up on the building's roof, smoking cigarettes and talking.

"What section are your parents in?" I asked.

"They work on the fifth floor."

I knew then to drop any more questions about what Dave's parents did at the Embassy. The fifth floor wasn't like the others. The other floors were open offices, people running around in a frenzy preparing visa papers, helping Americans in trouble, talking on the phone with Mexican authorities. The fifth floor wasn't like that at all. The elevator doors slid open into an empty hallway silent as a catacomb. On either side of the hallway were doors you needed a code to get in, a code that changed every few minutes. No one could enter who didn't work there, and even then, there was a machine that scanned people basically down to their eyeballs. The area was home to the CIA, FBI and DEA. I dubbed it the secret acronym floor. Dave's parents were spies.

On the roof one afternoon, over greasy Burger King fries and a Corona Dave stole from his parent's fridge, he asked me if I was a virgin.

"Of course," I said. "I'm barely fourteen, it would be weird if I weren't, right?" I'd only had one boyfriend, for a month, and we never did anything but kiss.

"I was fourteen when I lost it," said Dave.

"And now you're what, sixteen?"

"Almost seventeen," he said.

"So who was it with?"

"Suzie, my ex-girlfriend from Dallas. I so wanted to get it over with. Don't you?"

I was put off by his obnoxiousness, but I let him kiss me anyway. There was something different about him, something lost behind the big blue eyes. An hour later I went downstairs. The sun had gone down in an orange haze and my mother was chopping onions in the kitchen for yet another Mexican meal.

At school the next day, Dave introduced me to his friend Naldo, a dark-haired Argentine-American. Naldo's twin sister, Nina, was in my sixth-period biology class. Their father was president of a big international bank. I realized they were brother and sister when Dave and I went to Naldo's house in Lomas de Chapultepec after school one day and Nina was there, listening to the Pearl Jam CD in her room and painting her toenails silver.

"Our parents are going to Valle de Bravo for the weekend," Nina said.

Valle was a town on a lake where Sisley said a lot of the Fresas' families had vacation homes. "Why don't we have a party here?"

• • •

On Saturday night, half the school was at Naldo and Nina's. I was surprised, since I'd heard kids from school usually went clubbing because there wasn't an enforced drinking age. Parents-away house parties weren't even remotely a social staple like they were in all the American movies I'd seen about high school. This party was like that, with music blasting out of the two-story gated mansion. Nina and I played tequila drinking games with some guys I didn't know, by the time I realized a girl of ninety-five pounds probably shouldn't do five shots on an empty stomach, the living room was spinning and I forgot what Nina was saying soon as the words finished coming out of her mouth. I went to the kitchen and ate four pieces of bread out of the fridge, then found the twins' parents' room and collapsed on the bed. I felt like I was in a boat, rocking on the ocean, and thought it was still the tequila's effects until I realized I was lying on a waterbed. When I opened my eyes there was a silhouette standing over me.

"Are you all right?"

"Dave?" I said.

"Yeah, it's me," he moved out of the light he was blocking and lay down next to me. We started kissing but then he got back up, switched off the light and closed the door.

"Sleep with me tonight," he said.

"No. We've already had this conversation."

"Come on. Just you, me and this waterbed."

"I told you. I'm not ready."

"Yes, you are," he said, like he was answering an obvious question, as though I'd argued my hair wasn't black or that it was snowing outside. I got a bad feeling and stood up to leave, but he pushed me down, kissing me harder. I tried to get out from under him, but he was strong and I was still unsteady with drunkenness. His breath smelled of alcohol and he pressed into me, holding me down by the wrists, fighting back as I struggled, yelling but the music was too loud for anyone to hear, and he'd locked the door, anyway. After a while I stopped fighting and fixated on a dark spot on the ceiling. My mind began to drift and I clamped my eyes shut, willing myself out of my body, to fall asleep, to be anywhere other than there.

"Get dressed," he said when I came to.

"I'm going back out to the party."

The door opened, letting a stream of light and noise into the room, then it clicked shut.

I lay wrapped in the sheets with my eyes closed and I must have passed out at some point because I woke up to beams of sunlight poring between the blinds, illuminating tiny dust particles on the other side of the room. I dressed, stepped over sleeping bodies in the living room and flagged down a pesero, a small bus that cost a peso. The other people on the small bus stared at me, a rich girl in their eyes, and seemed to wonder what I was doing there.

I got off at the Zona Rosa and walked the rest of the way home. When my mother asked how I got there, I said Nina's mother gave me a ride. I went to my room, put my new Pablo Honey CD on the stereo and watched the cars going by and the people by the taco stand and the man playing guitar on the corner until the sun went down again and my mother called me out for dinner.

The news the next day said the peso was devaluating. It was three to the dollar, now it was hovering around twelve. The poverty level rose, the crime rate skyrocketed, and a substantial portion of the already small Mexican middle class was nearly destroyed. The streets became more dangerous. Tourists were robbed by taxi drivers. They would hail a cab out on the street instead of from a licensed stand, and it would be followed by accomplices. The tourists were driven somewhere, tied up and all their money and credit cards taken. If they had their passports on them, those went too, probably sold to counterfeiters. And if they were lucky, they would only be driven to an ATM and made to take out as much money as they could. Then they were left somewhere, stuck along some shady side of the Toluca highway where anything could happen. But you didn't need to be kidnapped for something fucked-up to happen to you here, as I was just beginning to find out.

Greg

Candice Brown

Greg is a boy.
I used to say: "my mother killed herself when I was young."
He would respond: "I wish mine had."
I would say: "I love red platform shoes."
He would respond in the affirmative.
I would say: "I want to become a whore when I grow up."
He would say: "And I will love you forever."

Greg is a man.
He would take off his shoes.
I would pick them up, and put them away.
The animal he loved would shit,
and I would clean it up.
He would say: "I will love you forever."
And I would be grateful.

The Long Way Home
Latiffany D. Wright

It was ninety-eight degrees in the Windy city when thirteen-year-old Pasha Armstrong walked out of the clinic. The clinic had air conditioning, so she felt as if she'd stepped from an icebox into an oven preheated to 450 degrees. The sudden change in temperature made Pasha feel more faint than she felt thirty minutes before while listening to the nurse. She headed to the library across the street from the clinic; it was where she was supposed to be. Getting out of Saturday morning housework was easier than Pasha thought. It was guilt that had really gotten her out of cleaning the house, but she did not know that. It started on Tuesday. "Ma," Pasha whispered softly. She did not recognize her own voice, and for a moment she felt disoriented. Her mother stretched on the brown suede sofa lazily, moved her arm that had been shielding her eyes and looked up at her daughter standing in the doorway. She could just make out the child's shape in the darkness. Only thing was that Pasha's shape did not look as if it belonged to a child. At thirteen, she had the body of a grown woman, and to her mother that could be dangerous. Pasha's mother drew in a deep breath and released it slowly. Right then Pasha knew her request to get out of the house would be denied. Her mother had come in the house earlier that evening snapping at her.

"Don't tell me you let Adam sit in this hot ass apartment all day long girl!" It was more of a statement than a question. Pasha's heart skipped a beat. Adam had not been in the house all day long, but he was supposed to be. Her mother continued before Pasha could think of what to say. "It's a hundred degrees outside and you didn't have sense enough to open a damn window or turn on a fan?" The tiny apartment was hot and a musty odor hung in the air although the place was immaculate. "I know what your ass been doing all day long." Pasha knew that there was no way her mother knew what she had been doing, so she started breathing a little easier. "You had your head stuck in these damn books all day." With that her mother swept her arm across a stack of Christopher Pike books and they fell to the carpet with a soft plop.

Slightly shaken, Pasha picked the books up quickly and took them to the small bedroom that she shared with Adam. She was stacking them on her desk when her mother entered the room. Her mother's dark brown eyes scanned the room to make sure that everything was in order. Then she focused her attention on Adam who had not moved from in front of the television.

He was playing his Sega Genesis. His mother and sister thought he was oblivious to everything around him. Just looking at Adam was enough to brighten Pasha's mother's mood. Adam, at ten years old, was a skinny ashy kid with big ears and a large smile. His dark eyes were a reflection of his mothers, and he had her curly long eyelashes.

"Did you eat today?" his mother asked. Barely looking up at her frame in the doorway he nodded. "Okay, lets try this again. What did you eat Adam?" His mother's voice was stern this time.

Pasha spoke for him. "He ate cereal for breakfast and hot dogs and fries for lunch." Adam looked up at his mother finally and smiled.

"Ya'll kids are crazy." Their mother shook her head and went to start on dinner. Adam smiled at Pasha before continuing with the colorful images on the television. He had not eaten hot dogs or fries that day.

Adam's day started early. He played basketball on the school's playground until noon. He used the money Pasha gave him and shared a large pizza with his friends Moon and Gene. By one he and his friends were chasing girls off the playground. He ended the afternoon chasing the girls back onto the playground and trying feel on them. He was home by four o'clock. One hour before his mom was due home, just like he had promised Pasha.

He was only allowed to play outside when his mother was home. It was July, he was out of school and he wanted to enjoy his vacation. By the time she got home she would say that it was too late for him to go out, so his arrangement with Pasha worked out well. Whatever Pasha was doing he did not care, although he suspected that she was up to something. He came home early one day to show Moon his new game cartridge. Pasha was furious and sent him right back out the door.

Adam remained in front of the television with his legs crossed Indian style until Gene came over and asked his mother could he come out. Adam was surprised she gave him an hour to play and raced out of the house as if he had not been out all day.

"Maybe he can start playing outside a few hours during the day. You could read at the playground while he plays," their mother suggested to Pasha. Pasha shrugged and went back to her room.

Later that evening, after dinner, Pasha stood in the kitchen looking out the window into the darkness. A cool breeze tickled her face. She closed her eyes and prayed for a few minutes. At thirteen she believed in the power of prayer.

Before her grandmother died, she took Pasha and Adam to church every Sunday. Pasha's grandmother taught her that it was important to have a close relationship with God. She told her that prayer was the best method of communication with God. Secretly, Pasha felt that when she prayed she was not only talking to God, but her grandmother could hear her and help her as well. She needed help during those times when she felt lonely and missed her father and her grandmother. She also prayed during the times she was sure that her mother loved Adam more than she loved her.

She stood in the entrance of the living room and watched her mother's body fill and release air. The breeze was also playing with her mother. She whispered in the voice that she could not recognize. Her mother, who had been resting with one arm over her eyes and one arm thrown over her stomach, lazily moved her arm from over her eyes. She took in Pasha's silhouette. Pasha's waist was narrow, and her hips were almost as big as her mother's. Her mother wore a size ten and Pasha was not far behind. Her breasts sat on her chest like two red apples and pressed against the t-shirt she was wearing.

"What is it?" she asked wearily. Pasha's body bothered her. She already could see the lust in men's eyes when she and her daughter walked down the street together. One man was either really stupid or trying his luck, when he called out to Pasha. She, Pasha and Adam were coming back from eating dinner downtown. They had just gotten off the bus and were headed down their block. Pasha's mother ignored the man after the first remark, but when he continued she turned into a lion. "Are you fucking crazy? This is my daughter and she's thirteen, did you hear that? I said thirteen years old, and you stay the fuck away from her!" People on the street stopped and looked at the scene. Pasha and Adam were embarrassed, not at their mother's behavior, but at the attention that they were receiving.

"Aw baby, I thought she was your sister. Can I holler at you?" The man was obviously drunk. His long, thin, body swayed in the wind.

She replied, "Hell no, and you didn't think she was my fucking sister. Stay the fuck away from her just like I said." But she thought, Stay away from her or she'll end up like me, two kids and no education or man. All of the men hanging out on the corner heard not what she told the drunken man, but how she told him.

Pasha's mother felt bad about throwing the child's books on the floor. Just because she had a bad day at work was no excuse to take it out on Pasha .The streetlight shined through the living room and Pasha looked into her mother's eyes.

"Can I go to the library Saturday morning if I clean up Friday? I read all the books that I have."

"Yeah, you can go. I'll call you tomorrow and let you know what time you and Adam can go out." They remained like that for a few minutes, daughter and mother staring at each other. Then Pasha went to her room where Adam's video game made colorful noises and he sat frozen Indian style in front of the television.

Pasha's mother lay on the couch wanting. She wanted to ask Pasha about her day. She wanted to tell her oldest daughter that she loved her and she appreciated her taking such good care of Adam. She wanted to ask her what was in those books and how did she read them so fast? Which were her favorite and which ones weren't. She wanted to call her back and almost did, but the breeze lulled her off into a deep sleep. She woke at two a.m. to the sound of gunshots in the distance. She crept to her children's room and kissed them lightly on their cheeks. She went back to sleep in her own room, alone.

On Saturday morning, Pasha left her house before her mother and Adam woke. She had not slept all night; She had stayed up listening to her stomach gurgle and throb. She prayed that the only heartbeat she heard was her own. Wearing yellow shorts and a white tank top Pasha walked slowly to the bus stop. Before she made it there a pool of sweat formed in her bra. She was looking for him. He told her that he might go with her, but she didn't see his blue Cutlass anywhere.

The bus came quickly. The ride to the clinic took almost an hour. She waited ten minutes before her name was called. After giving the nurse a urine sample she waited in the lobby until her name was called again. The words the nurse spoke to her did not hit her until ten minutes later while she stood in the air-conditioned library. She picked books that she had not read before by Virginia Hamilton, a book of poems by Gwendolyn Brooks and a handful of books by R.L. Stine. The books by R.L Stine were selections from the Fear Street series. She thought, with all these people dying on Fear Street, you'd think they had good enough sense and move. She almost laughed, but she still had a lump in her throat that formed when the Planned Parenthood nurse told her that she was pregnant. She checked out the books and left the library. The heat awaited her outside.

On the bus stop was an older woman, about five months pregnant. As if she had never seen a pregnant woman before, Pasha stared at her horrified. She ran back into the library and threw up on the floor. The librarian, startled, jumped up. "Are you okay?" she asked Pasha. Pasha clutched her books and shook her head.

"No, I am not alright. I don't feel good." She turned and ran back out of the library. She ran holding her books tightly, until finally she had to stop. She gulped the hot air and tasted the sourness of the vomit in her mouth. She stopped in a corner store and purchased a bottle of water. The Arab behind the counter eyed her body and flirted with her. She ignored him. Once outside she rinsed her mouth with the water and spat it back out on the ground. She was two blocks away from the store when the water evaporated from the heat. It was like it had never been there.

She did not know how she was going to tell her mother that she was pregnant by the local drug dealer. The same young man who had witnessed her mother cursing out a drunk man for daring to try to talk to her daughter. The young man approached her a few days later while she was alone at the corner store. He joked with her about her mother being so evil toward the man. She was trying to decide which chips she wanted. It was difficult to keep her composure when he kissed her softly behind her ear, and whispered that she'd get in trouble if her mother found out. His actions took her by surprise, but she liked it.

He was sixteen and sure she was a virgin. He was right. Two weeks later he gave her money to give her brother to get lost. Every time he came near, something in her stomach tingled and her breasts would swell. She had done as she was told and over the next two months he had come over two sometimes three times a week to have sex with her. It hurt the first few times, but the hurt was so delicious she could not have told him not to come back if she really wanted to.

She thought she loved him, he knew he didn't love her. It never occurred to either of them to use a condom, so Pasha Armstrong walked home thirteen years old and a little over a month pregnant. She had no idea how she would tell her mother or what her revelation would do to her, so she took the long way home.

She needed more time to think.

The Hymen Maneuver
darlene anita scott

first the blood then the boys.
the curse closes her knees so tight
they go numb.
when she doesn't
he says her name
and makes her aware of herself.

remembering is always the same:
begins with pain
ends with a smirk.
ahh, they sigh, umphh
they emphasize with
antics; sheaths for wordless words
hold the fragile seal in place
long after others come and go
pass through staying for hours, months, years
never forever.

the first piss made them wince;
thighs tight, making all movement
a deliberate act,
a decision more certain than
the yes-no-maybe creasing the brow
from frown to concentration;
from the near swallowing of her neck;
the prickly heat along the edge of her belly;
the smell of him in her hair

are secrets of the sisterhood.

the script warns they can talk you out of your socks
when you never planned to take off your shoes
implores you to move, get up, walk away,
not that these things make you stay
the same ones that make you come back.

Catholic Puberty: Lessons
Raina J. Leon

1.
My mother cultivated crossed ankle sit
demure knee press slant -
Your girly cloth will show.
No one would want to see that
thing underneath. *Coochie*
must always be clenched, closed.
She taught the eventuality of blood
through a blue-covered book, borrowed
from the public library;
I would have to return it,
she too embarrassed to go twice.
My mother did not prepare me:
bloody pillows born between legs,
how to dispose of red rag disgrace.
Secrecy answered in swoosh of flush.
Plumber pulled pads,
each branded scarlet streak on her face.
The wet tunnel hides nothing.

2.
My mother relinquished my sex education -
a book not enough for puzzled looks -
to Catholic school. I learned by rote:
Eve sinned, God punished.
Period.

Labor, labor pains.
One was bad but the other...
the Devil courted with handsome faces.
Labor without ring meant hell.
Enter the promised chastity belt of vows.
I prayed to enter the convent:
at least, the nuns, Brides

of Christ, ecstasy burned all the time.
No shame, no closet nuns:
rocking in church, Latin grit in throats,
they carried their rosary dicks,
crucifixes on their chains,
seemed immaculate still,
unsullied beneath the veil.
Intuitively, I knew convent cloisters
never would welcome me.
Perhaps it was the desire
for bodies over "body and blood."

My Right Hand
B. Lois Wadas

"I went out to get a dozen eggs. There was a man in the store. He showed me a hen. I told him that I didn't want no damned hen. I wanted a dozen eggs. He followed me from the store and turned my hair into chicken feathers."

My step-father is speaking in a low dream like voice as he strokes his hair. He is seated in one of the kitchen chairs. He has the chair turned away from the table. I am standing at the sink getting a bottle for my baby brother. I am scared. I am terrified. My mouth is dry. The only things moving are his hand, his mouth, the water running over the baby bottle and the second hand of the clock. I am stilled inside myself. I look up at the big faced clock over the stove. It is two-twenty in the morning. My little brother, six weeks old, is hungry.

Terror or no, I have to quiet this baby who has begun to cry tears that I cannot shed. My throat is dry.

I want my mother.

"Come here." He says. I turn to face him. He has stopped stroking his hair. His hand is poised above his head. I notice that his pinkie is crooked. There is something wrong with the first joint. His nails are dirty. Grimy. He looks up at me with weary eyes. "Feel my hair" he says softly. He is wearing his faded blue work overalls. There is a patch over his left breast pocket that says, "Giovanni's Park & Lock." He looks sad.

I can hear my mother's voice through the open window, "Deal the cards nigger!"

She is playing poker in my grandmother's apartment. I hear the tinkle of ice on glass and laughter cracks the night air. My grandmother lives one flight down from our apartment. Her kitchen window is catty-corner to ours.

I want my mother.

And hate her at the same time.

I wonder if I should go down there and tell her that Nick has gone crazy. He thinks his hair has turned to chicken feathers. I want to go down there and tell her that I am scared of him. I do not move. I discard the thought of descending the stairs. My mother would get mad if I interrupt her and her party. She would yell at me, maybe even hit me, or worse, tell me to stop bothering her.
I am also afraid to go out into the hallway.

I hate her fiercely now as I move toward the madman. I have the bottle in my right hand. I will hit him with it. If I have to, I will break his head.

I reach out to touch the tangled mass of reddish brown hair. His hair color is a result of the lye straightener he uses. The hair is wooden. It feels like straw.
I stroke his head. He smells like gasoline, tobacco and gin.

He closes his eyes. I say, "Are you going to go downstairs and play cards?" This is more of a suggestion than a question. As I say the words, I already know the answer. He never joins them in their card games. He does not gamble.

"I don't want to play no damn cards. I'm not going to give them niggers my money." He is snarling. My body stiffens but I continue to stroke his head, soothing him. His eyes drift closed. "Can you feel the feathers?" He asks. His eyes slide open.

I try reality. "Your hair is hair. It feels like hair to me." I say this in what I think is a reasonable voice. "You telling me you don't feel these damned feathers?" His eyehave become cunning slits. His tone is frightening. I am scared bad now.

Survival kicks in. I alter reality.

I decide without deciding to join him in his madness. I am very thirsty. I say, "I can feel some of the feathers." My voice sounds throaty to me. I have forgotten the baby bottle in my right hand. I have to contain this lunatic. I am eleven years old. I am ancient.

I say, "It's turning back to hair now. It's all right now." I say this gently. I am cooing. His slit eyes relax and close softly. He smiles. I continue a steady rhythm. I soothe myself. I dare not move or break the cadence of my hand/voice. I have to put him to sleep.

The baby bottle has gone cool. I can hear my little brother struggling around in his crib. He will wail soon. He will break the spell if I don't feed him...

My right hand stops in mid-stroke. I need to see if this maniac will continue to sleep. I am deer still. He sleeps. I back away. My bare feet are quiet on the linoleum. The tap is still running. I am scared again. I consider for a moment letting it run. I am afraid to go back to the sink. I am afraid the turned off water will waken the crazy man. I dismiss my fear. My mother will be mad if I leave the water running. She might yell at me or hit me or something. Her mad is worse than his crazy. I hate her again. I hate her for leaving me with her baby and her man. Her crazy drunk man. Her hungry about to cry hard baby. I wish she would come up stairs. Maybe I should call her from the window maybe...

I want my mother.

I cross the kitchen to the sink. I shift the bottle into my left hand. With my right hand, I close the faucet. He continues to sleep.

I go into their bedroom and get my little brother out of the crib. I grab a diaper and his powder and take him to my bed. I wonder what to do first. Should I dry his ass or fill his stomach? I decide without really deciding to fill his stomach. I wonder idly if the too cool milk will hurt him any. I hope not. I plug his mouth with the nipple. I have one ear cocked toward the crazy man in the kitchen. I can hear faint sounds of laughter from downstairs. Something crashes a bottle or something. Are they fighting down there?

My head has snapped up. A doe in headlights. I stare at the doorway to the kitchen. Muffled laughter seeps through the catty-cornered window.

He is quiet.

The baby has drunk more than half the bottle. He is sucking lazy now. I wonder again if I should change him. I wiggle the bottle a bit. He doesn't really try to keep it so I pull the nipple out of his mouth. I take off the soggy diaper and exchange it for the dry one. I don't bother to wash his butt. I throw the wet diaper on the floor. I pull him close to me and lie down with him. I put the bottle back into his mouth. He sucks. I am sleepy. I doze then wake when I drop the bottle. I am very sleepy now. I cannot sleep and hold the bottle. I prop it against my forehead. He sucks. I close my eyes. The coming sleep feels delicious. I am courting the edges of unconsciousness when I hear our apartment door as my mother flings it open. I am relieved now.

Mother has come.

She goes to her bedroom then comes into mine. She is in search of her baby. I pretend to be asleep. I watch her through my eye lashes. She flicks on my bedroom light then laughs. "That girl done propped that bottle upside her head." She says this over her shoulder. I feel foolish.

I hope she will take her baby. She does not.

The madman is telling her about his feathers. "Oh nigger, leave me alone," she says.

"I ain't got time to listen to your foolishness." Their bedroom door slams. I hear their voices but I am not listening to them.

I have a mother. She is not the mother that I want. She *is* the mother that I have.

I feel safe now. Mother is here. I drop down into the bottom of sleep. I dream. I dream of hens and eggs and snorting bulls...

Cornrows
Kesi Augustine

He'd asked why I wore cornrows to school.
So I began to wish that the Creme of Nature bottle
would transform my Afro into a flawless, vibrant canopy.
Long hair would make me pretty, I was sure of it.
The chemicals weren't good enough.
And when a short, skinny, light skinned local train would flutter by
his eyes would follow her into ether,
and I thought that my own weren't light enough.
He turned me off
going to school with a drawstring bag that cradled only
an unsharpened pencil.
He forgot things that took so much courage
for me to tell,
and he had the ability to make me question myself
when he barely had the ability to read.
But he turned me on
when I hugged him, I danced on cloud 546, 999
feeling like I'd digested butterflies
and I was glad that there was something in me
somebody else liked.
My affection has withered away and died
like the smoke rings between his parched lips.
On tomorrow's tomorrow I will wake up for school
tired and groggy with stress.
There will be rows and rows of braids in my hair,
and I will deflate under the weight of my book bag
ripping at the stitches because of my books.
I'll embrace the sun, as my skin gets darker —
I won't hold on to my Colorblends as tight —
And I will let my hopes of being stereotypically attractive fade.
Because I'm finally over him.

No Ignorance Here
Tina Pryce

She's known
Waters,
Vast and deep
Unforgiving are the waves
She's met
As they carried her love to the sea of war
And she never got to say goodbye

She's known
Earth tones
Seen them scattered
On Paleolithic cave walls
No different from her home,
The one she grew up in

4 years old
She was to lace paint the walls
With loud and cheap
Wax crayons
To drown out the sound of
Her daddy's voice
Mutilating the remains of her mommy's
Esteem

She's known
Battered ones
From Egypt to Iran
From the Americas to Australia
She's seen
The spine of sanity
Snap into reality
And break in insanity
The travesties
Have come in numbers
Only she knew the count

She's known
Lovers to come one,
Fall apart,
And be together
In dreams
That never came true

She's known
Leaders to rise
In a dead sun
And die in the darkness
From whence they came

She knows
The smell of death
As it sits
At the foot of her path.

Sacrifice
Sheba Karim

When I was young and had hair that met my hips, I would get high by riding my bike down the hill of our driveway at full-speed, my arms extended out like wings. After my uncle moved in with us, my bike rides seemed childish, and I decided to give it up. On my very last ride, as I flew down the hill, I lost control and crashed into the brick wall of my house. My mother came out and bent over my bloody, bruised knees, wiping them with the edge of her dupatta. She was about to scold me when we heard the honking, and looked up to see my father and Aftab Chacha, my uncle, pull up in a rented pick up truck with a goat in the back.

"Why do they have a goat?" I asked my mother.

She raised her eyebrows as if the question was ridiculous.

"To sacrifice," she said. "Why else?"

Aftab Chacha got out of the truck and walked around back. We watched him tie a rope around the goat's neck. He tugged the rope gently, trying to ease the goat off the truck. The goat bleated in protest. The more Aftab Chacha tugged at the rope, the more obstinate the goat became, walking to the far end and bleating louder. Eventually Aftab Chacha let go of the rope and got on the truck. He put his arms around her, lifted her with a grunt and, with my father's help, set her on the ground.

"Where should we put her?" my father asked, patting the goat on the back. She was dirty but cute, her whole body a ruddy brown except for the white ears that flopped down the sides of her face.

"Tie her to the pole in the garage," my mother said, and my father and Aftab Chacha began to pull the goat towards her new home.

Aftab Chacha, my father's younger brother, had been living with us for two weeks and nothing had been quite the same since. Whenever my mother complained about him to my father, she always referred to him as thirty-three and unmarried, as if one was made worse by the other. During the days leading up to his arrival, my parents fought like athletes, with an intense vigor and the occasional surprise blow. My mother wanted parameters, the length of his stay, the financial contribution he would make to the household. My father said Aftab was his brother and he had a duty to help him, no matter what.

"Help him what? Only Americans need to find themselves. Pakistanis don't get lost," she said. "Unless of course he thinks he's American."

When Aftab Chacha moved into our basement I looked for signs that he mistakenly believed he was American, but only found two: his brown leather cowboy boots that he wore almost every day, and the six pack of Budweiser he kept in a black plastic bag in his fridge.

Aftab Chacha spent most of his time in the basement, which offered two couches, a television, a kitchenette, a ping pong table with a broken net, and dark red paisley carpet. I spent a lot of time in the basement with him. Sometimes we watched Bollywood films together, mainly black and white. Sometimes we'd just talk. He liked to smoke Dunhills, sitting on the couch with his legs crossed, wearing cowboy boots and jeans with one of his countless striped button-down shirts. He would tell me stories, and answer my questions. I liked to ask him questions because, unlike my parents, he always gave me honest answers.

It was through Aftab Chacha that I learned that my father was once a romantic, a singer, and a wanderer, and my mother a thief. He told me how when my father announced to Dadi, his mother, that he wanted to marry my mother, Dadi locked herself in her room and refused to eat for two days because she wanted him to marry Sabeen, his first cousin, who would have been pretty had she been nice. My father stood outside Dadi's door and sang Hindi love songs from the 1940's and 1950's to try and explain.

"Did it work?" I asked Aftab Chacha.

"Your Dadi was a pragmatic woman. Once she realized your father would marry despite her protestations, she came out of the room and stared eating again. But she never forgave your mother for stealing her son."

Then he told me how my father, at the age of eighteen, threw some clothes in his rucksack, got on a motorcycle and left with a friend, saying he didn't know when he would be back.

"Where was my father planning on going?" I asked.

Aftab Chacha took out another cigarette from a silver cases engraved with his initials. He was always very kind to his cigarettes.

Before lighting one he would first smooth it with gentle strokes between his fingers, and whisper something under his breath I could never quite catch, an apology, perhaps, for the flame to come.

"He didn't know," Aftab Chacha said. "Anywhere. No where."

This was not true. My father always knew exactly where he was going. Before our road trips to Orlando and Toronto he would highlight our route on at least two different maps, circling and re-circling the relevant exits in black ink.

"I don't believe it," I said.

"Is it so hard to believe?" Aftab Chacha asked, and blew out a cloud of smoke so thick it masked his face.

The first night the goat spent in the garage she bleated for hours. She was tied to the pole with the rope, and there were newspapers spread out on the floor underneath her. My mother and I watched her for a few minutes. She kept straining at the rope, trying to break free.

"Poor thing," my mother said, and shut the door.

Aftab Chacha preferred to eat his meals in the basement, and every night, after I finished eating, I would bring him a plate of food that my mother had prepared. He always ate with his hands, scooping up the food with his long, thin fingers. I was able to stay with him for an hour, at most, before my mother would yell for me to come upstairs. Whenever she yelled Aftab Chacha would usually roll his eyes, and I would usually laugh. But tonight seemed different than the usual, and when Aftab Chacha rolled his eyes, I crossed my arms.

"I feel guilty laughing at my mother," I told him.

"It's a good thing," he said. "It means you're human."

"What else would I be?" I asked him.

"You could be a snake. Snakes feel no guilt."

I thought of the goat bleating all night. "What about goats?"

He considered this, rubbing his palm against the greenish-black stubble that covered most of the lower half of his face, chin to eye. "Did you know goats have almost 360 degree vision? No matter where they face, they can always see behind them. So if any animal were to feel guilt, it would be them, wouldn't it? They certainly have the eyes for it."

It took me less than a week to fall for my uncle. After he had stayed with us a few days and we had established our easy, frank rapport, I grew bold.

"My mother says you have no sense of direction," I told him.

"Tell me, wise one, where should I be in such a hurry to go?" he asked me, uncrossing his legs and leaning his elbows on his knees so his head was level with mine. "Should I go back to Karachi and get married? Should I move to a midsize city and get a job as an engineer? Should I move to an island and become a pearl diver?"

"I like pearls," I said.

"That is because you are a shehzadi, a royal princess. Only for you, my princess, would I dive for pearls." He did the breast stroke with his arms, pretending to swim. I pictured him diving into the sea, a giant, striped fish with a trail of cigarette smoke behind him, and knew then that I loved him, and would even follow him there, to the bottom of the ocean, if he would let me.

When I lay in bed that night I imagined Aftab Chacha as the star of a black and white movie, wearing his cowboy boots, shirt fully unbuttoned, a cigarette dangling from his lips, and me, the heroine, in a sleeveless black dress and heels and stockings, with warm, round breasts and soft skin that smelled faintly of jasmine. Aftab Chacha reached out his hand and pulled me close, and we kissed for a long time, my hair twisted around his fingers like a velvet glove. I felt a new kind of high, different than the one from bike-riding, like a deep, powerful wave that started at the core of my body and spread throughout my insides, lapping at the surface of my skin. Then came a strange, pulsating heat between my legs, and I knew it was going too far, that good girls should not be imagining such things. I forced myself to think of other topics, like what response I should write for my extra-credit question for social studies, until my body became cool and dry, and there were no more movies playing in my mind.

In the morning I checked on the goat. She was quiet now, and the food my mother put out for her was untouched. I reached out my hand to pet her on the head and she walked away, sitting down as far from me as the rope would allow. It made me angry, her rejection of my sympathies.

"Your last day," I told her. "How does it feel?"

She blinked once, and again.

I got on my hands and knees and began to crawl towards her.

"Tell me," I whispered into her snow white ear. "Can you see a world where I can marry my uncle and live happily ever after?" I willed her to open her mouth and speak, tell me of this world and how I could get there. But her sad, quiet eyes gave me a different answer. There is no place like that, they said. There is just this world. Only this.

I stood up. "What do you know?" I asked her. "You're just a stupid goat." But I turned out the light before I said it so she could not see my shame.

When I brought dinner down to Aftab Chacha he was not in the basement. I called out his name but there was no answer. Then I saw him outside, standing in the moonlight in my mother's rose garden, picking petals off a rose and putting them in his mouth.

"What are you doing?" I asked.

"Having a snack," he said.

"You can't eat rose petals," I said. And these were not petals from just any roses; these were my mother's roses, the ones she worked so hard to save each day from insects and deer and other admirers.

"Of course you can. I have since I was young." He handed me a petal, a deep, dark orange with a streak of pink. "Try it."

It tasted a little bitter, perhaps, but more like nothing than anything else. "Yuck," I said.

"You know what the problem with me is?" he asked.

There are no problems with you; you're perfect, I wanted to say. But I knew he would laugh.

"I have been infected by nostalgia. Terrible disease, causes depression and paralysis." He brushed the rose against the side of my cheek. "Umang," he said, and bent his head towards me. I did what I had seen in the movies, closed my eyes, angled my head upwards, and pursed my lips. It would be as perfect as he was; our first kiss in the moonlight surrounded by roses. Except his lips landed not on my mouth but on the edge of my forehead, the stubble on his chin scratching my nose. He took one step back and winked. "Tomorrow is Eid al-Adha. You should get some beauty sleep, my princess," he said, bowing and handing me the half-eaten rose.

I woke the next morning to my mother's face three inches above mine.

"Umang," she was whispering.

"Too early," I groaned, and rolled over.

She flipped me back around. I had never seen her like this, bottom lip quivering, eyes bright and straining with the weight of unwept tears.

"Tell me something," she said.

"Has Aftab Chacha ever touched you in a way he shouldn't?"

"No, never." I said, but there was guilt on my face, I knew, from the all of the places he had touched me in the cinema of my dreams.

"Well, he's leaving tomorrow," she said. "I told him last night. He has to move on with his life now. And you — I can't let you — " She could not finish, and I saw she was about to cry.

"But Ma," I began. "He never —"

"It isn't right, Umang, to let him stay." Then she kissed my cheeks, right first, then left.

"Eid Mubarak," she said.

After she left I decided to go downstairs and tell Aftab Chacha I loved him. I would not tell him I was in love with him, just a simple "I love you" spoken with an even emphasis, in a way that was not alarming but open for interpretation. Then I would ask him where he was going, and if I could go with him, just for a while, since I couldn't miss too much of sixth grade.

The kitchen counter was piled with food, two fresh chickens my father had bought from the local halal shop, potatoes, onions, okra, yogurt, basmati rice. My mother was talking on the phone in the kitchen, rolling flour into perfectly round chapatis, and frying onions all at once. I slipped away unnoticed and headed towards the garage, where I could hear my father and Aftab Chacha's voices.

They had tied the rope like a noose around the goat's feet, and my father was holding her body down. She was not putting up a fight, and lay still except for the tremors in her body. She was blinking rapidly, so fast it was making me dizzy to watch it. Aftab Chacha stood in front of it with a long knife in his right hand.

When he saw me I turned to leave, because I thought that was what he would want. But instead he nodded, approving, as though he was telling me to stay, so I did. When he raised the knife, I thought of what else the goat must be seeing, not just the Aftab Chacha and the knife in front of him but me standing in the doorway to his right, and our lawnmower and my bicycle to his left, and, behind him, our driveway and clear blue sky.

"Allahu Akbar!" Aftab Chacha yelled, and slit the goat's throat from one end to the other, then did it again, deeper this time, searching for the jugular. The blood began gush onto the floor, turning all of the newspaper red. It made me sick to watch it, but I refused to look away, and that is how I discovered that I was just as capable of killing as I was of love.

By the time the last bit of blood spilled, I knew I could no longer profess my feelings to my uncle. The curtain had fallen, the reel was up. And then I fell to the ground and started to cry, because now there was a dead goat lying in the middle of our garage, and I had never even bothered to say goodbye.

I am

Shaneka "Nekka" Brooks

I am a poet writing my pain

I am a poet living a life of shame

I am a daughter hiding my depression

I am your sister making a good impression

I am your friend acting like I'm fine

I am a wisher wishing this life weren't mine

I am a girl who thinks of suicide

I am a teenager pushing things aside

I am a student who doesn't have a clue

I am the girl sitting right next to you

I am the one asking you to care

I am your best friend hoping you'll be there.

to be a woman
Jennifer Karmin

to be a woman is to be a girl a girl a girl to wait to wait talked over interrupted don't raise your hand you have a penis and i have a vagina so you get to pee standing up and i have to sit down a ten year old girl in love with an eight year old redhead named julie herman who lives two houses away who you kiss and touch and we have no hair and her older brother found us naked and when we grow up we want to be playboy centerfolds but the curse i am a curse four girl cousins and then me and then my brother the boy the little man when my brother was born i said but where's the girl when i was born my grandfather martin came to the hospital drunk and said shame it's not a boy and my grandma jean told him he should leave or she was going to throw him out the window

On Sundays
Annie Dawid

I.

In the early morning stillness of a Sunday dawn, a shriek pierced the blue light of the house and shook the girl, who was dreaming the blurry dreams of adolescence. The shriek came again, louder, penetrating her sleep. "Help me." This voice, her mother's, unfamiliar now in its taut, tense pitch, an unimaginable register. "Help me. I swallowed a bottle of pills and I want to die..." The girl shivered out of bed, opened the door to find her older brother and sister huddled in the hallway, their bodies shaking in the January cold that clung to thin nightgowns and pajamas with icy persistence, like the fear gripping the girl's stomach. The father's voice then, brittle, barked, "Be quiet! Be quiet! You'll wake the children."

Her mother began moaning — unearthly, guttural noises.

"I don't care. I want to die." The moans drifted out through the space beneath the door. Moaning — primordial sounds issuing not from her throat or lungs but deeper, from a place foreign to the girl, who leaned against the hollow wall, quaking. The blue light turned grey. The brother went back to his bedroom and the two sisters stood helplessly on the landing, there beside the telephone table and pads for messages and the Yellow Pages. The father's sharp voice cleaved the silence. "What kind of pills did you take? Tell me!" he shouted, his words tinged with a panic that paralyzed the girl, her toes turning a pale shade of blue.

"Anacin. I swallowed a bottle of Anacin."

The response stemmed the girl's immediate fear that her mother was dying in the next room and that all she could do was stand there, outside, while her father stood inside, watching, powerless.

The father came out of the room with his overcoat over striped pajamas, said he was going down the street to fetch the psychiatrist who lived at number 27 and would the older sister please sit with the mother until he returned? The older girl hesitated, then crept inside, and after the father left she motioned for her sister to come in too. The mother lay on her side, facing away from them toward the windows now lightening with the cold glow of a short winter day. The younger girl saw her mother's large breasts silhouetted through white covers, a thin nightdress hiked around her mammoth thighs, the blankets down around her knees. The girl edged toward the bed, cautiously, as if this woman on the bed were a stranger, and pulled the blankets up around her mother's neck, seeing both their breaths. The mother would not look at either daughter, just toward the window, where the pale sky now emitted a watery light; and she sobbed a little.

The girl, just twelve, wanted to do something, to have some kind of effect, to transform the strange, weeping woman on the bed back into her mother, comfortable and warm, who had cookies and milk ready for her every afternoon after school, even though the girl thought she was too old for that now, and it upset her when her friends came home with her and found her mother sitting at the kitchen table with a glass of milk resting on a folded yellow napkin, and a plate of Lorna Doones. She would get mad at her mother then, when there were others around, but when she came home alone she liked to sit there and pat the dog and listen to her mother talk and talk. Often they drank tea with lots of milk and sugar, from a silver teapot which had belonged to her grandmother.

The front door opened, sending a current of icy wind into the vestibule and up the stairs to the bedroom. Footsteps, two pairs, mounted the thirteen steps, her father's light and familiar, the woman doctor's heavy and clumsy. The woman asked the girl to leave, gently, suggested she go back to bed because it was still early, too early to be up on a Sunday. The brother reappeared, dressed, said he was taking the dog on a walk. He leashed up the old mongrel with her black eyes watering and slammed the door behind him.

The younger girl sat on her sister's bed as the older girl dressed at the request of the doctor, preparing herself to accompany her parents to the hospital. She promised her sister she would come right back, and the father said nothing as they both supported the mother, heavy in her bulky coat and boots pulled on awkwardly by the sister —the mother refused to help — and the father went out to start the car while the three women stood silently at the foot of the stairs. The girl remained alone on the landing above, wrapped in a blanket, trying to stay warm.

II.

In spring, a year later, the girl sat on the ground by her mother in the backyard beneath soothing sunlight which stippled her dark recollection of previous months. The social worker was there, sitting alert on an orange plastic chair, sipping iced tea the mother had tastefully prepared and served in a clear pitcher with half-moons of lemon floating on the liquid's surface, sticking to the sides of the glass. The father was there too, and the sister and brother, all separated by green swatches of lawn, the father in a tie and shirtsleeves, stretched out on a chaise lounge; he had fallen asleep. The boy threw sticks to the dog and lingered in the far end of the garden, seeking solitude under the boughs of the immense, dying maple.

The social worker came once a week to the brick house on the silent suburban street. Usually she spoke with the mother alone, but sometimes the girl sat with them, drinking tea and eating cookies. This Sunday was a special occasion, a meeting for the entire family to discuss what had happened in the wavery time that had elapsed since that January dawn, a miasma of hospital rooms and drugs and torturous visits when the children came to see their mother in the psychiatric ward at the university teaching hospital. The sixth floor had locked doors, and when the girl came with her father, clasping his clammy hand so tightly with outraged fear, they had to be let in the massive white doors with their tiny eyes of screened windows by the nurse, and then again into the mother's room. The mother was always tired, her eyes floating in a tranquilized blur, vaguely acknowledging the gifts from home — a wicker basket filled with ripe bananas and shiny Macintosh apples. The girl remembered her mother's pink hairbrush resting on the nightstand, overflowing with brittle grey hairs.

In the garden, the social worker tried to bring the father around to conversation, to rouse him from the slumber he had fallen into from his sixty-hour week at the office, as well as the papers he pored over at home, always occupied with matters of law, of seeing the significance of the slightest details. But the father was so tired that he couldn't participate, and he snored loudly under the sun. The mother looked at the maple, dying, and the cherry blossom tree at the other end of the garden, now in bloom, shedding tufts of rose-colored flowers when a sudden wind came from the north every so often, sending the petals dancing like snowflakes over the green grass and into her hair. "This is a lovely garden, such a lovely place to sit," sighed the mother, barely tranquilized today, a tablet or two of Valium was all she took now, and that by doctor's orders. She reached out to stroke the younger girl's hair. The social worker was saying now that she couldn't come back anymore, that the state had assigned her another family now that this case had finished, and this would be her last visit. The girl looked up surprised, saddened, for she liked the pretty woman who seemed to make sense out of everything, who calmed her mother when she screamed about the shock treatments, about how she would never forgive the husband for allowing the doctors to mutilate her memories like that, but the social worker soothed her, saying the father didn't know, that he had believed the doctors who said electroshock therapy would help her out of the sinking depression she had fallen into that winter.

The social worker fished around in her handbag for a pack of cigarettes and said she had to leave in a half-hour. The mother merely nodded her head, watched the cherry blossoms float and fall, and the younger girl hugged her knees and wished the woman didn't have to leave, for she was the only one who understood, with whom the girl could let free her thoughts and listen to them unfurl in the quiet air of the kitchen after school. Once she told a friend about visiting her mother in the psychiatric ward, about the locked white doors and her mother so still on the narrow bed, but the friend had shrugged her shoulders, thinking perhaps of her own family — younger brothers and sisters in a shining new house — and shook her head, kept shaking her head; the friend had no words for the girl.

III.

The girl got drunk for the first time at her sister's wedding. She smiled at the bartenders, braces glinting, and they handed her deadly sweet whiskey sours without asking her age, which was obviously no more than the fourteen years she was then, on an uncommonly warm day in the middle of January, when all the ugliness of the past years slipped away into fraying memories and frightening dreams. She drank her drinks and then finished the ones forgotten or discarded on the table. She embraced her drunkenness like an old friend who could stay only a short while; she clung to it until she had to sit in her chair and hold her head, watching the dancing on the floor. Everyone drank steadily, especially her father, who usually spoke in clipped lawyer sentences and stayed mournfully sober.

On this day he drank whiskey and toasted the couple again and again, making jokes no one understood but everyone laughed at anyway, and he and her mother danced with the others, the swirling hands and chains of hora dancers, the sister and her husband sitting on stools in the center of the floor while everyone circled about them, clapping hands and grinning with elation and liquor, the mother too, glowing, with makeup she rarely wore and cherry red lipstick, the day blurring into evening with endless platters of food consumed and alcohol imbibed and dances danced again and again. The girl danced too, or tried, clasping the hands of strangers in a fumbly weave around the floor. But everyone had been drinking and nobody cared if she stumbled, for it was a wonderful thing, this wedding day, when smiles stretched across all faces, dozens of faces with teeth exposed, hands uplifted — to god or maybe to gin — in thankfulness of the opportunity, the excuse, to laugh and to drink, and the old men danced with young women, leering, some of them, and the lines of dancers snaked around the room to Israeli songs, coiling and uncoiling.

The girl sneaked into the bathroom to smoke a stolen cigarette and burned a hole in the center of her new dress without knowing it, sipping her drink on a red leather stool in front of the mirror in the great gilded ladies' room, smiling dizzily at herself, pleased and astonished by the bursts of happiness on her parents' faces, wondering where this joy had been hiding, knowing it would not last.

IV.

On Sundays, for as far back as the girl could remember, the house echoed with an unspoken anger, the unarticulated rage of the mother in her silence when she retired to bed early in the day, slamming doors, saying nothing, on this day that was supposedly a family day, the only day of the week when the father stayed home to relax, on this day her mother refused to speak cook or to smile and spent the afternoon fading into twilight alone in the huge bedroom, reading or dreaming. The girl fixed lunch for herself and her old father, cold cuts and soup, timidly knocked on the mother's door: "Mom do you want something to eat? I'll bring it upstairs," and the mother said, "No, I don't want anything," and the girl would hear a groan, her mother shifting her big body around on the blue bed where years before she had uttered those unworldly moans.

On Sundays the girl invented pretenses for leaving the house, leaving earlier and earlier in the mornings as she grew older and coming home as late as possible, for the days were like technicolor nightmares in slow motion, days she wished she could eliminate from the weekly calendar, for all other days were bearable; her mother would be gay and pour her tea after school.

This particular Sunday, in a March when the spring refused to arrive and the bitter winter to leave, the girl awoke to the sound of an early morning phone call and heard shrieks, her shrieking mother, "Oh my god, my forsaken god," and the girl in her bed under the covers gritted her teeth and knew another nightmare was beginning. The father got on the extension upstairs, saying into the telephone, "Quiet down — I can't hear what the doctor is saying," and the girl heard fragments: her isolated brother taunted by the WASP farmboys in his upstate college for being a dirty Jew, and by the chaos within him, running around the campus almost naked at three a.m. screaming, screaming his despair, and the security men cornered him and coaxed him into a car, like an animal escaped from the zoo. In the infirmary they drugged him and kept him in a white room with a locked door and these people, this doctor was calling to ask if the parents would come up and get him, to get him some professional help because something is wrong with your son, "Sir, Ma'am, something is wrong."

The girl heard her mother weeping in the kitchen while her father got ready for the drive. The mother stayed home and the girl had to flee the mother sobbing in the kitchen and the father opening the garage door. She was fifteen and acutely aware of her irresponsible flight but she fled anyway, to the home of a friend where she smoked one cigarette after another until her throat throbbed, telling this friend about this time and what the other time had been like, saying only,

"My brother flipped out," and knowing the friend would suppose it was drugs or drinking but no, it was far less tangible, unfathomable even for this friend who had known sorrow, and the friend apologized for her ignorance, saying, "I just don't know what to tell you." The girl cried a little, wiped the tears on the sleeve of her shirt and decided, pledged, that she would not be next, never, shivering with memories of locked white doors and the large stranger on the narrow bed and the zombie her mother had become with the Valium, Elavil and Milltown. Her mother had finally left the vials in her dresser drawer, only for emergencies, she said, and had stopped blaming (at least out loud) her husband for the lack of memory from electroshock; and now, the brother.

V.

Every spring the mother talked about divorcing the father and selling the house; spring was the best time for buyers because of the garden, because of the cherry blossoms speckling pink and white across the green. She'd say, "I want a divorce," and retreat to the small bedroom where she had moved when the younger girl took up residence in her sister's abandoned room, the sister who had fled, on those blue Sundays which remained the day for flight. The boy was home now, after so many psychiatric wards and doctors and diagnoses (paranoid schizophrenia, manic depression) and drugs (Lithium, Thorazine) and he stayed in his room all day and all night, eating and watching television, rarely washing or going out in the air and the girl felt poisoned by all of them, and by her guilt as well, for she was guilty of fleeing her mother weeping at the kitchen table and for never, ever visiting her brother in the wards where people screamed and sobbed. Sometimes she spent the weekends with her sister, who had flunked out of college and when she married, the father said she'd finally done one sensible thing. The girl could relax at her sister's city apartment but still she had to go home eventually, and Sundays were hard to get through everywhere.

The talk of divorce faded with the heat of summer but reappeared each spring when the cherry tree blossomed and spent its pink and white florets on the plush green lawn. The brother grew weary of his days and decided to see the country, leashed up the dog and stood by the interstate until a man in a truck pulled over and they disappeared in the West.

The girl sent her applications to faraway universities and the mother suggested she stay home the first year, only the first year, and the girl, terrified, insisted that the schools were no good in the suburbs and she had to go away (far, far away) and the father agreed, for the girl had good grades. When the acceptances came the girl picked the college that was eight hours distant by car and from where she would have to come home only once during the year.

VI.

The girl watched her parents leave from her perch on the stairwell of the dormitory, waving through the window, gripping the worn banister, feeling the staccato beat of her heart, observing other departures around her: girls anxiously hugging and kissing their parents, some of them crying, clasping their mothers in weepy embraces, and the girl wondered why anyone would view this day with sad eyes because for the girl it was a new life commencing, an opportunity to slam the door on that part of her life which had stretched like a seamless, surreal dream from that blue dawn until now, until this very moment watching her father and mother leave. They were almost out of sight now, slowly descending the hill in front of the building, the father in front, elongating the distance between himself and the mother with each step, he heading for the airport to fly back that evening, for it was Sunday night and he had to arrive at six-forty-five a.m. at the office tomorrow, as he had done every Monday through Saturday during the girl's eighteen years. The mother and father and the girl had risen early that morning and driven away in a rented car for the interminable drive over three state lines and as many changes in terrain, the house empty behind them, and the girl did not look back when they pulled out of the driveway, the father at the wheel and all of them in silence.

Now, the girl saw her mother turn and shield her eyes from the dying sun to scan the building's facade for her daughter's face — she couldn't find it — then continue her sedate walk down the hill and out of the girl's vision. The mother was leaving on the train, preferring the long ride alone to an hour on the plane with the father.

Shivering from the cold now settling upon the dormitory with the night, the girl returned to her room and looked at the bare walls, the ordinary cot and furniture mottled in the blackening twilight, and alone, she smiled at the prospect of liberation, assuming the nightmare had ended.

Nonverbal Communication
Rachel White

"Don't look so hopefully at me —
I'm only a lifeless desert,"
he seemed to say through
puffs of cigarette smoke.

"No, I see an oasis —"
my quick glance responded.
"— shimmering from
your eyes under
the afternoon sun."

Amidst traffic abuzz
on the far-from-deserted
street behind us,
he silently explained,
"It's just one of those
illusory desert tricks
to the thirsty traveler."

"Even though the glare
of your waters
nearly blinds me?"
I smirked back.

"My soul's water bottle
rests unfilled, forever
covered with sand,"
he shrugged, throwing
his burnt butt down onto
the sidewalk of 9-5 job life.

I smiled harder,
"...And crimson and yellow
seasoned petals bloom
from the dust of your earth?"

"The daffodil and poppy seed dreams
you scatter on me
will never germinate,"
he looked away in disbelief.

   "But I also hear the distant
   splashes of your soul
   swimming beautiful strokes,
   impossible to ignore."

When He Asks Why We Broke Up

Claire Mischker

I search every shadow in the museum
of our years together to see if somehow —
    before the broken windshield and lies to our parents
before kissing another girl in my bathroom
    before the closet door incident and attempted strangling
    before he bought that damn Mustang,
    before he suggested I have surgery to fix lop-sided breasts
and "get them augmented while they're in there"
      before he shaved his head
    before he stalked me to happy hour
and called me a cunt to watch my face crumple
    before he bi-polarized and voluntarily committed himself
      before he threatened that my face would be the precursor to
the bullet through his brain —
somewhere, once, we smiled.

Confessions from Outside Kenilworth, South Africa
Amber Hendricks

How her ink eyes haunt me to this day
just like the menthol smell of a perfect high
yeah, I heard her cry
she cried long and loud, too
but I had to
to keep from slipping away
she came when I was thirteen and never left
So I had to leave her
They say in town
a *doktor* say
that when you lay with her
she take away inside disease scent
and she would forget it somehow
among the smell of shit and urine
those *pikswart* eyes filled with love and then contempt
forget and only remember the alone
I felt when I birthed her in the world
on a semen stained mattress
smoke and bittersweet alcohol hung in the air
I would make her forget every time a gentleman called for me
But no
the walls closing in like a setting sun
these dying men they say
we do not want to lay with you
these men say
we pay for your daughter
I eye her
Silence at last
her graven ghost eyes alarmed lying on the pad
crying out suddenly
she knew, and will somehow forget
and see the walls
and the smell of shit and sweat
cry little one cry out

tell them how you're living
how mommy's not existing
cry little one cry loud cry out
I left her for twenty *rand* so she may not live to die
like the men who take her
she will not remember being cut or forced
to forget her one month memory and remember
what I am trying to forget
cry little one for I am unable to
cry for you or hear you
so that they will hear
and know that we
are not alone
in our tears

Pictoral
Mary Cate Hennessey

Introduction
The Cardinals made only one run and the city mourned as if we had suffered a great loss. I was dumbfounded at the degree of stupidity it took to throw yourself into a sport and obsess to the point that you find it impossible to discuss anything else. I pitied and envied ignorance at the same time; to have so few worries and to leave the racing thoughts behind in a nonchalant toss must be perhaps the happiest feeling in the world. I did a lot of baseball watching in the hospital, mainly to divert my attention from the nurses with cold hands and insincere smiles. The hands pricked my skin when they touched me; they were long, prying, and icy. I absolutely loathed the times when my blood had to be taken, the needle was almost more bearable then the psychological torture those hands seemed to cause me. The whole building caused a resentment and turmoil that I had never been able to place. Walking down those corridors made me get a vague feeling like I was walking on death row, scared and full of solitude, as if everything had ended already and I was simply witnessing my own demise. The fear made me find solace in mindless entertainment. I watched a few games, until I decided I'd probably rather wallow in my own pathetic-ness then pretend to be interested in a game I found rather ridiculous anyway. So I would sit there, staring at the television without actually seeing it, and pretend I was just too stupid to carry on a conversation with. If any other patient attempted talking to me, I'd simply get a blank expression on my face and act as if I couldn't hear them, or pretend to be mute. At times I felt like a rabbit being chased down into the burrow by a fox, and I secretly cursed God or Buddha or Allah or whoever decided to turn me into the epitome of self-loathe.

Human Anatomy and Physiology could have very well been the most idiotic class I had ever taken, and apparently I made my opinion quite clear. At the time I had expected my instructor to simply assume that I was another quiet one who bothered no one and who just didn't take up any energy seeing as how I never turned in one assignment. But, apparently, I couldn't have been more disrespectful by not jumping up and sprouting the differences between the epithelial tissues. She glared at me, and I glared back at her until she lowered her eyes and looked away. To be honest, I hated attention in the worst way, especially staring; it made me nervous and anxious, like they were somehow prying into me and attempting to read my thoughts, and know me. I didn't like the idea of being known. I guess people stared because, I figured, I was a stinking, ugly, despicable person who just happened to have come out cursing instead of crying.

I started my great quest at finding fault in everything early, and I had only one friend whom I tolerated named Amelia May. I felt just horrid for a person with a name like Amelia May, and she was loud and happy as I was quiet and spiteful. She had an outspoken manner that would usually anger me, but for some reason my surly disposition seemed to fit like a puzzle with her stupid one. Although she was obnoxious, at times she had the ability to be a good friend. She was tolerable, that's most likely the extent of my liking for her. She came from Nevada and looking at her hair was like looking at a vial of blood in the sunlight; slightly golden but mostly composed of an odd mixture of red and black.

There was a rustling in the distance, and I was instantly irritated at the prospect of my hiding spot being revealed. I often sat in the woods, on this log, in the seclusion of the woodland, and like a stone gargoyle, remained motionless and prophetical, entrapped by my own thoughts.

"Maria?"

"What?" looking for the speaker, irritated. God, here comes Amelia.

"Oh hell, how in the hell did you find it and what in the hell do you want?"

"What I want is for you to come to a banquet with me."

She ignored my first question, and was now angry for being yelled at.

"Why are you going to a banquet?"

"Valedictorian"

"Who's Valedictorian?"

"I am. It's also honoring grade point averages over 4.0"

"That doesn't mean I have to go."

"But I want you to, and it's a free meal."

She looked at me solidly. I didn't want to go.

"I can get a free meal at home."

She looked disappointed.

"I would just like it if you came-if you change your mind it's at the Demage, it's in the middle of the city. You know what I'm talking about, the huge old building? It's gigantic and has the ol-"

"I know what you're talking about". Fucking Idiot.

"Alright-Jesus calm down. Anyway, they'll be opening the doors around 7:30; it's in the banquet hall. Easy to find, straight ahead, basically."

"I'll think about it," I lied.

I most certainly wouldn't think about going to anything like that. I had no intention of sitting through a ridiculous meal that had absolutely no true meaning, no true accomplishments behind it. I was hungry though, and it was at a quite prestigious hotel-the food would most likely be of higher quality then a sandwich with bread that is rock hard. My mother wouldn't be back from work for hours, and she would come home and drink herself to sleep, so if I didn't make something, I didn't eat. I felt so tired and so lethargic that I wanted to curl up in a ball in the safety of the earth and moss and the fragrance of soil, and weep until I hurt. I, with the strength of a baby, started walking to the edge of the clearing to tread back to the house that I grew up in but, wasn't attached. I would go, I needed something in my stomach. I looked at my watch and realized it was already 6:42. I turned around and headed toward the hotel, until I the condition of my clothes. I went to change.

When I went into the house I trudged up the stairs, feeling as if my ankles were bound together by shackles, and stared blankly at my wardrobe, but not really seeing it. I tossed a nice shirt and an even nicer skirt on to the old quilt, and chose a pair of shoes I hadn't worn since my sister's funeral. I suppose I should feel guilty for not caring or mourning her, but I never felt the attachments sisters should share; the attachments were completely nonexistent. I just simply never formed an opinion about her, which in turn never left room for affection.

I sat on the old quilt and brushed my hair over and over again until my scalp was sore, delaying. The last thing I wanted to do was go to a ceremonious event that I was so obviously excluded from, and I felt forced, like a kicked dog. I was just so hungry. I sat with the brush dangling from my limp hand until I finally got the courage to unlock the door and step out into the hallway light, blinding and infested with faux happiness and disgusting sunlight. I headed toward the hotel to support a friend I wasn't particularly fond of and support an achievement I didn't give a damn about.

Home

When I arrived at home, I once more made the trip up the stairs in shackles, and I lay in bed for hours not sleeping at all. I suppose I should have humored her and fed her an ego boost, but to be perfectly honest, I didn't have a great deal of respect for any Valedictorian. It wasn't that I didn't respect them as a person, but it doesn't necessarily mean you're intelligent, it just means you're a very good worker. I respected the ability to be able to accomplish the hard working attribute, but as for their intelligence? I have no proof they're above average. It's just a title with no meaning other then to brag to each other how they surpassed societal standards. It made me empathize with some of those other lifeless beings I see wandering around school. As if the conformity and standards that must be met has crushed them for the last time, they're simply empty, simply gone, and simply dead. I see these people, these people who are remarkable and intelligent, being inflicted with one strike after the other, all because they dared to utter words of difference. These so called intelligent people at that school are the ones that are first to go in the world, they don't know intelligence out of structure. They're also the first to go in a school shooting. I surprised myself that I felt a deep sadness about those other people, usually I'm not bothered by anyone's suffering, but perhaps I connected with them. Finally when I got tired of lying lethargically, I wrapped myself in a blanket, made a cup of tea, and sat in a gigantic chair, looking out the window until the sun rose like a giant orange and the clouds parted with an unmistakable compliance.

School

Going to school with these people was like being a prisoner with the noose already tied. The more I would have to slump through the building, the tighter the noose would get, and one day, someone would push me off the plank and I would dangle as a shadow who once knew where the world would go. Every day seemed to shove me deeper and deeper into depression and the walls were trembling, any more weight and they would cave. If anyone would be at fault it would most likely be myself, perhaps I did something in previous life that I was paying for now. The voices were consistent too.

At a point, I was just attempting to decipher reality from my mind, so many times I ignored people, not to be purposely rude, but because I was completely sure that it was my mind playing tricks again. Often, I would hear screaming or cursing and my head would start swimming and I felt as if I was caught in a sandstorm, blinded, confused, and miserable. Sometimes, they would frighten me and draw me back from what was real. Johnny visited me sometimes, he informed me that the government had me planned as a test dummy, planned as a toy. He also explained that they wear green, so avoid completely anyone wearing the universal color. Of course I cut up and burned every article of clothing in my closet with even a speck of green; I feared it would attract them. But then again, I've always had an overactive imagination. I was just creative, and that was justification enough-when I was rational. At times of irrationality, the talking led to thinking, and I believed them. Especially Johnny, he could make me believe anything. He led me to the truth, he held my hand and told me what to watch for, who to avoid. There was a camera in the sea-colored gem of my silver ring I picked up at the drug store for a dollar-fifty. The book on my shelf was written for the simple reason to confuse me and leave an open portal into my mind for even a split second. The thoughts kept me awake at night staring at the patterned ceiling like an invalid until my eyes would become heavy and I could grasp sleep. It mainly depended on my degree of rationality at the time.

I had tried to make myself as least noticeable as possible while I walked through the hallways; I had gotten in the habit of staring at the patterned linoleum tiles and watching them swim and dance. They would form into almost fractal like shapes, but moving and swirling a deaf man's music. I would see all the identical females giggling and running their fingers through long, bleached hair, and I would fill with humor and pity. I had always wanted to ask them if ignorance really is bliss. Most of them were brunettes or redheads to begin with, but apparently beauty now lies behind the bottle of peroxide. Their shoes were identical and their clothes were the same shades of pink and brown and beige. It was impossible to tell them apart.

"Miss Langwerth." I snapped up.

"What?"

"Can you show us how to figure the proof?"

No, I couldn't enlighten them with my knowledge of geometry, a knowledge that wasn't ever there nor would ever be there.

"Uh, yeah." I walked up to the board feeling as if I was being dragged by a leash, and picked up a black marker. It gave me a headache just by inhaling the chemical, sour smell, and I started at the numbers and watched them swarm and spin like a tiny river of the number scale.

"I don't exactly understand how to do it." I admitted, really not caring.

"Then I suggest you start paying attention."

"I pay attention just fine, I just don't adapt well to some teaching styles."

"Talk to me later."

And thus he continued his feeble attempt to enlighten us with the power of geometry. So I sat there day after day and pretended to listen and pretended to make notes all the while writing incoherent scribbles and lines of poetry in the margins of notebook paper. I failed the tests, didn't do work, and, as a result, received another F, a letter which had a tendency to pop up quite often. I wasn't lazy, I was confused. I was no longer able to weed through my thoughts to develop a method that would work so I could concentrate. Another class I particularly struggled with was Biology. I enjoyed thoroughly learning about animals and how they work, how they survive, how they cope, but cells and genes lost me every time. I sat there while Mrs. Speil mumbled on and on about XX and XY and Down syndrome and other birth defects. I was scared honestly, because the prospect of all these things that could go wrong made me start turning into a true hypochondriac, I would find symptoms of all these birth defects in myself until I realized that both my mother and I would have realized years back if, in fact, I was defected at birth.

I attempted once more to listen wave of information until I felt my brain melting. It melted into a hot, stringy mess that ran down my back and puddled at my chair. There must be a hole in the back of my skull, I'll go to the doctor sooner or later.

Home

I had been robbed of the will to live and I just wanted it back. I vomited.

Truth

The hospital for Behavior Health had just hired a new orderly with blonde hair and white teeth named Janet. Her fingernails were painted spikes and she popped her gum so loudly that she could be heard down the echoing hallway yards away. The day doctor was an old man with green eyes and a kindly face decorated with soft wrinkles of age, his moustache white with specks of black peeking through. His hair was thinning and we wore the expression of a man who had seen too much too soon and had never found an answer. He looked at the new orderly with disdain and sadness, she wouldn't care for the patients with the compassion they needed.

The doctor led the new orderly around the ward introducing her to the patients' information and gave a summary and description of each case. He explained in detail the medication dosage and the importance of accuracy.

"Agnes Grett, 29 year old female with Multiple Personality Disorder. Diabetic, she needs meals ordered specially. Deborah Tate, she's 35, we think she has a case of schizophrenia, but it's hard to diagnose, she hasn't been here long enough and not enough tests have been ordered. We have her on a few anti-psychotics and mood stabilizers. Rita Villa. She's 47, an extreme case of Manic Depression; she's been assigned a number of medications, here's her chart sheet."

He continued to introduce her to the patients through closed doors, but skipped one. When she inquired about it, he looked at her with worry.

"That's a case we've assigned a specialist to; you won't have any responsibilities regarding that one.

She's a 17-year-old female who suffers from extreme delusions, it's plausible that she doesn't even realize she's being hospitalized, but, ironically, the only time she's left a hospital in the last 12 years is when she's been transferred to more intensive care. She watches TV sometimes, but doesn't move, doesn't speak."

Janet popped her gum again, and asked with apparent apathy, "What kind of delusions?"

"We aren't exactly sure, hence the reason it's so difficult to diagnose her."

He looked discouraged, as if the impossibility of this case saddened him.

"So, I don't do nothin' with her?"

"No, she isn't your responsibility. It's her nurse's."

Janet looked bored, and picked dirt from under those long fingernails. She scanned the room for a clock, then looked back at him.

"What do you think is wrong with her?"

"We have absolutely no way of telling that, the only words she's spoken in the last two years was to her nurse. Something about baseball and cold hands."

He cracked the door and instantly called for her nurse.

"Amelia, Maria threw up again, let's get her cleaned up."

Someone's Baby
Aysha Davis

I know now the truth
in patience is a virtue.
I only hope that I can keep that patience.
I was almost pregnant.
But I am not
my family wouldn't like it
Terrance wouldn't have said it was his
or want the baby for that matter.
He told me that I wasn't anything to him once we got back in school
no matter how much he tries to blame it on the three bags of weed he
smoked tries to say that he doesn't remember
I have a feeling that he knows
a little bit about what happened.
That was way before my mom even suspected
I might be pregnant.
My feelings were crushed from that moment at school
where it seems that all reality had faded away into completely
nothing.
I really had cared for him
he acted like he didn't give a rat's ass.
I had given him my virginity
my innocence
essentially the first part of my womanhood.
After that I was put on birth control pills
My parents said they didn't want to be grandparents.
I was someone's baby
'til I almost had someone's baby.

Come and Be Black for Me
Ethel Morgan Smith

I am the only African-American professor in my university department of fifty-odd faculty members. I reside in a world that is predominately white and male; a land grant, research state university with twenty-something thousand students, about 5% of whom are African Americans. And it is only during February, Black History Month, that everyone is looking for me, or rather, anyone who can come and be black for them.

Those six weeks begin after the holiday season. I come into my office early to work through my mail. My mailbox is overstuffed. Four other mail baskets have been placed on top of our regular mailboxes for me. I make two trips downstairs to the main office to collect it all. Most of the mail will be requests for me to represent "my people" for some worthwhile organization during the month of February and February only. Sometimes the tone is pleasant. I generally accept those. Most often the tone is not pleasant.

In my office I begin the process of grouping my mail into categories of "accept for sure," "decline for sure," "maybe," and "I'll get back to you." The first correspondence to go into the recycling bin is letters that point out (if not in so many words) that their tax dollars pay my salary and they rightfully deserve a piece of me and the least I can do, these letters imply, is come and be black for them. The requests that conflict with events that I must attend because it's part of my job are the next to go into the bin. If there aren't too many of those requests, I write notes expressing my regrets.

My telephone rings. A pleasant woman from the Arts Council needs someone to attend her luncheon/book club meeting at her house. One of my colleagues, who I haven't had the pleasure of meeting, gave her my telephone number. Her group is thinking of including a black writer on their reading list next year. She knows that I teach on Tuesdays and Thursdays. Wednesday is the day of the luncheon. I thank her and accept the pleasant invitation. It doesn't conflict with my calendar. I can be black that Wednesday.

The telephone rings again. A student from last semester wants to talk to me about her grade. I tell her my office hours, and thank her for calling.

Someone knocks on my door. A white male graduate student wants me to be a member of his thesis committee. A portion of his writing will focus on the impact of contemporary African-American women authors on American literature. He's a good student. I accept and thank him for thinking of me. I want to know when I can expect some of his work so that I can begin reading.

Someone knocks on my door again. An African-American female can't decide if she's angry with me or not. Last semester I thought she was being self-righteous (like I think many students can be) when she screamed at me in class for selecting a novel whose protagonist, a black man, was married to a white woman.
I blew up at her in class and asked her who made her God of Blackness? I don't think I apologized to her. She wants to talk about what do with the rest of her life. I suggest improving her grades. She leaves before I can thank her for coming.

The telephone rings. Someone is soliciting money for the United Way. I tell her that I gave already.

My mail is dwindling. Two more baskets. I start a pile of work for photocopying. In this stack of mail three students have asked me to write letters of recommendation for graduate school, and five more organizations have submitted requests for me to come (and be black). I am getting hungry, but it's too much trouble to go out in the rain for lunch. I take a break and eat an apple and two rice cakes. I can't find any more food in my office. I continue to sort my mail. Two rejection letters for two of my short stories are hidden in junk mail. I am disappointed. I'll decide what to do later.

The telephone rings again. Wrong number.

Someone knocks on my door. It's two white students, male and female from last semester's African-American literature class. They (well, *he*, since the male speaks for the female) liked my class and learned a lot, but thought they should offer me some advice for the future so that my classes would be even better. He tells me that the black kids, all four of them, wanted to speak too much when I asked for comments or specific questions about the text. I remind them that everyone was given ample opportunity to speak. The student tells me that it was also annoying that "they" always sat together. I point out that all forty of the white students sat together too. They leave before I can thank them for coming.

Someone knocks on my door. It's a colleague whose office is down the hall. He calls himself a folklorist. He too wants me to come and be black for his group even if it's in the month of March. He says he's sensitive to how I get exploited during Black History Month, but I should be thankful. I could be like him and never get exploited. I thank him but decline.

Two years ago, when I was new I accepted one of his offers. He coordinates one of the oldest conferences sponsored by the University. My folklorist colleague telephoned me at home that summer to extend an invitation to me to moderate the panel on "The African-American Experience in Film and Literature."

I go to the bathroom. Then I go downstairs to make photocopies and drop off some mail. The staff gives me candy. I'm glad; my rice cake and apple lunch has left me hungry. After the candy I go back to my office and drink a bottle of water.

The telephone rings. The bookstore tells me that two of my required texts are out of print, but due to be re-released next semester. I tell her that I'll get back with substitutes. I'll have to rethink my syllabus. When I first started teaching African-American literature I would begin my classes by telling the students how I couldn't get at least two of the required texts every semester. I asked what they thought about that. I stopped when students wrote on my evaluations that they wished I'd select books that they could get without problems. It was part of my job to do so. They thought that I should take some responsibility.

A week after my folklorist colleague called to invite me to participate in his conference, he telephoned again. This time he wanted to point out exactly what my job was—I was to keep time for the presenters so that the conference would run according to schedule. And I was to be lively. He said the real work, of the conference would be done by the scholars who were actually presenting papers.

Someone knocks on my door. A white male with a long red ponytail wants to bow to me for the rest of his natural life. I gave him a copy of Toni Morrison's *Sula* semester before last. Since then he has read all of Morrison's novels. I tell him he has discovered one of America's greatest writers. I like him now that he knows I'll only discuss literature with him. I thank him for coming.

Someone knocks on my door. An African-American female wants to know why I always pick novels that make the "brothers" look bad, books like Alice Walker's *Third Life of Grange Copeland*. I tell her that I'm sure Ms. Walker didn't have her "brothers" in mind when she wrote the novel. I thank her for coming by.

My telephone rings. Another request to come and speak. I decline. It's a conflict.

I file some of my papers. I find a box of old raisins. I eat them anyway and drink another bottle of water.

The panel I moderated for my folklorist colleague had an active audience of ten members hailing from California, Connecticut, New Mexico, Tennessee, Vermont, and, Virginia. Three presenters were scheduled to read papers. One presented. Two were absent. My colleague wasn't present after he'd promised that he'd be there because the conference was really taking a chance by including a panel on "my people." The one presenter's paper was about playing the "dozens" in the film White Men Can't Jump. The paper was titled—"French Toast and Jam: New Images of the 'Dozens.'"

Someone knocks on my door. A friendly colleague and I exchange holiday stories, and gossip about the latest divorce in the department.

Someone knocks on my door. Two African-American male

students from last semester tell me that they didn't appreciate me calling "Brother Mike" a criminal in class last semester. I point out that technically Mike Tyson is a criminal. I thank them for dropping by.

The telephone rings. The audiovisual division of the library has just received *Roots-The Next Generation*. I could expect the original *Roots* any day now. I thank the caller.

As moderator I had to make the panel work with one presenter whose paper was based on a film I hadn't seen. I introduced myself and talked about the kind of issues I encountered in my classes on African-American literature. I talked about texts and how students responded to them. I then asked each person to introduce him/herself, and speak about their interest in the subject. A retired literature professor from Virginia wanted me to know that he was glad to be there and happy that I was moderating the panel. He said he didn't have a racist bone in his body. He'd climbed mountains with pure Africans and was proud to call them friends. I welcomed him to our university and thanked him for taking part in the conference.

Someone knocks on my door. It's another colleague, white male who's fascinated with Africa and wants me to know that if I have any interest in seeing my homeland, he's the man to help get me there. I tell him that Alabama is my homeland. He leaves before I can thank him for coming.

The telephone rings. One of the staff members wants to know which graduate faculty committee council I'll be willing to serve on. I'd forgotten to give her my form. I apologize and ask which committee met the least during the term. She tells me, and I agree to serve on that committee.

Someone knocks on my door. A white female returns books of poetry by Gwendolyn Brooks, Lucille Clifton and Nikki Giovanni. She enjoyed them and wants to borrow more. I point to the poetry section of my library. We exchange a few pleasantries. She thanks me and leaves.

The audience blasted the presenter for using the film White Men Can't

Jump to make her point. Only one member of the audience had seen this film. They were sure that there were more sophisticated ways of her presenting scholarship. They weren't sure that a film called White Men Can't Jump was scholarly enough. I thought I did a good job of not allowing everyone to attack her at the same time.

Someone knocks on my door. An African-American female from the semester before last wants me to write a letter of recommendation for her. She's applying for a job. I ask if she has considered graduate school. She says not now. She is tired of school. She wants to live in a city. I ask her to drop off her resume and addresses of places to send a letter. I wish her well.

My telephone rings. Another student from last semester didn't receive a grade. I check my record and tell the student that I turned in a grade, but if she wants me to call records and admissions I'd be happy to do so. She'll get back to me after she speaks with her adviser.

Someone knocks on my door. A white male student wants me to write a letter of recommendation. I point out to him that he received a C- in my class. He tells me that was the best grade he received. I ask him what he wants me to say in my letter. He thanks me and leaves.

In my mail there are five other requests for me to come and speak. I check my calendar. I accept two. I stack all of the textbook catalogues in a pile.

I go to the bathroom and wash my face with cold water.

Someone knocks on my door. An African-American male student wants to know why I taught a book like *Giovanni's Room*. I tell him that James Baldwin is one of the most important writers of our time, and that I know of no other book written with more dignity and honesty. The student tells me teaching books about homosexuality should be against the law. I tell him we're all better for reading *Giovanni's Room*. He leaves before I can thank him for coming.

The presenter, close to tears, told the audience that she's really an apple — white on the inside and red on the outside — Native American. The only reason she was working in African-American literature was because Native American literature was too painful for her. The audience was silent. The retired professor from Virginia shook his head. I spoke longer than I should have about the main problem I have with teaching African-American literature, students find it difficult to place texts in a historical context. The presenter excused herself. The audience and I continued to talk about history and African-American literature.

Someone knocks on my door. A white male, wants a list of the books I'll be teaching in the spring. He tells me that everyone in his family is racist and this is the first opportunity he has to learn about blacks. I tell him I'm glad he's learning. I give him the list and thank him for coming.

Someone knocks on my door. An African-American female from last year who owes me a paper wants me to know that she's happy that I am on the faculty. She identifies with me since I embrace feminism and remain a "real sister." I tell her the way I dress and wear my hair is purely fashion. I want to know when I can expect her paper. She says soon and leaves before I can thank her for coming.

Someone knocks on my door. My chair wants me to be part of a new task force on diversity. I accept and thank him for thinking of me.

I have to get home. It's the beginning of "come and be black for me" season, and I need my rest.

The Only Black Girl
Roxi Trapp-Dukes

Now, I'm not tryin' to be silly, but let's face it, the same way that a white person may tend to get uncomfortable when they are the only one in a sea full of black faces, the same goes for the other side. What black person you know want to be around a whole bunch of whities. The whole bunch that's too many you know. I don't! And don't get me wrong, just like they got tokens, shit, I got a pocket full of change. I got more white friends than most, trust me. I mean, I was always that black girl. Always the only one. And always bad, smart I mean. Bad as shit. And versatile enough not to be isolated. Sometimes they were cool with that, but when they weren't, they weren't. I don't know what it was about the way I was raised, but for a long time I wasn't afraid of anything but some bullshit scary movie I'd seen in after school, but I mean even being the only black girl, or one of say six black kids I wasn't afraid you know. I'm telling you, the first time I came in contact with "the world's craziness" was when this little toothpick lookin' white boy in school called me a nigger and teacher told me I should be proud of it. And my dumb ass went along with that shit. Until, I went home and told my mama, and she beat my ass for being so stupid, while reading the definition of the word nigger to me out of the dictionary, which I had to furthermore write 100 times.

So, of course you could see how my comfort within these white institutions where I was attaining [obtaining] the supposed "best" education began to diminish with one word, manifested to describe my people..."A Negro, or a member of any dark skinned race — usually taken to be offensive, a member of a socially disadvantaged class of persons," According to Webster, but more accurately as my teacher had seen it, a nigger, you know the wild black beasts that built our country. And for the first time this feeling started to well inside me, you know, I mean all black or minority people have had to feel this at least once, when you see racism for the first time and feel it. And yeah, you get mad; you get so mad that you really do hate all white people. 'Cause it just seems SO WRONG, and SO STUPID! And you hate that even in the midst of this first feeling you're committing the same wrong. So needless to say, after this incident, I had some understanding to do, about how to maneuver you know, forgivingly, but not forgetfully. And I really thought I had mastered it, a crazy concept at 15, until I'm coming out of the shower at my boarding arts school where once again I'm one out of two, in my whole graduating class, and this bouncy blonde greets me at the door. She stops, right, and she's just staring, you know mouth open, lookin' real stupid. Like in a trance or some shit, and I'm wandering like what the fuck?

Like okay, I just got out the shower... and this dummy had the nerve to say, "Wow, you take a lot of showers, I didn't know black people could take that many showers. I always thought it did something funny to your hair." And suddenly my vision got blurry, and I got dizzy, and like a recording I started to hear all the dumb shit that some cracker had said to me....All the can I touch your hairs', how does it do that, all the I like hip hop, ya know my mom was a hippie, all the your soooo cools, and the you speak so wells, and all the excuse me mam is there something your looking fors when you know I'm just browsing like all the other muthafuckas in that store, and trust me that shit still happens, all of that shit. And I wanted to fuckin' explode you know, I wanted to say does you hair do something funny? No bitch, it gets wet! I wanted to say NO! Just stop. Stop. Stop all the pretentious bullshit that you do for yourselves. Stop thinking you have nothing to do with the problem cause it was just your people, you didn't actually enslave anybody. All the "times have changed" bullshit, when it still takes the federal government a week to supply aid to thousands of poor dying black people.

Just stop, and deal with your guilt. I mean I wanted to hold her up to the face of time and force her to be the representative of her entire race, right! But I couldn't, so I didn't and I'm safe.

Starfish — 2
Ching-In Chen

I don't want to remember
the secrets and half-truths I composed for my family
who said nothing

how I waited nights for you to come home
from driving all night to make rent
for businessmen who thought you didn't understand English
how many insults you swallowed

how every place reminded you of home
a place you ran away from
and migrated back to nightly
a location existing on your tongue
in spice and song

how you decided to hurt me
you calculated how much pain I could withstand
you couldn't tell your family
you were in love with a woman
whose lifelines and ancestors did not match yours
and you couldn't tell me

and then how you stopped talking to me
days when words lived in your cheekbone and ridges of your eyes
and how desperately I wanted to grab them
seize them
breathe them
hold you in my mouth
those days when I talked to no one
and slept in silent enclosed spaces

the words wouldn't spill out
and grew root at the corner of your mouth
how my words formed stairs
then mountains
until whole poems grew from our silences
this poetry you wouldn't listen to
because you knew it was glazed with pain

how I left because our hearts held vacant spaces

how I wondered about this numb foreign object called my heart
whether I would miss it if it were

torn out
lost
replaced

Beautiful Passions
Alicia M. Greene

BEAUTIFUL PASSIONS
SO LONG I HAVE SUPPRESSED
ALONG THE BUSSOMS OF MY BREAST.

LOVE HAS NEVER TASTED SO SWEET
LIKE THE BATTLES OF DEFEAT.

ALTHOUGH THE STORMS ARE STRETUROUS THAN EVER I
WILL
CONTINUE TO LOVE THEE FOREVER SOME MAY THINK THIS
FEELING IS A CURSE BUT MY LOVE, THEE I NURSE.

MY HEART HAS NEVER FELT SO FREE
SINCE THAT DAY YOU CAME TO ME
EVEN IN DEATH YOU STILL REMAIN
IN THE CHAMBERS OF MY DOMAIN.

MY HEART BEATS FOR YOU EACH PASSING DAY
REMINDING ME OF WHEN YOU WENT AWAY

BEAUTIFUL PASSIONS SO LONG I HAVE SUPPRESSED
ALONG THE BUSSOMS OF MY BREAST

OUR PASSIONS IGNITE FAR GREATER THAN THE HEAT
LIKE MANY BATTLES FOUGHT IN THE STREET.

YOU ARE DEVOTED TO YOUR LAND
AS I DREAM OF HAVING YOUR HAND
OH! HOW YOU HAVE CHANGED MY LIFE,
I'D BE HONORED TO BE YOUR WIFE.

MY HEART HAS NEVER FELT SO FREE
SINCE THE DAY YOU CAME TO ME
EVEN IN DEATH YOU STILL REMAIN

IN THE CHAMBERS OF MY DOMAIN.

BEAUTIFUL PASSIONS SO LONG I HAVE SUPPRESSED
ALONG THE BUSSOMS OF MY BREAST

MY BRAVE WARRIOR, YOUR WOUNDS AREN'T AS DEEP AS
MINE
FOR I HAVE WITHSTOOD THE HANDS OF TIME.
WATCHING, WAITING FOR YOUR RETURN.
EVERY MOMENT THERE WAS CONCERN.
HOW CAN I EVER THINK OF FINDING ANOTHER
WHEN I HAVE LOST MY ONE TRUE LOVER.
I CAN NO LONGER SEE HIS FACE
OR FEEL HIS WARM TENDER EMBRACE.

MY LOVE, MY HOPE, MY HEART, MY GLORY
THERE IS NO END TO OUR LOVE STORY

BEAUTIFUL PASSIONS SO LONG I HAVE SUPPRESSED
ALONG THE BUSSOMS OF MY BREAST

MY HEART HAS NEVER FELT SO FREE
SINCE THE DAY YOU CAME TO ME
EVEN IN DEATH YOU STILL REMAIN
IN THE CHAMBERS OF MY HEARTS DOMAIN

Choosing the Path to Healing
Christine McFarlane

The Canadian government had a practice or removing large numbers of Native children from their families. These children were then adopted by white middle-class families. This occurred through most of the 60's, 70's and early 80's, and was commonly known as the "Sixties Scoop." Under the Indian Act, this led to interracial adoptions of which the government didn't consider the consequences.

When an historic apology was issued by former Indian Affairs Minister Jane Stewart to the First Nations people of Canada on January 8, 1998, she singled out native residential schools as the most reprehensible example of Canada's degrading and paternalistic Indian policies. She did not apologize for the equally assimilationist strategy that followed: the widespread adoption of Aboriginal children out to non-native families.

I was a part of that "Scoop," and this is what happened to me. At six months I was taken from my biological parents, along with my other siblings and put into a foster care group home. At the time, the Child Services in Winnipeg felt that my parents were unfit to raise children. My biological father was a very jealous man, and abused my mother. He was also in and out of jail for breaking and entry. My mother was an alcoholic.

This government sanctioned abduction of First Nations children from their families had many repercussions. When adopted into a different culture, where you are not allowed to practice your traditions or speak your language, you grow up with a sense of lost identity and a insecurity that something about your background is wrong. I am now finding out that I am not alone in fighting the insecurity and the pain of being separated from my biological family. There is an entire generation of Native children who have lost their legacy, culture, language and sense of identity.

My biological sister and I were adopted together by a Scottish white family in the province of Ontario. There was emotional, physical and spiritual abuse. The abuse started shortly after my sister and I began school. It was at this time, that I realized how different I really was. I was a nonentity to them. I was locked in my room on a daily basis, with a deadbolt on the door and an alarm that went off as soon as I would touch the doorknob. Food was withheld from me, and I would get beaten at the slightest provocation. To my adoptive parent's three sons, I was just a shadow in the background. The only reprieve I got was when I was at school. This is where I learned to pour myself into books and write. The attention I received was from teachers. I believe they knew something was wrong, but could not really do anything because I refused to talk about what was happening to me. If I came to school with any marks on my body, I had the ready remark that I had fallen or bumped into something.

At the age of ten, I was given up by my adoptive parents. They kept my sister and their sons. Their reasoning for giving me up was that I was not wanted. I had to grow up really fast. I was the youngest in the group home that I was brought to. I went through a lot of emotional anguish, believing that life wasn't worth living, if even my parents didn't want me. I still remember going to court and hearing my adoptive father say that I was not wanted. Shortly afterwards, I became a Crown Ward of the Roman Catholic Children's Aid Society. I lived in the group home for one year, and then went through three different foster homes. I did not get out of Children's Aid until I was nineteen years old.

At the age of 13, I started high school, and that is when my eating disorder started. At the time I had been placed in a new foster home outside of the city. Someone had commented that I was fat. I internalized that more than anything else. I slowly cut back on foods, until I reached a point that I would only touch certain things. My foster parents at the time didn't understand what was going on with me. At the suggestion of my social worker from the Children's Aid Society, I had to go to a family doctor every week. While at these appointments, I had to be weighed and I had to show a food diary. I thought that I had the doctor fooled when it came to writing down my food intake, but he wasn't. I had started to lie about my intake because I didn't feel comfortable going to this doctor. Yet, inside me I couldn't stop the behavior of not wanting to eat.

At the age of seventeen, I moved back to the city to attend college. I was away from the friends I made, and the only foster parents who had given me a sense of stability. My mental health began to falter. I was still suffering from my eating disorder, but with the shift from being around a stable environment to an environment of living independently, things started to take a toll on me. I went from being protected from seeing my adoptive father to all of a sudden having him in my life again. The very first day that I moved back to the city, there was a letter from him waiting for me.

I started going through a lot of intense anger and a lot of self destruction. Issues that had been festering inside of me for years had begun to start haunting me. I self-harmed in a lot of ways. I would take pills to numb myself, use knives and scissors to cut myself, and attempted suicide. Even though the cuts I made on myself were superficial, it was a way to get that pain I was feeling outside of me. At the age of nineteen, I ended up in the hospital for the first time. I spent much of my twenties in and out of the hospital for psychiatric reasons. I was put on medication to help me through the depression and anxiety I was suffering from. I am still struggling with disordered eating. I went from being extremely underweight to being overweight. Going from one extreme to the other is not healthy. I am struggling with taking the weight off, without going too far and getting unhealthy again.

Even with all my difficulties, part of finding out who I was, was doing a search for my biological parents. This was my legacy. I met my biological mother in 2002: when I made a bus trip out to Winnipeg and was introduced to her. I found out from her that my biological father was dead. He was murdered on December 18, 1990. Both of my parents had a rough life. I felt really sad that my father's life had ended the way that it did. I will miss never finding out more about him. Spending most of my life without the influence of a mother, I had grand expectations of what my mother should be like. When I found that she didn't fit these expectations, I found myself distancing myself from her, until finally I stopped contact with her. I know now that wasn't fair of me. What happened to our family was not her fault.

Along with my search for my biological parents, I found that I had a rather extensive family out West. I went from having really no family to having a number of people in my life. I don't have regular contact with them, but knowing they are out there is in a way comforting. Knowing they are there makes me feel less alone.

I have struggled to have a relationship with my adoptive father. Since last July, I stopped contact with him, when I realized that it was a relationship that was unhealthy. He refused to acknowledge his part in the abuse that went on in his family and with his first wife and that left me feeling empty.

I felt that I always needed his approval for things, and that if I didn't live up to his expectations, he would withdraw his support from me. Having no contact with my adoptive father has lifted a weight off of my shoulders.

My adoptive father has custody of my biological sister's youngest daughter. I worry that she won't understand why I stopped contact. Stopping contact has also meant that I can't be in touch with her. I am hoping that as she gets older, she will know where to turn to, if she should want to find me.

My sister has had a rough life too. She doesn't have custody of either of her kids Her oldest daughter lives with her father and his new wife. She also has a new little sister. I have found that my love for these kids has increased tenfold. I try to be as constant as I can, because I know that that would have been something I would have wanted at their age. I know that, by missing out on contact with others at that age, it made me feel empty inside.

Changing the legacy of my family is important to me. I still have a long way to go in my path to healing, but it is in me to start things anew.

Sleep Well
Anonymous

Tonight all I can feel
is his hands [between my legs]
Palms pressing [outward]
As though he is praying [backwards]
Kneeling in front of my
[naked] body.
And then it shifts
The camera blurs as the scene changes
A shadow [man]
Over my bed
Not now [Daddy], I'm trying to sleep
But his hands are covering [my mouth]
My voice [inverted]
My eyes fixed [robotically]
On the seam where wall meets ceiling
They hold the darkness [in]
But I can still see
My legs [bent] in front of me
[and him]
My toes have become [permanently] curled
Even though this is not the first [night]
That I will try [to forget]
I can feel an instant
Of pain with each push
And then he is walking [out the door]
Removing the towel
That carries the blood [he] took from
        [me].
Sleep well, pumpkin.

Defenses
Laura Still

Lie in the bed you made
my stepmother would say
(though she was a restless sleeper,
forever pulling her sheets loose
in spite of hospital corners
she tucked in tight every morning).
I know what you are! she spat;
knowledge soured her tongue.
The seed of my mother's unfaithfulness
produced a bitter herb that flowered
in darkness — too early I felt
the rising of shadow, knew
drop to the ground, seek cover,
melt into the underbrush. Shrapnel
picked up in those early skirmishes
sometimes erupts through my skin
in spite of careful layering of scar
and callous grown to keep it in.
Beneath the surface the covert war
continues undeclared; I fight on,
relying on guerrilla tactics.

The Seasons of My Deceit

Jessica W. Giles

SPRINGTIME, 1998

Shannon awoke alone in the apartment and wondered if it all really happened. She has been here before, it seems, in another life. When things made sense. When people were predictable. The sun is low in the sky, and it pierces the windowpane, leaving the wall behind her bathed in an orangey glow. This morning, the sun shining in the window is not her sun. Not any sun she has ever known.

I've gone out for a run, the note said. But if not for the dull pounding behind her eyes, the bruises on her wrists and thighs, the blood caked on her lip, the uneasiness under her skin, she might have believed that things were so innocent.

She eyes the key that she knows to be above the doorframe, wondering how long she has before he returns. And what might happen if he came back to find her gone.

They had spent the evening at a martini bar, surrounded by other young urban professionals yearning to escape. There were drinks and drinks and more drinks. Lights dancing, smiles jumping, drifting, fluttering. The street felt cool and damp, a nice place to rest her head. A call, a shout, laughter, coming closer now, and songs seem to ring out from all around. She is lifted, carried in his arms, and she remembers thinking that he is strong, happy, brilliant. Her friends giggle and run in circles around them. And then they are gone.

Now, entering his building, the stairs seem endless, mocking her. Then she is inside the apartment, thinking a glass of water would be nice. It is a small closet of a room, like so many others downtown. You can sit on the toilet and watch dinner being made. The bed is in the living room which is somehow part of the entryway. And this reminds her of songs sung in summertimes past. *And the green grass grew all around all around and the green grass grew all around.* And there is no way out. There is nowhere to run.

The radiator hums and like the ones she remembers from her childhood it is white and you get the impression it would be hot to the touch. There is a towel, striped blue and white, hanging over it to dry. The bathroom door has been left slightly ajar, so a slice of light from the light bulb hanging overhead leaves its mark on the living room floor. Aged hardwood, cold, stark. He brings her the water, ice clinking in the glass. *Come here*, he says.

The dark closes in, furrowed, muffled, frenetic. It is as if she is struggling underwater. A blur, punctuated by stills, scattered photographs of hours rather forgotten. Words drift and are thrown into the darkness. *Slut. Whore. Bitch. Fuck.* It is all gray, wooly, but for the blink of the green clock on the microwave. As if the power had gone out. So mundane, so trivial compared to this. And then the blinking is a tide to sail away on.

She met him through a mutual friend, and in the early days of knowing him it was all laughter and chasing and smiles. Singing and joking and yelling out into the night, dancing in the middle of the street to songs no one else heard. And she felt that she had always known him. And since she trusted the mutual friend who introduced them, a dear boy she had known since she was thirteen, trusting this one was not a decision so much as an instinct. Sometimes we are so blinded by what we cannot yet see.

Lying alone in his bed that morning, she decides that she should probably leave. Not just leave the apartment, but leave town. Head up north, where no one knows her. Where he won't find her. And yet her feet are firmly planted, glued, and she is immobile, like the dream where you cannot run but the monster is chasing. Her eye drifts back to the key above the door. *How hard can it be to just get up and walk away?*

And then, the sound of a key in the door. His key, not the spare. She sits up fast; she knows she is too late. But he bounds in, inexplicably, with a smile. *Top o' the mornin' to ya, Shan!* And the shocking thing is his smile: it is a sincere one, a kind one. And she looks into his eyes and thinks, *My God, he has no idea. He has no idea what he has done.* And another thought, on the heels of the last, *you allow him his power.*

He tosses his baseball cap onto the coffee table, the coffee table that doubles as the dinner table. His hair is sweaty, messy, and he brushes it back with his hand. *Wanna go get some breakfast?*, he asks, almost playfully. *Are you kidding?* she says aloud.

His name was Jason.

WINTER, 1997

That wasn't the first time things got weird. Not the first time she doubted what she knew about this man. It was winter, frost still and white on the ground. The phone rang at two in the morning, and he was supposed to have gotten in late from a business trip. She thought it would be him, since it would not be unusual for him to call at that advanced hour. And she was happy to hear from him, and they talked about his business trip, they both talked about it, but sleep was thick and confusion easy. And so when the conversation turned south she began to wonder if he might not be who she thought he was. Years later she would understand that she was right, not because the caller was a stranger, but because this man had another side.

His breath is heavy and slow now in the receiver. Hot, it seems, over the line. *Take off your panties, Shan,* he said. *Show me your pussy.* She hesitated. *Who is this?*

Shannon, who do you think it is? he crooned. She could almost hear him smiling. *I bet you like to touch yourself, don't you, you little slut.* Raspy, like a whisper, threatening, growling, low. *I wanna come fuck you until you bleed.* In her memory, a lone yellow streetlight shone in through the window. So mundane, so trivial compared to this. A window that had flexed and breathed and danced its way through the fiercest of storms. A window that seemed so fragile now, like no protection at all. Like ice, like nothing.

Fear, in her throat and in her lungs. And then he is gone. The phone hangs limp in her hand. She hurls it away, as if it were the phone itself that had created those words. Silence. Except for her heart, pounding loud and hard in her chest, and a ghost, whispering in her ear. She will come to hear its voice in the quietest of places.

Shaking, she dials his number, not knowing why or what she will do or say. His voice on the line, sedate.

"Jay?". she says, shaking.

"Oh, hey, Shan, what's up." There is a ruffling, as if he is arranging papers at a desk.

"Yeah, um, did you just call me?" she asks.

"No..." he says, *"why?"*

"Well, someone called, and I thought it was you."

"Why would you think it was me?"

"Uh, well..." She fusses with her baby blanket now, worn and faded. She has a habit of weaving it through her fingers, like a rosary, when she needs to be soothed.

"Well, you... the guy... uh... well, maybe he didn't..."

"Didn't what?" he presses.

"Didn't say his name."

"Well, did you talk to him? "

"Yes."

"And what did he say?"

"Um, really kind of disturbing things."

"So what did you do?"

"I don't know..."

"Shannon, it was probably just a guy making prank calls. Go back to sleep."

"I'm too upset to sleep."

"Well, try to relax, everything is okay."

"It's just that I was sure it was you..."

Her confusion is thick, and she is tangled in his web. Ignores the details of the business trip, the delayed flight. Files them away until spring, when they will tug like ribbons at the back of her mind, some gently, some insistently.

She takes deep breaths, looks around the shadowy room. Empty.

She pulls up the blind and scans the yard. Alone but for the wind rustling the leaves. A search light in the distance, seeking, mourning. It's been a while, she thinks, since this fear visited me, but certainly, we've been bedfellows before.

SUMMER, 1989

Danny and Shannon were both virgins and they were 13. Let me repeat this for emphasis: they were 13. The first two times he tried to force her to have sex with him, she was too strong and his will too weak. And nonetheless everyone around her knew it, knew she had been soiled. His friends believed he had gotten her to do something that their girlfriends would not. Put out, as they say, in the parlance of our times. Sure, she made out with him willingly in the past, let him put his hands up her shirt, let him put his fingers inside her. And she never said she didn't enjoy that. But she did not, steadfastly did not, want to have sex with him.

The first time, in her bedroom one afternoon, he held her down and tried to put his dick in her mouth. *Let me go!* she cried. And then with the shorts, pulling, tearing at them. Tugging at the button, the zipper. *Please let me fuck you,* he whispered, *I need to.* She still hears the *no* that followed, the steady, unending stream of *no's* coming out of her mouth. And had it not been for P climbing into her second story window, implausibly, it might have been gone just then. An odd twist, like from a screenplay no one buys.

Then, that night on the phone came the apologies. *I never meant to hurt you, Shan,* he whispered. *I don't know what came over me. I will never do anything like that ever ever again, I promise.*

The second time he managed to get her pants off. They were alone in his bedroom in the middle of a weekday, his parents at work. And she didn't know how to stop him, did not know what his limits were. *I'll still tell them I fucked you no matter what,* he shouted. *I've got to prove it to them, I've got to prove it to myself...* Over and over, that mantra, *I've got to prove it to myself.* Since they were still about the same size (he was thirteen, after all), she put up a good fight. As he struggled on top of her, she hit him, kneed him hard in the balls, and somewhere in her memory she stores an image of biting him on the shoulder, recalls in some vague sense the metallic taste of his blood. Then he is off her, panting, and she's running out the door. And it's the end of summer but still so hot and she doesn't manage to grab her shoes by the front door before she gets on her bike and the pavement is so hot, hot sticky hot and then she's pedaling like the wind away from this place away from this boy and she's crossing the railroad tracks and she doesn't stop until she reaches her best friend's house. *I think,* she pants as she struggles for air, *I think he tried to rape me.*

It is the first day of school and Shannon is the word on everyone's lips. She was thirteen and in the eyes of her peers she had already given up what so many of them had not. And thus what was indeed still hers, not by choice so much as by luck, was not really even hers. Her virginity, her youth, now owned by everyone. Out there to share, to have a laugh over, to gossip about. She passes two girls standing in front of the library, whispering, pointing, *I heard they did it twice. I heard she blew him.* In line at the cafeteria, *that's the girl who did it with Danny Maelstrom.*

So the third time, she just let him do it. Let him have his way. Let him make her bleed. In some strange guy's bedroom, with two other people in the room, watching but trying to act like they weren't. *Everyone thinks I did it anyway,* she tells herself. It's hard for her to use the word *rape* in the telling of this story, in the telling of any story about her life. Mostly, she tells herself she was to blame because she kept coming back, kept telling herself it would be different this time. These are the lies we tell ourselves so we can get through the day. Lies that have their consequences nonetheless, especially if you have the time to wait around for them.

AUTUMN, 1983

It starts here and this is the first thing. She is eight and he is tying her to the chair, binding her with a rope that cuts into her skin and her soul. And she's crying *please, please let me go* and he's cinching it down tighter, tighter until she bleeds and she's calling out his name and she does not understand she does not know why.

And she wants her grandparents to come back and she doesn't know why they left her here with him and she doesn't know how to make him go away.

And she is eight and he is tying her to the chair. And she doesn't know why he would want to hurt her or what he is doing or why her back feels wet but it does and she wants to run and hide but she can't she can't get out of this chair, out of this horrible dream.

And she's eight and she's tied to the chair and where are they where did they go when are they coming back will they ever come back and the tears feel so hot and they won't go away and he is laughing at her, laughing and dancing around her.

She almost forgets over the years and it fades, but she could tell you if you asked, only no one ever did. She could tell you about the red flushed heat of his skin, his white t-shirt with the sleeves cut off, the sweat dripping off his hair onto her skin, the heaviness of his breath, which chair at which table and what was on the table and that the front door was eerily, implausibly ajar.

What does it do in there, in the back of her mind? Does it seep into other memories, blackening them? Does it compel her, like a magnet, launch a cascade of stories like a broken record? Or has this always been it its very own thing, alone, separate, affecting nothing, affected by nothing?

His name was Joshua.

Epilogue

Shannon is like me and maybe she is like you. She is weak and strong and blind and numb. She is plagued and she is free. She loves and desires and dreams, and sometimes these things scare her. She follows, but does not entirely trust, her heart. She forgives them before she forgives herself, long long before.

These are the stories of many women, and these are the stories of just one. They are tragic, but not so tragic. For ultimately we live and we survive and we sink and we float, sometimes just barely. These are but the stories of an ordinary girl, in an ordinary world. These are the seasons of my deceit.

Homecoming
Amy Sturm

For the first time
my arms are stretched
wide enough to hold
the earth's fullness.
I am content in knowing my
location on the map.

The compass rose transects
my body north though south,
and again, east to west.
The longitude of my spine measures
the distance from last year.
The poles are balanced in perfect tension.

These hills, my ancestors
no longer quarrel,
divided among themselves.
I sleep in the stories of five generations.
I rest in the safety of my father's home.

classifieds.
.jade foster

iii

I want my mother to yell at me like when I was a kid,
"stop crying before I give you something to cry about"
I want my mother to call me downstairs, order me to wash the
dishes,
sweep under the table, wipe the counters
I want my mother to pop me for failing pre calculus,
ignore my excuses and take away my phone

I want her to scream like I'm not right in front of her
ask, "what did you just say?" like she didn't hear me
order me to stay out of her closet like she stayed in mine

I want heaven to part like the red sea, her voice burning in a bush
I want to wait by her grave, just in time for resurrection and tell her
'it's September 6, 151 days, you almost missed my birthday'

ii

I want my mother to call everyday while I'm in new york
make surprise visits because we've never been apart
I want my mother to take me shopping for my dorm room,
splurge on Fendi shoes because I don't have a pair
I want my mother to be in the front row at graduation, scream "that's
my baby"
wear white just because I had to
I want my mother to take hundreds of pictures at prom, offer to be
my date
I want her to help me pick out my clothes, tell me if I look cute
I want her to give me gas money, tell me not to ask for anything else.
I want to succeed Babel's people and reach her, send a dove to find
her
I want to wait at her grave, just in time for resurrection and say
'it's been forty days, what took you so long?'

i

I want my mother to check in my room while I sleep
I want my mother to yell at my father about child support
I want my mother to ask do I have a boyfriend
I want her to wear slippers when she drives
I want her to dye her hair pink, then change it back when she runs
out of matching outfits
I want her to gossip on the phone, burn corn on the cob, be late for
church

I want to wash her feet with my tears, wipe them with my hair
I want to grow impatient at her grave, for her to resurrect and say,
'3 days was way too long.'

Safety in the Arms of Strangers

Lauren Dudley

My slippery fingers were as far back as they could go and the cookie still wasn't coming up. How was I supposed to sit in class knowing I didn't purge? Kneeling over the toilet, with a panicky push, I shoved my fingers back down and willed my malnourished body to dispose of the food clinging to my insides. The choking, watery eyes, and shortness of breath didn't bother me one bit because as I cleaned up and composed myself to return to class, I knew I was holding onto a secret that no one else could touch.

The constant binge and purge cycle lasted for five demanding years until one day I couldn't keep up with myself. The emotional and physical demands of an eating disorder left me in a state of exhaustion where all I wanted was sleep. It was during my sophomore year, I noticed my grades, my ambition, and my will all on the decline. In a lot of ways it was either live or die. I decided to live and turned to the support of my parents. As I walked up the stairs one night after fighting with them over grades, I collapsed into tears, "Do you even know what's going on? I'm still sick and I threw up blood today. I can't even think straight anymore and I can't seem to care about anything enough to feel." After a certain point an eating disorder becomes more then any single person can handle alone; it stops being a conscious choice and instead becomes an unconscious habit. With my mother and father's help I began to take the first of many needed steps towards recovery.

That very next day I remember being called out of class and my parents picking me up for a meeting at Renfrew, a treatment center for women with eating disorders. It was decided I'd move in the next morning. Walking up the pathway, I can still feel the way my heart tightened as my parents and I walked pass the other residents sitting down to eat breakfast. I could feel their eyes on me, judging me, comparing their bony frames to that of my own battered body. My first few days went well. It was a little unsettling to be woken up every morning at five to get my vitals taken, weight checked and body inspected for cuts; I was put on mandatory water intake where they watched me drink sixteen ounces a day. I was dehydrated. My days consisted of group therapy, nutritionist appointments, therapy appointments, psychiatrist appointments, and more group therapy. I got along really well with the other girls and the center itself made me feel safer than I had in a long time. It felt okay to be different; most importantly, it felt okay to eat.

While at Renfrew, I was forced to acknowledge the years I spent struggling to be heard, the need to reach the expectations I thought my parents had set. I was yearning for approval and in the end all that mattered, I learned, was approval from myself. Did I like the person I had become? The girl crying in the bathroom at lunch? Exercising manically in the middle of the night? Could I live with myself if everyone around me left? No. Actually, letting my guard down and allowing the program to work had it's own complications. Giving up my eating disorder is one thing, but having to change the way I viewed myself in this world and realizing there was a place big enough for me to fit in is another. The food or lack there of was my crutch.

After two weeks, I was homesick and struggling. I didn't feel "sick enough" compared to the others. I purged a few times and finally broke down in a group and through tears admitted to the others the secret I was keeping. I was so skilled at my years of lying and putting on such a façade of smiles, no one had the slightest idea, but then aren't all eating disordered individuals practiced liars? I was put on suicide watch and made to sit in the dayroom where I was supervised from morning until night. I sat there with the other self mutilators and dayroom women. It kind of made you restless after a while. I did a lot of coloring and a lot of art therapy. The art gave me a voice and helped me realize what I wanted to say through my eating disorder all along. It was simply "pay attention."

After realizing what I wanted, I promised myself I'd really make it work, for myself and for my parents. I couldn't see my father cry one more time or see the helplessness in my mother's eyes. I was their oldest and also the one that put them through more than their share of worry. I decided I'd make them proud of my recovery. I didn't have to be the most popular, thin, sick, or smart to have them love me or even me love myself. I grasped that conviction and jumped into my recovery in full swing.

Sitting amongst a group of women, all with different stories yet all facing the same disease, we relied on each other and even though we only had just met. We knew one another's hidden secrets better then our friends at home knew them. I believe that would be one key element that makes Renfrew so effective, the bond shared between the women that are treated there, at least for a time. We all swore we'd keep in touch even after our releases, but in the end everyone goes back to their own life.

The day I was released was one of the most exciting, yet terrifying days of my life. I was leaving the world of meaningful discussion, quiet reflection, and patient understanding, and in turn stepping forward onto a new path.

For the first time in my life I was entering a public school, in the middle of my sophomore year at that, but at least I was prepared to accept each situation life presented. I was growing increasingly comfortable and confident with myself, a new feeling for me.

The crucial decision I made to actually embark on the road to recovery by being admitted in to Renfrew still affects me today. Nowadays I am able to live life and look beyond the surface of any difficult and triggering situation presented to me. My recovery has allowed me to connect with people I wouldn't normally connect with and see human nature from different perspectives by openly communicating. By the end of my sophomore year in high school I had already formed a support group for my peers who dealt with depression, drugs, cutting, even schizophrenics were involved. I hope to one day help steer women away from the ideology of having to be thin, pale, androgynous females in order to obtain beauty. I hope women will stop buying into pro-anorexic companies that glorify the image of nutrient starved woman. A woman's body should be celebrated in each curve that shapes it, for it's with these bodies that life comes forth.

Motherless Child

Tashamee Dorsey

Mommy's dead........ and I am tired of people telling me that when I need her...I can some how conjure up what she would say...
I became a motherless child at 30 and I am not over it yet... two years later....though I think I am expected to be...
I hurt when I think of her
Even when joy comes at memories...sadness inevitably follows....
I can not conjure up what she would say.
I want her here saying it,
period
end of discussion...
I don't want to have to remember and pull together pieces of advice like a shredded letter...
My momma's dead and I don't want her to be..... I hurt all the time......... and a lot of people pay for that pain....... I don't know who I am anymore........ I was my mother's daughter............ and now I float through the atmosphere looking for somewhere to land........ somewhere familiar.......I've been looking for some time and I haven't found anywhere left that I belong..............don't know who I belong too anymore...........brother had family before mom died...........I want a family...........But I don't know who I am so I don't know who to present to the woman I love...........because of that she gets my representative...............a pale facsimile of me...........she doesn't like her...............neither do I.............momma would hate her....................
but I don't know who I am.................and I am not sure how to be...............and sometimes I don't want to be at all anymore..............
but only sometimes.................everyone has dark places..................that's mine...
I cope.................but right now
I want my mommy
I am tired of coping
I am tired of being a grown up......
I just want to be my mother's daughter again...............I want to know where to land

The Lunchbox

Dinh Vong

The lunch line snaked its way out of the cafeteria's tall double doors, wrapping itself around the building and trailed into the hot sun. Near the end of the line, I looked through the smudge-pressed windows, where children had rested their foreheads and hands, and watched the rows file neatly past as tables were gradually filled. My calves began to itch as I sidled my weight from one scuffed brown loafer to the next —ugly shoes I wished weren't so comfortable in order to spite the practical Auntie Eight.

Suddenly a brilliant herd of children raced by. Ignoring the line, they ran straight through the doors. My eyes followed them past the dirty window, as they made their way to lunches lined neatly along the stage. They opened brightly colored boxes, ate with the vigor of play, and drank out of the caps of their thermoses. I felt a livening of my senses. I was witnessing something important that I needed to take to heart.

Once inside, the aroma of baking bread with top notes of dishwater wafted around me. I made my way along the formidable steel countertop, clutching the pale green tray in my hands as food was plopped from great big spoons into the separate compartments. Some of the servers' fingers were jammed hastily into the wrong holes of their plastic gloves. On my plate, the vegetable broth bled into its neighboring borders, soaking the bottom of my bread.

Lunch was turkey cutlet, a white roll, canned green beans, carrot cake, and a carton of homogenized milk. I waited a moment, and when I discerned it was safe, took a bite of my roll. I longed to dip my bread in the gravy, but everyone agreed that the turkey was terrible and at most took mincing bites. For this same reason, I could not eat my green beans. It was always a challenge, this ritual of eating and not being allowed to eat. Every meal was deemed sub par among the crowd who brought their lunch. For the rest of us who relied on the cafeteria, it was a guessing game between what was accepted and what was scorned. Levy Neelen had given into temptation and stooped to lick the sauce from his tray. He was met with taunts and hardy shoves. I feared the horde and forced the dry bread down.

Good thing no one ever turned down cake. I relished the white frosting, rolling it along my tongue. I imagined Auntie Eight's face scrunched up as it was every time she ate an American dessert; it was always too sweet for her palate. She was used to fresh fruit and azuki beans, pound cake with more egg in it than sugar, dried tamarind and plum with the pits still intact.

On the first day of school, I made the mistake of polishing my plate clean. The children at my table stared at me in contempt.

"Tastes better than gook food, doesn't it?"
Back home, the idea of pickiness was unheard of. I ate everything I was given, even if I was allergic to it, for what was an itchy tongue compared to a stomach filled with air? My parents would beat me before they let me leave the table with food on my plate —such an oversight was mocking fate itself. For there were periods in my village of drought, poor harvests, accursed soil.

But here, one threw perfectly good food away. Food I secretly relished, because it was American after all, and I had never experienced such things as sloppy joes, ravioli, and grilled cheese. It was always with regret that I dumped my half-eaten plate.

I looked away from my tray so as not to tempt myself. It was then that it occurred to me; If I brought my lunch to school, a world would open up. One in which I could eat what I wanted, and wear bright cuffed socks, and have my hair plaited neatly in two braids down my back, instead of cropped short like a boy's, the way Auntie Eight insisted on having me for the prevention of lice. Boys would chase me on the playground and girls would link arms with me. My transformation would begin with obtaining a lunchbox. That was key.

• • •

We always ate together as a sign of respect. If anyone spent a few minutes dallying after Auntie hollered, "EAT RICE," she would look sinisterly at the late-comer and mutter, "I didn't know we had royalty among us! How spoiled we are in this country, where we have to beg our children to eat." Everyone had a job to do. Uncle wiped the table clean. I set out the chopsticks, soup spoons, and napkins. Au brought out hot plates of food, and Seng scooped the bowls of rice. When he was lazy and skimmed from the top, Auntie would say, "break it up first. We don't want bad luck. Take rice from all edges of the pot."

That night at dinner, I embarked on the subtle erosion of Auntie Eight's will.

I shoveled down my first bowl of rice and ran to the kitchen for seconds.

"Slow down," Auntie Eight said. "You're going to hurt your bowels."

"You're right about American food. I haven't gone in a week." I came back with a double portion.

"Gross!" Cousin Seng said, food smeared across his fat cheek.

"I'm trying to eat," Cousin Au said. When I sat down beside him, he gave me a hard pinch.

"Au hit me!"

"She's lying!" Au said.

"Get the belt," Auntie said.

"It was an accident!" Au said.

"Let's not spoil a good dinner," I said.

Auntie always believed me, even when I was lying. I learned quickly to be merciless with my cousins, who aspired to be WWF wrestlers and often used me as their opponent. Once, I saw my cousins pee into an empty coffee can, draw a dollar sign on its lid and place it in the parking lot, lying in wait for some dumb innocent. I dragged Auntie Eight out to witness them, crouched behind a tan Pinto and sniggering. They went to bed that night with huge welts on their thighs.

"Lily, I told you. It's all that junk food. Bread can't fill anyone up," Auntie said.

"I can't help it. Lots of soda and sugary cakes at school."

"You're nuts," Seng said.

"Is that what they're feeding you? It's no wonder everyone's so fat," Auntie Eight said.

"Pizza and burgers — not fit for a pig!" Uncle Yiu roused himself from his copy of Song Moi to pipe in.

"How can you taste your food with your mind in two directions?" Auntie hated that Uncle read and ate at the same time. Uncle ignored her.

"Auntie. You're always saying I'm pale," I said. My chopsticks lingered over the steamed fish.

"Don't be rude," Auntie said, and waved my hand away.

"It's because you're a weakling," Seng said.

"Should we take you to Dr. Eng?" Auntie said.

"Nothing drastic. I could bring my lunch to school from now on," I said.

This time I studied the fish before reaching for the best part. The meat under the gills was the most tender Auntie shook her head in disapproval. I was greedy to pick the best for myself instead of taking what was closest.

"Let's think about it. See if you poop tonight," Auntie said before raising a piece of daikon to her mouth.

Auntie Eight is calculating, a hard liner. She never throws anything away even past its salvageable point and she never buys anything new unless it's necessary. This was how she survived as a boat person — with her wits and frugal nature. As the Viet Cong advanced, forcing the capitalist Chinese out of their homes and businesses, Auntie was forced to leave behind her wedding apparel shop that she had scraped for all her life, and soon found herself floating in a rickety boat to nowhere. It was Auntie Eight who hoisted the group's sagging morale and did not stop chanting her prayers. It was Auntie Eight who rubbed grease into the faces of the women to lessen their chance of being raped and kidnapped by pirates. It was Auntie Eight who instructed her people to spread ice cream on bread after a large American ocean liner brought them to refugee camps in Singapore.

And it was Auntie Eight who took me in, though she had two boys of her own. My parents were waiting, working, saving money, and would join me later. The truth was they did not have the foresight or the wedding jewelry Auntie Eight had sewn into her undergarments while the Viet Cong raided her home. She sews a money pouch in her underwear to this day. When she pays for something, she flips the waistband over.

Auntie Eight is also convinced that it is because of her vigor and intelligence that she brought forth boys, while my poor mother was relegated to four useless girls. In Vietnam, raising a daughter is like pouring water onto the ground; after putting her out of the house, you never get her back. But because she loved her sister, her childhood friend who she told her deepest secrets to many a humid night, she treats me like her own, with the same intermittent acts of kindness and cruelty.

• • •

The next morning, I found my lunch prepared, packed in a metal container, the same kind Uncle Yiu took to work. I knew what was inside —last night's leftover fish, rice, and stewed daikon —entirely unacceptable if I wanted to live another day. I shoved it into my bag and caught the bus to school. When lunch came around, I stood in line as usual, awaiting cold French bread pizza and canned corn. Everyone at the table picked off the pepperoni, including me.

"Feeling better?" Auntie Eight asked when I came home.

"They didn't let me eat. They said metal is dangerous. I might throw it like a Frisbee and kill someone."

"Ludicrous!"

"I need a plastic lunch box that comes with a thermos to carry soup in."

"How much?"

"$2.99 at Woolworth's." I knew because I had circled the store the last time Auntie had gone to buy food for her goldfish. She keeps ten of them in a small tank in our living room because fish bring money and luck. I taped a picture on the back of the tank, one I ripped out of a National Geographic Uncle found at work. It's a picture of a giant squid. I was surprised that Auntie Eight approved of the decoration and never removed it, even long after the edges had rolled up and the Scotch tape had yellowed.

When I was seven-years old, I arrived at the Oakland International Airport in my best clothes and a cardboard box containing all I owned — some ow yays, a doll, and a comic book I filched from my sisters. It was our favorite from a series, about an old man and his fat sidekick, their failed jobs and botched romances. I was thin and worn out from the plane ride, gazing intently for a familiar face. There was Auntie Eight and my cousins wearing jeans, which I had thought only farmers wore, ready to take me home.

It was Auntie Eight who provided the warmth of a woman, who helped me pick my American name out of a phonebook. "Lily. Good for girl," she said. It was Auntie Eight who haggled over my ugly, but comfortable shoes she bought at a flea market, and lectured me on the benefits of sea cucumber soup. She made sure I ate all the rice in my bowl so that my future husband would not have too many pimples, and she was not satisfied until my limbs plumped out into healthy proportions. But the protective Auntie Eight could not follow me to school. On the first day, I wore a mixture of my cousins' hand me downs and didn't say a word. Because of my tube socks and short hair, I was mistaken for a boy, and during recess, was relegated to the outskirts along with the interminably shy and weak. Because I could not speak English, I was barred from forming any cohesion even among those undesirables. For weeks I played alone, erecting miniature versions of Hanoi in the sand, swinging from one monkey bar to the next, sitting against the fence so no one would see me cry. I was the youngest, but the strongest, my father said. I would bring the rest over — such a weight to carry on my small shoulders.

There were times when I wanted to write letters saying, "stay where you are, I'll come to you." For it seemed I had traded my poverty for loneliness. All of a sudden I looked different, smelled different, tasted different. Even the ability to speak was taken from me. I missed my village, the bicycles winding to and fro, the dolls we made out of sticks and old cloth, the stories my sisters and I dreamt up every night. But I could not forget my pride as I boarded the plane.

How important I felt to be airborne, and how everyone had made such a fuss and cried over me.

So in a letter, I wrote:

Dear Family,

I'm doing fine. How is Mimi? Does she still sleep at the foot of my bed and howl for me? I don't think I'll everfind a dog like her ever. Auntie says animals are vermin and we can't have any.

We have television in our home, and radio! No more long treks to the gas station if we want news. There are lots of sidewalks, but people don't walk here. Everyone has a car.

Seng and Au are always getting into trouble. I'm glad we have no boys in our family. Tell Nan that I hid her doll in the medicine chest. I forgot to return it before I left.

I've grown fat and round and have made many white ghost friends. I am getting all A's in school.

My English is coming along fine. I'm obeying Auntie.

Sincerely,
Lily (my new name — Auntie helped me choose)

My goal was to forget the past and my old friends, forget the noises of the street vendors peddling outside my home, forget their carts of delicious steamed pork dumplings and long noodles. I worked so hard at forgetting that I often wept while doing so, believing the tears to be memories leaving me. One image, as my shuddering chest lulled me to sleep, were my sisters' arms gathering me inside their secret circle, singing a song I can no longer remember.

For months I worked at improving my position. To learn the language better, I sat in front of the television, soaking in the street lingo. I would then practice on Seng and Au.

"Kiss my grits!" I said.

"Shut up dork," Seng said.

"You son of a gun!" I said. And there he was, standing on the arm of the couch, with his elbow positioned toward me. He arched in the air and I rolled quickly out of the way as he descended.

After many hours in front of the tube, understanding dawned on me and Auntie Eight could not pull me away from my favorite shows. Somehow there was an underlying gravity to Mr. Belvedere, Nell Carter, and Jack Tripper. There was a mystery tucked away in the bright clothing, leg warmers, ponytails tied tight to one side of the head. Madonna. Michael Jackson. George Michael. The more fluent I became, the more difficult it was to keep up with Auntie Eight's conversation.

"Where is Seng's rollerskate?" Auntie Eight would ask.

"In the garage-ah!" I said.

Communication with Auntie became *"Kitchen-ah! What-ah? Cruel-ah!"* To Auntie's horror, I began tying scarves around my forehead and jeans.

"Will you be my lucky star?!" I sang.

"This is what whores wear!" Auntie admonished, hiding my scarves, whipping me when she found clothes I had deliberately tore holes in.

Though Auntie disapproved, she would not take away the small black and white television, which was a luxury, a symbol of wealth in our previous life. So I continued my daily absorption of mass culture.

Then a stroke of fate to speed along progress — at school, it was discovered that I had a knack for catching softballs. I was standing over in far left field where my team always placed me so I wouldn't cause much damage. Joseph Garcia gave a crack to the ball and was running past first, past second, confident of making it home. The ball was headed straight towards me. I knew I had no choice but to catch it, as my team's murderous eyes watched on. Luckily, I had practiced numerous times with Seng and Au in Auntie Eight's garden with unripe lemons. I caught the ball with two hands cupped to my chest. The captain patted me on the shoulder and said, "good job, chink." After that, they invited me to join in their games of tetherball, jump rope, chase. I was strong after all, and a fast runner. It wasn't my fault I was fresh off the boat. At most there was a daily "ching ching china sittin' on a fence." All in good humor. I smiled while they sang it.

Life got better after that, and I was happy. The only problem was food. For Auntie Eight, only Chinese food was food. We lived on a diet of various roots, fish, durian and taro flavored soft drinks. American food was too expensive. American food was not healthy. American food gave people cancer.

• • •

We run off to the white ghost aisle of Wang's Supermarket and bring back large boxes of neon green cereal.

"No," Auntie Eight says.

"There are vitamins, Ma."

"No good thing in the world is that color."

"Look, A, B, C, potassium, riboflavin — "

"You love rice porridge."

"We're sick of porridge."

"Since when? Last time I bought you a pizza, full of grease and salt.

I'll never stoop so low again. In this country, one pounds their taste buds with a hammer. They don't know a meal is a means of conjuring memory and emotion. There's subtlety in the rice flour wrap, the earthy aroma of bamboo shoots, the way in which seaweed melts on the tongue. This is my love for you — a bit of the past wafting into your nostrils."

"That's such old fashioned thinking, Auntie," I say.

"How you hurt my heart! I can't bring myself to tell my sister that her daughter has become a stranger. How terribly jarring your Cantonese is now. Our conversation has become like a dog speaking to a monkey, incomprehensible."

• • •

There was no Smuckers and Skippy. No Miracle Whip. No Oscar Meyer. No Juicy-Juice. Instead, there was Hong Van Grass Jelly Drink, Golden Dynasty Egg Roll, Panda Oyster, and Siracha Hot Chili. I was determined to find something I could mold into submission. I scoured the kitchen, flung open cabinets, looked behind bulk cartons of soy sauce. And then I saw it: Instant Kung-fu noodles. I thought it through, then pounded the raw noodle to bits and ate it in the living room like a bag of chips. Another time I threw away the sauce packets, boiled the noodles, drained the broth, and squirted ketchup over the top to simulate spaghetti. When Auntie discovered my concoctions, she exhorted me about the terrors of diarrhea and forebade me to cook.

But I continued in secret, sneaking the food into the coat closet, along with the bottle of chewable vitamins that I popped like candy. It was as if my eyes had been opened, because I began to see the shrimp chips, the mango pudding cups, the lychee flavored juice, in a new light.

Over the course of the next week I addled my guardians with the determination of a monk and spent extra time on the toilet reading comic books. When Auntie discovered for herself that a lunchbox was not an expensive thing, she purchased one at Bartell's —— a mauve lunchbox with a unicorn on its front and a matching thermos inside. I didn't recognize the illustration but was satisfied with its gleam of newness.

"I'll pack my own lunch. Don't worry about me, Auntie."
That night, after I had placed my first school lunch inside the refrigerator, I dreamt of my father.

"Are you American yet?" He said, floating by on a cloud.

"Going to be," I said. And then he was sliding away from me. I stood up in panic, my weight falling through the sky.

At noon, there was my lunchbox waiting for me. I galloped toward it, along with the rest of the children. My fingers grazed the white handle when James Callahan snatched it up. He was big, handsome, and mean.

"That's mine," I said.

He frowned at me and I wondered if he had not understood.

"That one's mine," I said again, reaching for it, but he held it out of my reach with such confidence and anger, that I wondered if perhaps it wasn't.

"Anna, I got your lunch!" He called.

"That's not it." A voice clear and bored came out of a blond, shiny head.

Instead of handing the box to me, he looked at me in disgust, and then ran back and set it with the others. I walked to it, picked it up, and by this time the front of the table was filled. I made my way towards the middle and observed the others. They brought forth gleaming apples and sandwiches made with thick white bread. I feared my counterfeit lunch would be exposed but the weeks invested in preparing for this moment gave me courage. I took out my thermos filled with lychee juice, which I poured into the lid and drank. No one seemed to notice. I then took out the mango pudding, looking around as I scooped the jelly into my mouth. Again, no one looked up. I was nearing the home stretch. I rested my elbows on the table like everyone else. They were not so fearful after all. I whipped out my container of spaghetti and began to eat with a plastic fork.

"What is that?"

The words stung me, thick as the fork pressing an indentation in my hand. Perhaps it was a mistake. I looked up at the eyes filled with horror and smiled like I meant to.

"It's spaghetti," I barely whispered.

"It's cat brains. Chinks eat cats."

"I don't eat cats," I said.

"Yes you do."

"They eat dogs and rats too."

"No we don't," I said.

"No wonder you always stink!"

Shame pressed heavy against my face and shoulders and sucked itself into the pit of my stomach. I covered my meal and put it back into the shiny new box. I stared at its handle and dared not raise my eyes until the bell rang. My ugly shoes felt heavy against the rungs of the table.

At home, Auntie Eight had prepared steamed chicken with crushed ginger and fish sauce. I sat down to eat, relishing the moist chicken mixed with my tears.

"Why are you crying?" Auntie Eight asked.

"No reason," I said.

"Tell me." And because Auntie Eight wanted to know, I cried even harder.

"Come here," Auntie said, pushing my small head against her bosom.

I clung to her needfully.

"What's wrong?"

"Auntie, do I stink?"

"Let's see." She pressed her nose into my hair and took a deep breath.

I could feel the outline of my mother in her.

"You smell like candy, and the sun."

"I want to go home," I said, letting out my great secret.

"Is that all?" Auntie said.

Hip Hop Haiku

Jocelyn James

#1

We don't love dem hoes
but Brother, we are ALL one
so who do you love?

#2

class and gender war
fought in rhyme, backed by dope beats
fame's casualties

#3

hip hop weeps, suffers
like those who create the art
searching for relief

The Whinings of a Cum Laude Seven Sister College Graduate Working Bored as an Assistant
Nana Ekua Brew-Hammond

Do you know how many ideas pass through my mind a minute?
Just give me 50,000 dollars a year and I'll make you feel bad for how
little you compensate my talent
I'm overqualified to be your assistant
Which is why I'm at home writing this
I'm gonna be rich
I'm gonna write this book and sell it
Chapter One? You're listening to it
Remember that promotion you never gave me?
The real reason I quit?
Yeah, that story's gonna be in it
It's the ultimate tale of office politics
A demonized boss threatened by young intelligence, long legs and
big tits
That sounds hot right? This is legit.

I didn't know you were supposed to play along with it
My parents stressed preparation - education, a good interview suit
- they're immigrants
But come to think of it
Mammy - I mean Mommy had to deal with her own corporate
dynamic
But speaking of, she got an Oscar for it
Say what you want, but that's in the history books, critic
Smiling and filing, over-timing, - Mommy got a trip to Paris out of it
We all went
To the Champs Elysées, kid - I just wanted y'all to know I have a
pretty good French accent
Daddy, thanks for setting up a payment plan, paying my tuition bit
by bit
I'm sorry I couldn't just go to law school so you could brag about it
Those sacrifices you made gave me the luxury to do this

Oh yeah, I'm not rich

Yo, the job market doesn't care if I'm a cum laude seven sister college
graduate
I need a good-paying job, like now, but my resume says I'm only
qualified to be an assistant
Right about now, I'll take any job I can git
Thank you so much for giving me this internship
You won't regret this
You just tell me where to go and I'll gofer it
I mean it - if you throw it, I'll fetch it
Anything I can do so when that assistant job opens up, I'll be the one
to get it
If I can't be Malcolm, I'll be Martin, she-it
Wait, both those cats got assassinated
Listen, I just wanna get my work out there and get paid for it
Well, that's not it
I also want a house on a private beach with an office facing the ocean
on the second floor of it
And my Pulitzer and my Oscar propping up the pictures on my desk
of my husband and my kids
Is that so selfish?
I mean, when we have our clambakes you're all invited
And I'll write consciousness-raising works as my community service
- that's my commitment
What do you want from me, I'm a member of a generation
somewhere between Y and X
And I'm getting up there - about to turn 26
Something has got to pop off now and I don't mean this zit
Father, I'm trying not to be anxious
Okay, so I'm being a tad melodramatic
And I did get the job - once again, I'm somebody's assistant
Mommy and Daddy, I promise you - I promise myself
- I'm gonna make that $100,000 degree worth it

Eenie-Meenie
Roma Raye

"What I need from you is space to think about this issue as well as your agreement to look at your own accountability for getting us to the place we are currently at. Your recent decision regarding your sexual orientation," he continued, "as well as your decision to end my marriage is a great example of how you are a victim of yourself. I tried to love you and you wouldn't let me. It's not my fault you cannot be sexually pleased by me. That is your issue. I have offered you numerous opportunities to amend your misconceptions around sex and intimacy. Maybe you are broken."

Minee-Mo

"I hear you," she replied to him casually. "I will integrate the information you have shared with me and reflect on your observations." She didn't need to engage in his hippy-dippy-therapyland-bullshit-man game. She had responded well and could just walk away at this point. As she turned to leave she caught a slight smirk start in the corner of his right eye and travel around his mouth.

Catch a tiger by his toe

She glimpsed toward his crotch as he quickly and subtly adjusted himself. She knew that his own words had made him hard. She also knew that at times like these he gets anxious to go into the basement ("my office" he calls it) to listen to Enya, smoke pot and jack off to internet porn. "Have fun down there," she called to him, "if you find any decent girl-on-girl sites, let me know?" He dismissed her with a wave of his hand so she called to him one last time. "Hey by the way," she said, "I'm not broken — I'm a dyke. It just took me a while to figure out that the pussy I want in my life isn't you." His shoulders hunched as he spun around to face her. Red-faced and trembling slightly, he opened his mouth showering her with spit and hate. "Fuck you, you fucking cunt! Maybe if you learned to fuck like a real women we wouldn't be having these issues!" Curling into her body, she began to rock to a familiar rhythm: Ifhe hollerslethimgo ifhe hollers lethim go if he hollers let him go if he hollers let him go.

Eenie-Meeni

She sprang to her feet, pinning him to the wall. "What are you doing, you crazy bitch?!" he growled at her. She leaned into him. The anger rumbled through his chest into hers, raising her up to reach his ear with the breath heated by the fire in her belly. "Minee-Mo," she replied coolly. His eyes clouded over and his words faltered. A look of understanding circled his face as he realized in the process of his stumbling, he had hung himself. The seduction of her heaving breasts and trembling hips was masked by the violence in her eyes, "my momma told me to pick the very best one and you are not it."

Sunday's Mondays

Eunice Alicea

Monday morning had everything to do with thick unmanageable hair.

No Monday morning had everything else that I was supposed to be doing but couldn't do. No, no no Monday mornings were queasy, bottomless stomachs of all the things I didn't know how to do and all the places I could not fit into and the people I could not please. My second grade teacher made me so nervous I would pray, pray, pray that she would not be there every Monday morning as the bus turned into the school. If that God, that god the formless growing sensation in my closed eyes would just hear me, I would find one day of peace. Because I never had good hand-writing or a mother that came to PTA meetings; and I knew it was because she never wanted people outside of the house to try to decipher what she was saying in English. I would cry every Sunday night at home and pray every Monday morning on the bus. My teacher was only ever absent once. Although somewhere in the middle of the school year my older sister came in and had a conference with her. That day she called me to her desk, grabbed both my hands in hers and told me that I never, ever had to be scared of her. I don't remember having to pray again after that.

Or the Monday mornings of fifth grade, praying praying praying Monday morning that I would not be so off. That I would be named Alona or Michele (with one "L") or Kristi. That I would not find myself in the lowest reading level even though I understood everything at the highest reading level. Monday mornings in the fifth grade, walking into school and with each step feeling the tightening of my stomach and the increase of moisture in my palms. It had been like that ever since I looked around and noticed there was not one place for me there. Everything, wrong. The clothes I wore, because I didn't care for pink yet. My big, bossy, black hair. No curls, no blonde, no braids, nothing but bangs. Wrong the way my voice grew louder when I did an Elvis imitation, which still to this day is probably the best short chubby Puerto Rican girl Elvis impersonation. Being loud, that was always wrong.

Signals crossed though. Between Mondays and Sundays, signals cross. Sunday's were shouting, singing, laughing all out loud, all over the night, throughout a preaching, agreeing to the promises of redemption and the freeing of the Israelites. All of it hovering over me, pulsing, getting absorbed, Pentecostal osmosis, Sundays.

A scene grows from a blur, lying back on a wooden benche, eyes closed but not darkened. Instead that sort of closed that responds to movements of light. And the hard bench underneath me, the lights in my closed eyes, and the sounds of people signing all around me and people singing songs about their awe of God, or their knowledge that God is bigger than anyone knows, songs that magnified God in the heavens and shrank the peoples of Earth. Me, lying flat on the bench with voices filled with prayers all around me. Floating right over singing, crying, crying out, crying in, crying over me, voices filled with the certainty of God and the uncertainty of life floated past me. And these people all around me changed the way I thought of things, changed the way I heard things, hearing their honest supplications hearing them become bare and speak out. Speak out in Spanish, speak out to God, speak out in Spanish, and in tongues but no English, transported me, transformed me, transfigured me, because it was only me on that bench hearing them; hearing them and wondering if God heard me.

Different. A Pentecostal church, a former bowling alley turned supermarket with low ceilings, an altar lined with green shag carpeting and a pastor with a day job. Not conventional, not mythic, merely a space — a place that mirrored the working class congregants — every one of them somewhere in the middle. A generation apart from warm Puerto Rican beaches and generations away from total acceptance, total understanding, mainstream anything. Four times a week, twice on Sundays, filing into the building with brown hair, brown eyes, brown skin, old and young, male and female walking into the same industrial building, and with their presence building a church. And there I went, under my mother's hand, behind my sisters, filing into this building, participating in building a church as it participated in building me. Faith reciprocity throughout a childhood.

And as I walk in again, as an adult, walk in with all of my new skins, with all of my solid beliefs, with all of my nuances in thought, in maturity, in hindsight, none of those opinions seem present or clear.

I walk in so as not to alert anyone of my entrance. Hard to do, especially hard to do with the creak of that heavy metal door, painted dull brown on both sides, the silver bar across the inside and window frame painted over. It shuts behind me and suddenly outside and inside are not the same times, not the same by years, not just the seconds of distance between opening and entering. Time decreases in matters of personalities, hairstyles; who you were and who you are walking in as. It has to do with memory and being a girl and being in between, in between everything. It has to do with trusting what you loved, remembering yourself and smiling while trying not to cringe. It has to do with hearing the voice of God before anyone told you what it was. It has everything to do with being alone in a crowd of people that watched over you, with hands raised and songs sung and tongues spoken. Everything to do with what faith does to a girl growing up.

That's how it would happen, as though it had never happened before. That door would creak open against the wind outside. That brown painted heavy metal door would open and my mother would guide me into church. There would always, always be a song already and people clapping. Some would be clapping too fast, like a doubled up marathon runner or the thin ropes of double dutch tapping the concrete. There would be some clapping slowly, as the beat within their hands dictated rhythm. Some would be clapping at leisure, sometimes emphasizing a word: librè [CLAP] Cristo [CLAP CLAP] refugio [CLAP cry CLAP CLAP CLAP]. And they were all on time, all present, synchronized without trying.

It would begin to grow there. The accumulation of wonder within the walls of my rib cage would begin when I walked into the door. Hearing the words sung into the air, voices out of tune, muffled sounds through crunchy old speakers. My legs and back on the hard brown bench, once again, and I would lift. The out-of-sorts ways of Mondays I'd begun to believe were everything there was to me. Lift a bit higher as I would close my eyes and look up at the fluorescent lights. Take that first breath enraptured in the glow of prayers, or singing, of Spanish and broken English and languages of the sacred. This was never unfamiliar and it was not ever wrong. This wasn't me being wrong.

And at some point calm would settle on my back, over my

shoulders; settle into the part I imagined the soul to be. A calm with color, sound, with inspirations and indulgences, a calm that felt like skin, like your very own skin wrapped around your body. It never overtook or burdened, never forcing me into belief or to tears. It welcomed me into my own.

Sanctity. Maybe that's what bends times when the door opens and the walls are still eggshell white, the linoleum on the floor still cracked, and the wooden benches are still divided into three sections so there isn't a middle isle. Not the stained-glassed cathedrals of many other Puerto Rican childhoods. No doll eyed saints looking down, blank upon all those that gathered. Frozen, still, rigid. Nothing moves, nothing breathes, nothing fallible among ornamental altars and starched collared priests. The congregation quiet, respectful, fearful — full of reverence, lacking voice. The Catholic church paled in comparison, it faltered. Its stone face never allowed people to cry out, to form their voice in speaking to God, to use their own words. The scripted prayers that turn over and over and over around once, twice, three times, around into the same days, one into another never yielding for the newness of struggles, the emergence of new identities, differences.

And Monday: quiet classrooms, don't speak to your neighbors, although we're supposed to love them, and not so loud in gym class when the boys are watching the quiet girls twirl their hair and act like they can't throw a ball. Quiet in church meant reverence. Quiet in school meant discord, and I was out of tune.

Or the other Mondays. Or Tuesdays, weekdays and weekdays full of everything that I could not feel good about. I could not feel above. I was in it. I was in it and not there at all. Weekdays of working through what was so wrong with me. Weekdays full of waiting for something bigger, greater, more. Every beginning of the week, of the school week the beginning of askew, crooked, the hem of a pant missing a stitch because my mother used to sew some of my clothes and I was proud about it until one day I was told not to be. Or the fast clapper in a room of moderates, sounding sometimes on the beat and sometimes off, but always present. There were moments when being there and not being there seemed interchangeable. Moments when I'd talk, inside, talk to me inside while I looked at everything outside and try to quash that burning. Burning, like the bush burning and it's voice saying, whispering, saying, calling, telling me: this is not all there is, this is not all there is to you, this is not all there is for you, this is not at all where it is.

Never. I could never prove that anything was said, or heard. And when empty and awkward and wishing wishing wishing and praying praying praying so hard that I would wake up and be thin, or blonde, or thin and blonde and named Melissa, or Janet, or even Rachel, like my mother had originally wanted, I knew I had made it up. I knew, especially by Thursday or Friday — end of the school week and the disaster of upside down stomach flips and attempts at being quieter, having straighter hair, eating less, buying acid wash jeans and L.A. Gears, that voice, those words, never were.

Sundays was who I was and who I was becoming by the songs to God in other tongues, and it was me learning how to talk to God. But it had nothing to do with being everything else I was told to be. It had nothing to do with being told what to do period. Because so much of everything else had to do with being told what to do. Being told what to say and what to wear and what to act like when in the presence of strangers, those that were not Puerto Rican, not dark-haired, some white, all better.

Or maybe being told what to be or who to be or how to be. Being told the way to understand math and science and reading and Christopher Columbus and being told to be comfortable with not being comfortable. Being told that the world outside is logical, clear, simple. Things felt different on Monday morning. There were no moments that were safe enough to close my eyes. There were no moments that weren't warm enough, enlightening enough, moving enough, within my chest, in my soul, there weren't those moments. There were moments of wrong. Very, very wrong in every capacity. Wrong hair, wrong size, wrong sort of name, wrong family dynamic all wrong. Or if not wrong, at the very least, off.

Faith; inextricably a part of the definition of self — lack of, adherence to, abjection with. The where of it not as important as the what of it. What it did, what it does, what part it took in sculpting the inner portions of who you would become, who you are, who you are told you can not be, who you always were. It is grace, the unmerited favor to become the person you saw within the lights of your own eyes, the voices you translated as your own, the damnations you rejected, the salvations you procured for yourself, within yourself. Unapologetic and unrestrained, this *duende*, a fantastic and illusive portion of you planted somewhere within the grounds of adolescence will rise up at the times when you are most undefined, most ostracized and possibly most questioned and labeled as other. Because its formation lies in the languages of your youth, the hand gestures of those around you that resembled you the most, the voices that cried through similar struggles, alienations, the prayers of girls, women, men, boys that went out those doors into their weekdays and prayed prayed prayed for change. Prayed to be ignored or seen, prayed for better hair or clothes, prayed for a voice or a listener. Faith forms in the substance of things hoped for, not in the specifics of them. No matter the grandness or weakness of everyday, of the Monday and Tuesdays.

And so that is why, wherever life has turned and bent for me, wherever my greatest pains and triumphs have collided, walking into the off white and brown church of my youth brings with it every single fixture and creak of who I am most. Those doors open and I walk in and sit on the hard hard brown bench and a glee, a joyous outcry from those inner walls begins to form. It, like faith, grows up and pushes out the me, the woman, the girl, the imperfections, the everything that I have become, that I was, that I have not even yet begun to imagine. It pushes beyond the slight scarring of second grade or the bruising of fifth, it glides passed the shortcomings of being short, being fat, being loud, being on unmanageable hair and pours forth a song of possession and self fulfillment.

Who Needs Friends?

Vanessa Seay

I was always moving around and never really had friends that were my age. I usually would have to move from town to town, so I never really had a place to call home. In middle school at the end of sixth grade I had to leave and go to a new middle school again. I wasn't very shocked because I knew I was going to have to move sooner or later. But this time, I was kind of scared to make new friends and start over. I had one friend that was going to the same school as me but she was one year older and one grade higher than me.

I couldn't even imagine what would happened to me on the first day of seventh grade, all I know was that I would be shy and have no one to talk to. The summer went really fast and the next thing I knew it was the first day of school.

When I first walked into the school it was just how I thought it would be. My friend Aliza had to go to her class with all her friends and I was left alone with all these people my age that I didn't even know. The whole day no one talked to me except my teacher.

My last class of the day was P.E. and there was another new girl that just couldn't stop talking and already made one new friend. She looked my way and asked me if I was new.

"Yea I'm new," I said kind of nervous.

She said "really, so am I! What's your name?"

"Hannah," I told her.

"Oh my name is Emma and this is Marie," she pointed to the girl that she had been talking to.

The next thing I knew she was calling up another girl that was sitting alone on the bleachers.

"Hey are you new too?"

The girl just nodded her head in response to Emma.

"Come over here," she said while waving her hand toward her.

The girl got up and walked down the bleachers to where we were.

"So what's your name?"

The girl kind of looked down shyly and said "my name is Naomi."

"Ok everyone get a group of friends and stand in line in front of the table so we can give you your gym lockers," one of the teachers yelled out to everyone.

"Want to be in my group?" Emma asked to Naomi and me.

"Sure," Naomi and I said.

After that day of school I started to talk to Emma and Naomi a lot more. I guess you could call us best friends. I started to talk to other people in my class and I became friends with them too. Suddenly school wasn't as bad as I imagined and I made friends really fast. If you see me now at my school you would say that there is no way I'm a shy person. I have many groups of friends and they really help me in life, especially when it's rough.

Right now, things are good. My mom has finally recognized how happy I am here and has decided to stay in this town. I even started a new advice column for anyone now who has been feeling low. Now I have been living in the same town for quite a long time and I'm still best friends with Emma and Naomi. We are going on to high school soon and we hope to have a great time there just like in middle school.

Who needs friends? We all do.

serah's birthday wish/prayer/song
Tracey Rose

fingerprints emblazoned on skin,
touch affirming the existence of this new & old life,
found on the edges of
a smooth, round, honey-colored world
a young womanchild laughs and cries along with us

she breathes in our calm
as we take off our shoes
and lose ourselves in the cool, fresh dampness
of God's green earth
and when we lay hands upon her
we hope our sorrow and our blindness is not contagious
that she won't inherit the demons
that plague her mother
the rise and fall of spirit that rode down
in her grandmother's blood
and rose up in the blue-black marks
that tattooed her skin

ay, we lift her up in our voices,
the woman-centered sounds that we pray
will guide her down different roads
may she cling to the fearless, adventurous spirit
that will be hers upon arrival
and the self-absorbed grace that won't allow her
to entertain thoughts of inferiority in her early days

we'll clothe her in loving, wild song and
never allow the disease of fear to manifest itself in her skin
we'll feed her the milk of sky-blue dreams
and wash her in baths of water-colored poems
we'll steal stars from the night sky,
crush them, and sprinkle their magic on all her days to come
we'll fashion her wings to venture upon clouds,

and the laws of gravity will be her only limits
we'll shelter her in the world we built for her
and she'll dance on the walls of our prisons
and sing freedom into the hearts of all those
within her reach

Oriental
**(Dedicated to the victims of child sex tourism that
dominates the Asian world and beyond)**
Togtokhbayar Ganzorig

She could hardly remember her little hut
With its slanted door and beat down windows
And her little brother, with his sly smile
And joyful glee
He use to be bring so much empty happiness when it stormed the
whole village
Oh so much empty happiness....
But memories always seemed to be strung together
White and black and white and black and **black** and **white** and black
and *white* and black....

He came offering jobs
A lot of money he said
And she'd be perfect, twelve years old
With *slightly slanted almond eyes*
Thick black hair
And signs of womanhood peaking between *her thighs*

Yes...yes...

She'd be perfect

A fair skinned fantasy

Slightly slanted almond eyes...
Thick thick black hair...
Untainted...
Oriental...
Twelve...

Value was not measured by her soul
When money was on the line

Her spirit broken in half
And her purity stolen like her youth
Measured nothing to the value of the crinkled American dollars
Her heart trenched in mud
And her future battered with whips
Her past wiped like an eraser
No...
Measured nothing to the *moaning of a blue eyed blonde haired 40 yr old man's*
Crinkled American dollars

She could not feel the inside of *her thighs*
Or the tenderness of her *growing breast*
No...
She could take hour long baths and wash her thick black hair over
and over again until her scalp hurt
But it's been so long
Thrashed against a wall of blood
With her broken spine
And broken soul
Over and over and over and over again...
No...
No....
The value of her words
The value of her treasures in her mind
Her soul
Her being
Could not measure up to the *crinkled American dollars...*

Slightly
Wet

Undoing the Dress

Kimberly Cosier

We moved to Howard City at around 11:00 p.m. on the night before I was to start seventh grade. The next morning, in typical Cosier family fashion, we were running late. My mother, digging desperately through a mound of unmarked boxes to find toothbrushes and underwear, would hear none of my plaintive protests against her decision to make me wear a dress on the first day of school at my new junior high. I was devastated. After having recently survived a year and a half of fashion oppression under a Baptist school dress code, I had been looking forward to presenting myself in a wardrobe that more closely reflected my '70s tomboy tastes and sensibilities. I had my first day outfit laid out in my mind since the day we went school shopping: a satin-trimmed cowboy-cut denim shirt paired with dark blue bellbottom corduroys.

If my mother had set out to doom me to the sidelines of Tri County Junior High School society, she could not have devised a more effective weapon of mass destruction than the dress. I am not at all clear about how we came to be in possession of it, but I can conjure as plain an image of it today as the day I first laid my horrified eyes on it. The dress was made of limp, off-white cotton, generously sprinkled with a cloying pattern of tiny, indistinct floral bouquets. The tightly clustered little bunches of blue and purple flowers were meant to be feminine and sweet, I suppose, but in a time when hot pants and halter tops were in, they clinched the fact that the dress was utterly outside the realm of acceptable fashion. Not only were the fabric and its pattern loathsome, the construction of the dress (a potato sack loosely gathered at the wrists and waist with thin strings of elastic) was equally unappealing and unflattering. In that dress, with my pursed-lipped mother walking nervously yet purposefully at my side, I approached Tri County Junior High as the early Christians must have come to the Coliseum.

That dress was the kind of garment that telegraphed difference. It was plain to see that any unfortunate soul who wore the dress would be an outsider in all, but the most conservative settings. It trumpeted: "Under no circumstances should any self-respecting adolescent person befriend the wearer of this dress." As a matter of fact, though I didn't know it yet, an announcement of sorts had been sent. Before we get to that, I guess a little background information is in order.

We landed in Howard City at the end of a 57-mile spiritual journey, which my parents had undertaken with a small band of like-minded religious zealots. Of a different mind altogether, I had been dragged along on this little trip for the past three years. In its first decade, my life had been wildly happy and enormously satisfying. We lived in a neighborhood full of kids at a time when children could still roam freely until called for dinner. Our house sat high on a hill. In front of it was a lake where we fished and swam and skated on ice.

Behind us, woods, with grapevines that grew in tangled masses high up into the trees, forming jungle gyms and secret spaces.

Church was on Sunday then. And Sunday was the only day I was made to wear dresses and shiny shoes, which was as much as I thought I could bear at the time. Each week my Dad broke the law on our way to services. Keeping an eye out for the police, he sped madly in an attempt to make up for time lost by the rest of us. My mother stroked the back of his head in a roundabout apology as my sister and brother and I breakfasted on maple leaf sandwich cookies or pecan sandies in the back seat. The little country church was built of yellow brick, with a stubby white wood steeple that humbly pointed heavenward. Upon arrival, our parents slinked to the front pew to the tune of *The Old Rugged Cross*, while we kids trotted off to Sunday school. Our Sunday school teacher, Mrs. Vink, drew sadistic Calvinist pleasure from scaring the bejesus out of us with stories about innocent people killed by sinful children who dropped bowling balls from overpasses. After church, children rejoined parents and sidled up to old Mr. Van Eizenga, who would produce thick, pink peppermints from the pocket of a worn suit coat.

But when I was ten, my parents became part of a new "church" and my life took a turn I did not care for in the least. As I write this, I realize I have no idea if the founder of the little congregation had any pastoral credentials whatsoever. As near as I can figure, he found his calling at a lunch counter somewhere in Texas, after some other business ventures fell through. My parents (children of alcoholics, both, and suspicious of formal education) cared nothing about credentials. Drawn in by the lure of ecstatic spiritual conversion they joined the group, which held regular Sunday meetings in the preacher's mother's shag-carpeted living room.

The members of the little band believed in a thing called "baptism in the Holy Spirit" which is most notably proven by *glossolalia* —or speaking in tongues. They believed in other supernatural gifts of as well: the "word of knowledge," which gave its receiver psychic ability, discerning of spirits, faith healing and other miracles, prophecy, and interpretation of tongues. Luckily (and inexplicably), they did not believe in the gifts of drinking poison and handling snakes without harm, which are mentioned right next to those other gifts in the Bible. My mother received the ability to discern spirits. This would come as no great surprise if you knew her. In my eleventh year, she discerned the Demon of Rebellion in me for the first time —a diagnosis she has made many times since.

From the beginning of their charismatic conversion, I squirmed. Watching my parents become enmeshed in the culture of the church was enormously uncomfortable. It was a far cry from the congregation at the little brick chapel. There my parents had been the redeemed offspring of well-known town drunks; here they could be pillars of a spiritual community. They began to pepper their sentences with "halleluiahs," and "praise the Lords." About a year into it, they decided to give over their lives (and mine) to the church. They sold everything we owned, save our clothes and some small personal items, and gave the proceeds to the church. In the interest of full disclosure, I admit that they did take us to Disney World —a fact that my youngest sister, who was born later, has never really gotten over. Following our last hurrah in Orlando, we left our former life for good. After a failed attempt to save the "downtrodden" in an inner city mission, the adults in the group decided to purchase a farm in the middle of nowhere and live communally, in harmony with God and nature, which brings us to Howard City and the announcement I mentioned earlier.

The part of nature that was human in the little town did not understand the holy impulses that led to the arrangement. Certain that the town's newest residents planned to engage in any number of illegal and immoral activities (wasn't the word "commune" synonymous with smoking marijuana cigarettes, organic gardening, and wife swapping?) they had circulated a petition to block the purchase of the farm. I didn't know about the organized opposition of our little community as I made the excruciatingly awkward trip from our van to the school building —but the other kids did. I didn't know that something even more damning than the ridiculous dress had marked me.

It turns out that the students themselves were generally not opposed to smoking marijuana or sexual promiscuity per se, (though they were probably suspicious of organic gardening). But they weren't about to haul out the welcome wagon for a girl like me. Difference was not well received in the mind-numbing homogeneity of this town. People who were different were "weird," certainly not to be trusted. So, before I ever got a chance to utter a word, meet a single person, or even catch the eye of a potential friend, I was branded an outsider.

I recall, with sickening clarity, our approach to the dilapidated, soon-to-be-condemned two-story building that housed the junior high school. Since we were running late, there were relatively few students in the schoolyard. Those who lingered outside eyed me warily as I dragged myself and the horrible dress closer to the nearest entrance. My face burned with embarrassment as we reached a dimly lit stairwell that led to the second floor. A girl, who I later learned was named Norma Rose, was standing a couple of steps from the bottom of the stairwell. Her hot pants were so short they revealed the lower quarter of her butt. To complement the shorts, she wore a turquoise and white striped tube top that barely contained her already substantial breasts.

My mother gasped in horror. She then pursed her lips so hard I was afraid she might begin to make a smooching sound. I let my head sag the rest of the way to my still undeveloped chest and tried to prepare myself for our ascent past the girl. Norma was screaming obscenities at someone who turned out to be Andrea "Andy" Mitchell. Andy, who could not yet be seen, but was easily heard, returned Norma's verbal abuse with an equally colorful string of epithets. At thirteen years of age Norma already looked like she'd been (as the cowboys say) "rode hard and put away wet." As I squeezed past her, wishing with all my might that I would miraculously vanish into the sour smelling, dusty air, Norma stopped her tirade, leveled her Robins Egg Blue eye shadowed gaze at me and asked pointedly, "What the fuck is your problem?" I didn't respond and prayed hard that my mother's mouth would remain sphincter-like and silent. Thankfully, it did. We were halfway up the stairs when Norma, who had just seconds before seemed to detest Andy with a passion that was reserved in those parts for hatred, called up, "Hey! Mitchell, do you see this? What the fuck is that?"

Welcome to seventh grade.

It took months before I made much headway in the coarse, countrified world of Tri County Junior High. Even after I ditched the dress, I was pretty much doomed to the farthest outskirts of society. One day in mid-November, when I had simply taken all I could stand, I snapped. It was Debbie Northrup, a heavy-set, bulldog of a girl who was looking for a way to augment her own meager stash of cultural capital, who pushed me over the edge and out of the margins. On that day as I walked out Miss Yankovic's English class, the only class I almost enjoyed, Debbie glowered at me from the second floor. Fate must have led me to look up and meet her eyes. "What are you looking at, you little piece of trailer trash?" she spewed. Without reply, I threw my books to the floor and took the stairs two at a time. With tears of anger and humiliation burning my eyes, I reached the top of the stairs and charged at her.

Although she outweighed me by at least fifty pounds and probably could have taken me under ordinary circumstances, the look on her face changed from contempt to terror as I bore down on her. I drew my arm back as I ran, then slugged her substantial middle as hard as I could. The momentum of my approach must have added considerable energy to the punch. Debbie doubled over on the floor, gagging.

For the first time since I had left my childhood home, I was unaware of myself in relation to the rest of the world. Focused exclusively on exacting my revenge, it seemed to me that Debbie Northrup and I were the only two people alive. But when I took an unsteady step backward, I noticed the considerable crowd that had gathered around us. Being as hopped up on adrenalin as I was —and savoring the metallic taste of vengeance for the first time — I didn't care what they thought of me at that point. To my amazement, it began to dawn on me that the hooting and hollering was all in my favor. I had broken through a social barrier. I had learned to do as the natives did in this harsh and unyielding place. Violence was not only acceptable at Tri-County Junior High; it was the preferred style of communication.

At the height of ruckus, I discovered another, heretofore unknown, emotional capacity when Tina Sorensen (the most popular girl of the "Partiers" in the school) put her arm around me. Thinking fast, I said, "Damn, I thought I was gonna lose my arm in all that fat!" Tina and her disciples roared with laughter. My heart thumped madly in my flat chest, first jump-started by hatred and now by, what was this? I had a crush! On Tina Sorensen!! She spun me away from the scene of Debbie's social de-pantsing, and ushered me down the hall.

Still Life
Sonya Renee Taylor

I remember Trea
like a Renoir
almost moving
lovely
still

Remember wishing she would stop
living in the grey of his words
the same mouth
full of ibis
and vultures

The first time he crashed into
her delicate face
with the steel beam of his knuckles
she sat suspended
like the air between each blow
certain she had dreamt this fury
sure it would fade in the morning
like moons

Sometimes we write I Love You's
in between the lines
In the grey shades
of sweaty sheets
pieces of skin
under our fingernails

wipe our bloodied noses
with the thin white petals
of orchids
brought to us as penance
for yesterday's transgressions
Let them love us hard
as fist to jaw
sharp as knife to gut
Love us like a

gunshot

to the memories
of a first kiss

Sometimes Trea left like spring
only to return season
after season
when his angry winters
promised to melt
to warm
to return soft
as forgiveness

This time she left
like all the pamphlets said
like the 800 hotlines walk you through
packed her shirts, her shoes
and left
Not like spring or seagulls
She left like hope
She left like a bird with nowhere to
return to

leaving is not always enough
in this world of paper processes
and conundrums of laws that protect you
after you're hurt
after he breaks you like a sparrow's wing
after his love
like
a knife

a fist

a

gunshot

leaves you still
as paintings

I remember Trea like a Renoir
almost moving
not like the placid cold
dead of a woman
laying hollow
on her apartment floor

a single bullet in her head
mouth shaped as if she meant to
tell him she could
still
love him like
spring

He shot himself
I think he hoped to follow her
forever like
autumn after summer

And this is how I remember Trea
like summer
waiting on the breath of May
to bloom
remember her like a swan
bowing to meet the water
I remember her like seasons

and birds
but they
die

So I have to remember Trea
like a timeless painting
like a Renoir
beautiful
still
and
almost
alive

Life Without Love

Faye-Symone Pompey

Life without love, can you imagine?
Can you even imagine not having love ?
I don't have to imagine
I've lived life without love.
No unconditional love, none at all.
No love from a father figure.
no love.
What does a child do to not deserve love?
How can I explain not knowing love?
Do you know love?
If you do can you show me love?
I never had it .
I never felt it.
I never even seen it.

How can I *Possibly* mean it?

The Day Linda Died

Piper Anderson

I am writing this from my bathtub in the dark. I'm sitting in an empty tub in a dark bathroom because it is the only place at this moment where I can find privacy and silence. I've just had the final fight with this particular live-in lover and this is where I've come to make sense of how I got here. How I ended up in yet another destructive relationship with another person that I realize that I have no business being with. The realization always comes entirely too late. After we've signed a lease together, professed endless devotion, and even introduced the family. Nine months later I realize that it was a mistake. Unfortunately, not before being left with bills that may never get paid and an apartment I can't afford. But this time I've decided to give myself a "time out" so I've come to the bathtub instead of continuing with the volatile exchange that will only go where I've been way too many times before. I had no intention of fighting, but then again I never do. Yet some how I'm shoved against a wall, the pot of food that I was cooking has been thrown on to the floor, names are called, and I have a bruise beginning to turn fleshy purple on my leg. So I retreat to the bathroom while on the other side of the door I hear apologies being moaned and cleaner applied to the stained walls. I ignore the apologies and wait for silence on the other end to signal that my adversary has retreated. I am not afraid of violence just tired of it.

Earlier that day my mother called me just as she does each week. In her uniquely practical way of demonstrating motherly concern she runs through her customary list of questions. "Do I need anything? Money? A warm coat? A bus ticket home?" But this time she had more to say. As her thick full voice cracked open grief spilled out and the words "Linda's dead", ripped through my eardrums. Just as quickly as the cry was there it was gone and my mom's voice returned to its normal even alto explaining the details of her death. "It was an ex-boyfriend... They'd been together on and off ten years... She wanted out... He threatened to kill her... She didn't report it.... He came through the upstairs window.... The one with the broken lock.... Stabbed her to death.... Her son, Askia found her body...You remember Askia.

Well he's grown now. 21... Taking it hard... I'll let you know when the funeral arrangements have been made..." We hung up the phone and I was left to decipher her tone and measure how much I could allow myself to feel. I've always looked to my mother to determine just how much feeling is enough. She is the stoic barometer that never registers a reading above calm detachment. You can either call it a Zen approach to living or the disassociated tendency of a trauma victim. I think it's both. She is an expert on surviving. I've watched her at work perfecting the art of survival and served as her apprentice.

Before Linda there was Stephanie...
I was fifteen when my mother called me into her room at 1am.
She was on the phone long distance with my Uncle Leon receiving the news that my cousin Stephanie had been shot to death by her husband. He turned the gun on himself after he shot her. Stephanie's marriage was deemed the model of perfection in our family. Finally, a woman in our family had found a man who would marry her (the more common alternative being single motherhood), buy her a house and a car, and stick around even after their two children were born. So when Stephanie began to complain about his jealousy, dominating nature, and eventual death threats, she was told by mothers, aunts and cousins that she was lucky to have a man and she had better not give it up. She couldn't possibly deprive her children of their father. Stephanie was told to stay despite fearing for her life because of the house, the car, and the financial security. After nearly a decade of marriage in the end she lost everything including her life. When I walked into my mother's bedroom that night her voice cracked open spilling out grief much the same way that it would ten years later. I began to scream uncontrollably. Loud shrill painful screams hysterical and confused. How could this be happening? Before the painful leaping shock inside of me could reach its climax, I heard my mother's commanding voice rise above my screams and tell me to be quiet. I abruptly stopped screaming and turned to watch her. How should I respond? I thought. How do I deal with this? With the phone firmly pressed to her ear, she listened silently to hear what needed to be done to deal with this tragedy and hung up the phone. Her face revealed nothing. She was stoic and still. The funeral arrangements were made

in the next few days, but we never had a conversation about why this happened. Why was Stephanie taken away from us? Was this kind of thing normal? Does this happen in everyone's family? I silently cried myself to sleep and I never asked any questions. But the murder of Stephanie rocked me in so many ways. It taught me that as a woman, a black woman, my life could be taken away from me and no one would truly mourn, no one would cry out against the injustice done to my body, my soul not even my own mother.

Who is my mother?
My mother is a woman who wakes at 5am on Mondays, Wednesdays, and Fridays to drive herself to a dialysis center where a machine completes the process her kidneys cannot. She has maintained this routine for ten years as she waits for a kidney transplant to relieve her of this time consuming task. On one of my monthly visits to Philadelphia to visit my parents, I went to pick her up after her one of her weekly dialysis treatments. Standing outside of the dialysis room watching her amongst the room full of patients, each lying back on a chair with an IV in their arm connected to a machine cleansing their bodies of impurities stored up over the two days since their last treatment, she is the one that seems oddly out of place. Most of the other patients look old and bewildered by this process. But than you see my mother and she looks tranquil, if not revived by this routine procedure. But I know better. I've traveled with this woman enough to know how she got here. The stress of a marriage to a bi-polar alcoholic husband by night and caseworker to dozens of mentally ill adult substance abusers by day she refused to acknowledge that stress relief was a skill that needed to be learned. So one day at work sitting at her desk big bruises started to rapidly appear all over her body. She was rushed to the hospital. Hypertension had now transformed into kidney failure. I was twelve years old when my mother joined the list of thousands of people waiting for a kidney transplant. Till this day she refuses to acknowledge what sent her there. No one did. Because to do that would mean that she would need to leave my father for good.

My parents have taught me everything that I know about love. When I was born my father was married to another woman. While I don't know how my parents met, I do know that they had an affair for several years before I was born. I came into the world as my father's first marriage was unraveling. At 27 years old and pregnant with her first child, my mother had already decided that she would be a single mother and do it on her own. She was more than capable of it to. Back then she was a schoolteacher and marathon runner who ran races up until her eight month of pregnancy. I have vague memories of my mother taking me to the track to watch her train. At three years old I started running with her. At three years old my mother's goal of raising her child alone was thrown away. I remember when I realized that she was a prisoner to my father. The day he broke down our front door chasing her up on to the roof of the house that my mother bought and paid for on her own in North Philadelphia. He dragged her down the stairs out of the house and into his car. For a while she resisted his attempts to dominate her. She fought to get away, to keep her sanity, her life. But soon he wore her down. Killed her spirit using a deadly combination of mental and physical abuse. The last time she tried to escape I was a sophomore in high school. We secretly moved to the outskirts of Philadelphia; some place that he would never find us. And for a while we were safe and happy. But six months into our new life she called him. Six months later we were moving back to Philly to live with my father. To this day, I don't know what triggered that phone call. What made her willingly turn her life over to him for good? When I asked her why we were going back? She told me "I needed too much stuff". I was hurt because not only did I look up to her and depend on her example, but I was also her confidant. I was the one that she plotted escapes with and mapped out the future. When my mother stopped fighting I learned that love was a war that no woman could win. Because if my mother, this brave, strong, powerful woman could not resist a life of violence than no woman that I knew could.

For better or for worst, most of my life I have followed the example of my mom. She walks through life with the stoic demeanor of a Zen Master. But upon hearing the news of my cousin Linda's murder, I realized that I no longer possessed the will of my Zen Master. After

25 years of faithfully following her example, I allowed myself to feel the full extent of my grief. I sat down and I cried openly, publicly, in Washington Square Park on a bench in mid-day as roller bladders, bicyclists, nannies with full baby strollers strode by me. NYU students sat on the grass painting themselves into the picture of this beautiful winter day ignoring the disconcerting nature of my release. I cried and big hunks of tears fell out of my eyes. I trembled and I held myself and felt the grief that I'd been holding in for years. In that public display of stored-up grief, I felt all the pain that I had never allowed myself to feel before because I was taught that it was an inappropriate, unnecessary, foolish, useless waste of time. I grieved and I didn't care who saw or what my mom would say or whether or not I'd be able to pull myself back together once the tears began. I was just tired. Tired of keeping it all packed in. I was in desperate need of healing and change. There is no way that I could continue to follow my mother down this path any longer. I don't want to be the next woman in my family to die at the hands of a lover. I don't want to see all my dreams and my health slip away because I chose to stay with a man whose love for me is expressed through violence. It's time for me to choose life. Surviving is no longer enough.

So here I am sitting in my bathtub in a bathroom locking out a lover who has proven to be just as volatile as others. Just as volatile as my father who turned a free spirited woman destined to carve out her own beautiful legacy into a chronically sick 52 year old too disabled to work. My mother. A woman who only dreams of getting her PhD and going back to teaching, but may never believe in herself enough again to actually do it. Just like Linda's former lover who decided to take her life rather than live without her. Just like Stephanie's husband who murdered her in her bed and than turned the gun on himself. I have lived with violence for much too long. It has cut out the air all around me making it impossible for me to inhale freely. I want to be free from violence. Free to become the woman that my mother would have become. The woman who will leave this bathroom tonight, walk out the front door, and never look back.

Between Cooking and Dancing

Zoraida Cordova

Mami-Leja said
learning to cook came second
on the list of things a nice girl like me
needed to accomplish.
Finding a nice Hispanic husband
was first
because who would eat all the food
made during the day?

I told her I wanted to be a painter,
write novels and plays,
run naked through the Amazon,
have an affair with a beautiful
Irish man
and order take-out.

No! You learn real Ecuadorian food!

I did cook a *Seco* once—
chicken served with yellow rice—
when Mami-Leja was too tired to move around
and sat on a stool in the kitchen
to criticize while I made the *refrito.*

Cut tomatoes
—*No, too fine!*
Chop cilantro
—*Your fingers swollen, girl? Faster!*
Slice peppers
—*The green, not red!*
She looked to the ceiling asking Saints Gregory
and Bernard, and Mary herself

Why, why my granddaughter no cook!

I let the chicken cook in the *refrito,*
had to ask the neighbor for a Corona
and explain it was for the chicken, not me.

Mami-Leja left to the living room
to watch the soccer match on *Telemundo:*

Ecuador vs. Argentina

and I wrote in my notebook on the kitchen counter,
the new Salsa and Merengue radio station just loud
enough for me to still hear the score.

Then I saw smoke,
and Mami-Leja smelled burning rice,
rushing to the stove—
bad leg and all— to see my disaster.

Ready for the lecture:

I learned to cook when I was nine
and your Ma was 10
and your cousin's only 12 and she never burns the rice!

But she remained quiet,
reaching for the radio and
turning the volume up.
It was our song, the one about the gypsy woman.
She moved her shoulders
because her legs weren't as fast.
I took a step to the side
and spun on my heel.

Mihijita,
At least you can dance.

Rice. Determines When You Get Married.
Maikong Vue

"Get up. I have already run to the market and back and you not awake yet!" My mother whined, intentionally making me feel lazy and guilty. I got up to realize the aroma of freshly cooked rice. Now I am feeling more guilt that she not only ran to the market and back, but also cooked rice. In my culture, the girl is never to wake up late. She is always to wake up early and cook for the whole family.

I felt a fast burst of anger as she said softly, "what kind of a daughter-in-law will you be. Mother-in-law will probably send you back. Say that you are lazy. Not cook for your husband's family." Pretend I *had* woken up early enough to cook rice. She would then find a reason to hate the rice that I've cooked. "Not enough water in your rice. Rice is too hard." Or "Rice is too soggy. Too much water in your rice." She would speak as if the rice I made was going to determine when I would get married. If you were in your mid-twenties and unmarried, that meant that you did not cook good rice.

I had a way of expressing my anger. I slammed cabinets. When I received lectures it was always in the kitchen during my cooking. Since she cooked the rice. I MUST cook the vegetables. At least then I would get a little respect for waking up late. In the kitchen there was an unlimited supply of cabinets. Every time I reached in to grab a bowl, I slammed it. I never talked back to my mother. Not only will the lecture get worst, but she was my mother. *She* ... was always right. For every cabinet door I slammed, she blinked her eyes real hard as if it would shove me down the side of a mountain and say, "don't you be so stubborn. A good daughter does not act that way." She always had the power to make me ask myself: "Am I raised to be a successful daughter, or a good daughter-in-law?"

I knew her answer: "You will be a successful daughter and a good daughter-in-law." That's all that is important in Hmong society. I want to tell her that I don't want to marry a Hmong man. I am going to marry a white man and move away from here. I mean it. I mean it to get her angry. I want to tell her I will be a successful woman. The "daughter-in-law" portion will come after. I don't tell her any of this. She is my mother. *She* ... is always right. On her part, that is.

We Couldn't Ignore It
Carissa Kiepert

The first time I had seen my dad in a year and a half, he was wearing a forest green jumpsuit and handcuffs. I was standing, trembling at the door of the courtroom. I slowly walked into the room and stood by my place, in the front row on the prosecutor's side. The bailiff opened a heavily bolted door, and in walked my dad. I abruptly sat down as he walked past, clearly intent on not looking at me. My half-sister sat in the front on a hard plastic chair, not even 15 feet from the man that had ruined both our lives. My own flesh and blood, the man that had acted as my half sister's father for most of her life, sat stone-faced in his chair.

The judge walked in and everyone stood up. As we sat back down, the trial began. The D.A., Sandy Williams, sat next to my sister. Behind them, I sat wedged in between two of my sister's best friends, each holding my hand. On the defendant's side, my dad sat next to his lawyer. Behind them was my step-mom and many other people I had known my whole life as family. His family, to be exact.

The judge said a few opening words and gave the floor to the DA. She said a few things and then started reading a statement from my mother. I didn't listen that intently because I knew if I did, I would start crying. After the D.A. read the letter from my mom, my half-sister started to speak. When she started off her sentence with, "Mr. Kiepert..." tears started to come. I quickly blinked them back, but I had finally realized that this was actually real. I don't know what I had expected her to call him. Certainly not 'dad', which she had been doing for the past 14 years of her life, but by hearing that I felt isolated. That was my last name. That was my dad. I didn't know how to react. Apparently, neither did my dad, because he sat there, staring straight ahead, barely even blinking and he certainly never turned around. He didn't speak at all until it was his turn to address the court.

When he finally did speak, he turned to the side, facing my half-sister, and started uttering an extremely insufficient apology. All apologies would have been insufficient at this point, but his two-minute speech wasn't very moving. During this "speech," my sister sat stone-faced, looking towards the front and barely blinked, doing something I know she had been wanting to do for a long time: Ignore him.

This was something she could never do in the past. She couldn't ignore him while he was telling her to take off her clothes. She couldn't ignore him when he made her sit down as he took pictures of her. She couldn't ignore the pictures he made her look at of children, some as young as six, in degrading pornographic poses. And she couldn't ignore it when he told her to copy those poses. If she did ignore what he said she would get hit, and then, so would I.

No one else could continue to ignore what was going on at this point either. Not the judge, as he was shown some of the pictures brought in for evidence. Not my step-mom as she sat, crying, on the bench. And finally, I couldn't ignore what had happened any longer; I started crying. Then the judge gave his decision: 18 years in prison. My dad couldn't ignore it. He was finally being punished for what he had done.

Now, six years later, I'm still ignoring him. One parole hearing has come and gone, without success for my dad. Another is looming in the distance. I choose not to write a letter to the parole board for the first hearing and I am not planning on participating in the second. I feel like I should continue with my life and not worry about what happened in the past. I've suffered enough because of him, and I don't think he is worth anymore of my time. A lot of people wonder why I don't write something to try and keep him in jail. They think that because he hurt me so badly six years in prison isn't a long enough consequence for the lifetime of change and suffering I have endured. I don't really know why I don't want to write something. Sometimes I feel like I'm still pretending it didn't happen. Other times I feel like I just want to go on with my life and as long as he doesn't bother me, I don't care what happens to him. Regardless of the reason, I still maintain my original plan of ignoring him. It took me 10 years to do it, and now that I am able to ignore him successfully, I don't want to try to stop. If I let him creep back into my life, I just don't know if I would be able to push him away a second time.

Visitation Hours at Kershaw Correctional

Christina Owens

I.

The first time I went to see my dad in prison I almost missed the entrance. It was on a lonely road with an empty field on one side and a sign posted between the trees on the other, "Kershaw Correctional Facility." Up above the official signpost there was a piece of particleboard, spray painted in orange, "Jobs Here ."

The facility itself was a low, squat complex of white buildings, white power poles, white fences and white razor wires rolled together like tumbleweed, perched high to the sky. All around this were the greens and rusty oranges of pine trees, standing guard in regimented rows and columns.

I parked my car and sat there for a few minutes. My stomach was feeling strange, like either I needed to eat or sit on the toilet for a long time and wait for something to come out. The entire trip there, I kept reminding myself to stay cognizant and engaged, to breathe and concentrate on my surroundings, and what I was about to do and what I was willing to give.

In the prison parking lot, I watched all the other people getting in and out of their vehicles. *What are their loved ones in for? Do they come here every weekend to visit? What's that like?* My mind wandered. This is my worse coping mechanism: auto-pilot dissociation. *Take your time. Don't speed up out of fear. Look at the barbed wire, the razored fences. Sit in the car for a few minutes before you go in. Breathe.* I had to coach myself through the movements.

In the line, there was a whole family standing in front of me, mother, sister, lover, children. The officer glanced at my blank paper with the ID number at the top, *"Is this his number?"* *"Yes, it's his".* Somewhere along the way I had forgotten that prisons and numbers are gendered.

I went through one door, which was locked behind me, then another, locked behind. A corridor and another door, then there was a woman sitting at a desk eating fast food. I looked at her, puzzled, and she pointed to a window. The woman behind the window came over to stamp my hand with invisible ink. I gave her the printout with my dad's name on it and she pointed to the side hallway. The door labeled "Visitors Entrance" buzzed and, as I stepped through, I heard her announce over the intercom, "Lavern Owens, report for visitation."

The visitors' hall was bright and bustling, with concrete covered in white tiles. I walked in, not sure what I was supposed to do or where I was supposed to sit. A man in khakis, an inmate helper, caught up with me halfway across the room,

"I'll seat you. The people over there usually do it but today they gave me the job."

He collected the printout with my name on it and led me to table number 12. "He'll be out in a few minutes." I sat there, looking around, wondering which way he would come in, if he would know which table I was at, if I was allowed to go to the canteen by myself beforehand, if I would be able to give him a hug or if there was a rule against that.

There was no rule, or at least it's not enforced. We hugged. He was nervous, couldn't eat, and couldn't stop talking. I was reminded of my first few months living in Japan, where every weekend became a race for unfettered communication. Five days in our rural Japanese towns and we were bursting with words in English. My dad had been in for six months and I was his second visitor.

"Where am I at? Where is this place? When they brought me from the Kirkland prison I could tell we went a long way on the interstate, then we got off and made lots of turns before we got here." The piquancy of the questions struck me—to know with certainty that you are going nowhere and yet still wanting to put yourself on a map, to feel somehow less lost.

It took us a long time to come to the issue of him and what got him there: criminal domestic violence, perpetrated against my stepmother while I was halfway around the world in Japan. It had happened almost two years before and I had spoken to him only once since. He offered apologies and heaps of self-degrading commentary on his own mistakes and short-fallings, lots of excuses of why he "lost control." I have nothing to say to any of this. I've heard it before.

At one point he began to cry.
   "Don't give up on me now."
   I held his hand.
   "I haven't. That's why I'm here."
That's the only statement, the only signifier of emotional commitment that I feel comfortable offering. As always, he wants me to help fix his problems, explain where it is that he went wrong, how to recognize his destructive patterns and break them down. "Maybe you can help me work it out. If anyone knows my problems, you do," he says. And he's right. I know my dad better than anyone else in the world. But it's not my place to tell him how to become a better person. I can't be his therapist. I'm not sure if he'll ever understand that though. As long as he keeps asking the question, I'll know that, like him, our relationship is in lock down, a stasis that goes nowhere.

II.

I went to see my dad almost every other week for the whole four months I was living down South. The round trip to Kershaw was seven hours then the visit itself was four hours long. It was a full day's lonely agenda, with me all by myself in the car, listening to Japanese conversation CDs and wondering what he and I would have to say to each other.

The first few hours were always easy. He would talk about life inside, prison culture, the tenor of daily routine. He's happy to go through the diet line, where at least they give you fruit. Inmates have to buy their own butter, salt and pepper from the canteen and carry it to the cafeteria everyday. They only allow you five minutes to eat and then kick you out.

At night, groups of people pitch in together and make "set-ups," big tubs of microwavable rice mixed with specialty canned food from the canteen. The cheapest and most popular is canned mackerel. My dad prefers beef stew. He rarely takes part in the set-ups. I think he's afraid of feeling too much a part of the group. He was never supposed to end up in prison, after all. He was supposed to be more "in control" than that.

There are a few people he talks to, mostly older white men like himself. From our assigned table, he looks around and points out the bullies and the loudmouths, other men from his yard, other men from the hometown. He tells me about this one old man in his wing who met his son inside. He missed out on the boy's childhood, but now they're cellmates.

I begin to notice some of the same people there every week: the Latina girl visiting her boyfriend with their baby; the elderly white couple with the bespectacled, tattooed son; the African-American mother who offered advice on visitation procedures; the girl who looks like my cousin Naomi. We are in the line-up together every week, waiting to take off our belts and shoes and go through the metal detectors. I look around from my little, square table and watch their visits.

At 3:45 the correction officers call a count and all the inmates have to line up against the far wall. By the time my dad comes back, we only have an hour more to go. He's still nervous around me and can't muster an appetite for the whole visit. He fidgets. I'm still anxious and guarded, not sure what this relationship is supposed to be about.

In the last hour he wants to talk about life outside, his life, what got him here and his prospects after release. "I hope Mary doesn't come around and bother me when I get out," he says. Mary is my step-mother, the so-called "reason" why he is here and this is an old habit for my father — making himself into a possible martyr and conveniently forgetting his whole history of stalking.

"I'm sure she feels the same way about you, afraid that you'll come around and bother her," I reply.

Predictably, he counters my objection with a list of Mary's infractions, how I don't know her as well as he does. "She was coming around the house everyday, toying with me, asking for pills. I should've known back when she started going to see Lisa. I'd go with her sometimes and they'd be back in the bedroom doing crack and meth. Everything went downhill from there. You don't know Mary, Chris. She's a different person now."

"I don't care if she's a different person. What I care about is you taking responsibility for yourself." I'm screaming these words on the inside while on the outside I'm giving some stilted argumentative account of his violence. I am tied up in knots and there are only twenty minutes left in our visit. I'll never get untangled.

In the last hour of the next visit he wants to know why I don't want to be around him anymore, why I move to far away places, across the country to Seattle, across the world to Japan. "I always tried to do right by you. But being in here, I have lots of time to think and I realize I wasn't perfect. Last week I said I've always been a loser in my life. That's not what I meant. I've always been a failure, not a loser. A failure. What happened to you down in John's Town—that was my failure. I should've known about Chucky touching you. Back when I was spending all that time with Rachel I thought about you growing up and how I should've done things different. I could've spent more time with you. I could've done better. I'm sorry I wasn't as good as I shoulda been, but I always thought I was doing what was right. It hurts me that you don't even wanta be in the same state with me."

Five minutes before five, the correction officer announces the end of visitation. People stand up and hug. My dad and I walk slowly toward the far wall, still caught up in the knots. When we get to the red line, we stop and he stammers something that breaks my heart and I hold his hand.

"I'm sorry I upset you when you come here. I don't mean to. I put my foot in my mouth and then I beat myself up about it for the rest of the week."
"No need to beat yourself up."

"Please come back."
"I will."

III.

Two weeks later I did go back and I decided to lay it all out. "Don't interrupt me. Don't try to defend yourself or give your side. Don't say anything. Just listen. After this visit we don't ever have to talk about this again. This is for this space, right now. If we don't talk about this, if you don't hear me out, if I don't speak my mind, then this kind of thing will keep coming up every time I come here and I don't want that. Here's a pencil and some paper if you want to write things down, but please don't interrupt me now. Just listen."

The sentences came out in spurts with tortured pacing and slow, awkward pauses. I kept reminding myself that if I don't talk now, then we could always get caught up in the unsaid, the unheard. My dad would always leave the visitation room afraid that I would never come back, caught up in imaginary power plays where I withhold visitation as punishment and he is defenseless in my wake.

I talked for almost two hours. I talked about growing up with him, about the love and the price for love, the expectation that I should love him over anyone else. My dad didn't hit me as a child. Instead, he convinced me that he was perfect and infallible and all the horrible things that he did to my mother and his girlfriends were their fault. All downfalls, break ups, setbacks, lay-offs, firings, bad decisions and lost causes can be and were rationalized away. As he so often says, I was the perfect child: perfectly programmed to project the image of himself that he wanted to see.

But projections are not reality. Reality is in relationships — the intermittent outbursts of stalking, hitting and beating, the constant manipulation. When I am feeling generous I tell myself that he has too much love that he doesn't know what to do with and too little self-esteem to know that he can be loved back, without coercion and manipulation, without illusions and false ideals.

I know the story of his abusive grandmother and our alcoholic family. I know the weight of traditional masculinity and working class capitalism. Still, none of these things absolves responsibility, none of them decreases the value of recognizing the patterns in our own lives and knowing that we have no control over anything, but ourselves and our reactions to what the world throws at us.

"I moved away to all those far away places because I thought I needed distance to get perspective. It took me three years in Seattle to face your imperfections and three years in Japan to face your humanity and see you whole again. You should've been a nursery school teacher instead of a welder. That's what my friend Sarah said when I told her this story. When I told her about you raising me as a single father, babysitting two-year old Rachel for three months straight and crying at every sappy movie you see. You should've been a nursery school teacher. I never would have thought about it that way, but it might be true."

You, my father, lover of small children, sentimental man with gnarled, working hands and too little self-esteem. Maybe you could have learned to weld your love into patterns more fruitful, more beautiful, than the bars you've put yourself behind.

I said all of these things and more, with innumerable stops and starts, rephrasings, clarifications and examples. He fidgeted with the pencil I gave him and looked down at the table. Every now and then he would quietly interrupt to deny something, like Teresa's black eye or my mother's bad knee. My mom tells me of a time when he beat her so badly she could barely walk. She went back to her father's house for help, but he spat at her feet, "You made your bed, now sleep in it." It has become a story of condemnation for both husband and father. I first heard her tell it when I was a kid and have no reason to doubt its truthfulness. I do doubt my dad's understanding and memory of his own violence. We agreed to disagree on examples and I kept slowly talking through the issues. At five o'clock the corrections officers called time, so we hugged and said goodbye.

I saw my dad one more time in Kershaw after our talk. He drank apple juice from the vending machine and raved and laughed about how good it tasted. He told me about the strip search they go through at the end of visitation, how another guy from the hometown snuck a watch in once. Sometimes he gets the hometown newspaper from that guy and reads about what's going on. We talked about the pictures I sent in the mail, letters he was writing to old friends, technicalities for a parole hearing in March.

At the end of our visitation he paused, "I know you said we don't have to talk about it again but I've been thinking about what you said for two weeks now. I don't agree with everything you said about me. I don't think I'm always trying to live up to images. I just want to be a good person. But that doesn't matter. Maybe it is true. You always have been smarter than me anyway. But by saying it, by telling me what you think, I know you love me. To sit down and say all that stuff that's so hard to say, I know you love me."

True to character, the man who loves tearjerker movies cried a little. And that's all he said about it. And we haven't had to talk about it since. The relationship that I imagined was in stasis, locked down, has moved on, at least for now.

SHE WAITED TO EXHALE

Tanis Kwanette

SHE SPOKE...
WHEN SHE FELT IT TIME TO SPEAK
HER VOICE...
SOFT CONCRETE WAITING TO SET, EVEN AND NONCHALANT
UTTERED...
VOLUMES REACHING MANY AN ACHING SOUL, I KNOW
THAT SHE SAVED
A LIFE THAT NIGHT.
SPECULATIONS OF SEXUALITY
AFFIRMED.
REJECTION IN HER MIND...
EXPECTED.
HATE LETTERS AND DEATH THREATS MIGHT TAKE SOME
GETTING USE
TO.
TEARS...
THAT WONT STOP FLOWING, A METAMORPHOSIS OF ELATED
BLISS,
FALLS INTO A POND OF LIQUID SADNESS.
ALL BECAUSE...
SHE CHOSE TO LIVE, DREAM, COME OUT, SPEAK,
EXHALE.

Bursting the Umbilical Cord
Tess McCray

At 18 years old I stood behind my mother in her kitchen. My world. The woman who had trapped me with the kind of love that slowly, quietly sucks out life. She tirelessly stacked sandbags, shoring up the walls of the umbilical cord she wanted forever connecting us — keeping us close — keeping me safe.

In her nylon nightgown, she stood at the stove cracking eggs on the side of the skillet and sending them sizzling into the pan. She was perfect... she never spilled.

"Mom I'm a lesbian." I sent the words sailing out to the back of her head.

Egg in hand, she paused for moment. The floor was cold on my bare feet as I stood waiting for her.

She tilted her head to the side, and in a voice devoid of persecution, but also devoid of love said, "How do you figure?"

The million answers I had stored up seemed to leave me at once. I had spent hours working out responses and reasons, but at the moment I needed them most they all seemed to slip away. I looked out the window, and my mind became a swirl of memories: first kisses, yearnings, truths. Finally, I centered on one...

Mrs. Bishop was my fourth grade teacher. She was allergic to chalk and nuts, and always parted her hair left of center.

I have never noticed so much of a person so quickly before. She commanded a reaction from me not only visually, but through all of my senses. The first parts of her to jump at me were her temples. They had this almost imperceptible way of moving in and out when she chewed or spoke. I remember always wondering if she would mind me placing a solitary finger there while she talked to the class. Her hair was limp, short, and blonde. It stopped just above her ears, so I began to use the class scissors to cut off bits of my hair during recess.

Unlike my mother, she never wore makeup. I would get lost in the reality of an unpainted, female face. She had slight freckles and a small mole above her lip. When I noticed it, I began to understand why my mother said Marilyn's mole was a symbol of sexiness.

Crow's feet surrounded her green eyes, but I enjoyed that. It made her seem so real to me, so different from my mother. Her eyebrows had a high pitch to them, like the crooked silhouette of a bird's wing. Her mouth was slim and of almost the same color as her skin. It was hard to notice where her skin left off and her lips began. I would watch them move, wondering how her words found their way out around her tongue. Her voice was deep and raspy, and I could hear it at night when I closed my eyes.

Her body was covered in a thin layer of white hair. When she stood by the window the light would play off the hairs and make her appear as though she were some celestial being with a divine aura. The lines of her body were so different from any other woman I had known. Her cheek bone was profound and sloping. Constantly she wore these sleeveless, floral patterned dresses. I remember noticing the curve and dip of her arm. The sweat always seemed to collect there, in the hollow place at her elbow. She was tall, thin, and strong. I was embarrassed of my fat mother, of my fat self. Her fingers were long. She constantly used her hands while talking, and her wedding ring would slip up and down, up and down. When she came to my seat to point something out on my paper, I would study the teal veins on the back of her hand, daring myself to reach out to feel them.

I was compelled to be her favorite, and at the book fair I used my allowance to buy four books so she would be pleased. I would sit in the far reaches of the corner at recess. Pretending to play cards, I would watch her swing the whistle around her three middle fingers. If she smiled, I smiled. If she laughed, I felt an incomprehensible swelling in my chest. If she was absent, I felt sick. I was addicted to her.

During tests she would sit at her desk and slip her shoes off casually. From my seat in the front row I could just see her naked, white feet. Though unremarkable, they were her feet, and that made them more interesting than anything in the world. I knew better the shape of her ankle than my weekly spelling words. When called up to her desk, I would hold my breath until she leaned far enough over her papers for her dress to fall away from her neck. When it did I was able to catch a glimpse of the cups of her bra. It was black, with a lacy floral pattern that reminded me of my mother's crocheted doilies.

The tops of her breasts were pure white and my interest in them confounded me.

My mother would pick me up from school, and I would run into the bathroom and close the door. There I would stare at my naked self in the bathroom mirror. I would touch my breasts and stare at the plane of my stomach, my legs, my vagina. I would wonder how Mrs. Bishop's body would look in a mirror and then wonder why I cared.

Finally, my mother would bang on the door and surprise me into fear, and I would shove those questions down, very far down.

The sizzling of the skillet brought me back to reality, and I realized my mother was still waiting for me to explain just how I knew I was gay. I wished that I could articulate my childhood feelings to her. I wanted her to understand the way I saw Mrs. Bishop. I had indeed loved her, as pure and primal a love as only children can have. At that time I had no concept of homosexuality, but she awakened in me the primitive beginnings of my sexual identity. But I knew I could not explain that to my mother.

I did not have the words and even if I did she would not have understood. I wanted to be able to console her, to tell her it had nothing to do with her or how she'd raised me. Yet, I wasn't ready to do that either. I felt I could not honestly say she was not some part of it unless I could separate her from those first memories, and clearly she was still a big part of them. Somehow, I think she knew how big a part of my sexual identity she might be.

So instead I responded with, "I don't know how I know, I just do," and left it at that. I watched her tilt her head to the side and switch her weight to her opposite foot. A few moments went by and she didn't say anything. Instead she put her hand on the stove handle as if to steady herself, and used the other one to crack the last egg on the side of the skillet. Except this time she let some of it run down the side of the pan onto the burner where it boiled into nothing. With that I understood that she wasn't going to say anything. That just as the egg had leaked onto the counter, so had the shores of the imaginary umbilical cord that connected us. She was through shoring it up, and so was I.

Sherisse's Poem
For Sherisse Tucker from Ms. Younge
May 30, 2003
Jewel Sophia Younge

"Let's meet here after 2nd hour
that'll be when we fix up our lockers.
Right before we eat."
Sherisse informed Tucker.
Tucker just shrugged
and pulled out a mirror
from the drawstring bag
she had made for Mrs. Wheeler.
Sherisse had too many notebooks
to carry anything but tape.
Tucker had been smart
and used that extra space
for pictures, and mirrors,
memories from their kid years.
Tucker nodded nervously,
"Okay, Sherisse, right there."

As soon as they're in the door
Sherisse goes left, Tucker goes right.
Hugging arms. People running.
Not 15 minutes in, the first fight.
Where went Tucker?
Where went Sherisse?
Tucker.
Sherisse.
Tucker. Sherisse.

Tucker walked over to the fight,
watching the crowd more than the blows.
Two freshmen, "trying to get a rep,"
like the old school rap song goes.
Tucker thought of summer at home,

hearing DJ Needles say, "peace,"
as she got ready for...well, hanging around the block,
waiting for Sherisse
to come back
from one of her Stars and Heroes things.
Bell rings. Crowd breaks up.
Tucker stops daydreaming.
Caught up in summer,
she was hella late.
If she had magic powers
she'd've told time, " WAIT!"

    Like good people,
Sherisse had gone to class.
Most people were there,
though she thought she had passed
EVERYONE in the building
standing around the fight —
same old skating ring, set tripping, B.S.
Something real last night.
Sherisse sighed deep and got ready for class.
The bell rang.
A crowd rushed in from the hall
and found seats fast.
Tick. Tock. Tucker.
Tick. Tock. Tucker.
The teacher repeated her name 4 times
"Maybe, probably she got lost or something," Sherisse volunteered.
Tucker was never this bad at the junior high.

All they did was cross the street!!!!

Where was Tucker now?   In the bathroom.
Hiding.   I'll just wait a second. I'll go to class soon.
...no! I can't go back, she thought.
The teacher will think I tried to skip,
but, I am skipping. The very first day.

The very first class. Ain't this a blip.
Who's that in there?
Mice pissed on cotton.
Damn all the trouble
being in the wrong place had gotten.
Come out. You hear me.
At the Senior High we do not play.
Whoever this lady was, was fussing at Tucker.
Caught. The very first day.

Science would be fun,
and even easier than last year.
While the science teacher was talking
Sherisse wondered, "Who all is in here?"
She discovered she shouldn't have been nervous at all.
Hardly any of these faces were new —
sophomores who she was at JJH with,
neighbors, one or two.
Same old faces everywhere,
friend of cousin's sister's brother.
A reunion, but everybody first day cool,
everybody except old dumdum Tucker.
OOOOOH! And, PLUS, she had Sherisse's locker stuff!
Where the heck was she?!
All Sherisse's pictures of Omarion?
Her baby Tracy McGrady?
...and...and...and her program from 8th grade celebration!
It best not be messed up either.
Sherisse thought, and then frowned, concluding
or it's like that for Tucker.

Sitting in this office
for some shit I didn't do.
All this drama for watching a fight?
I hate this stupid school.
Mhmm, all them people watching the fight.
Ain't none of them in here, I see.

I hate this school district, and they stupid rules.
Know what? It can't be me!
Tucker walked out that office,
like she was grown and bold,
out the doorway, out the block,
to Jennings Station Road,
before she realized she had Sherisse's stuff in her bag.
"Dang," Sherisse would be truly mad
if Tucker went home with almost all the stuff
that either of them had,
plus she ought to go back, but...
naw. If she went back she'd get in trouble, but...
she was already in trouble, but...
she really wasn't in the mood to get screamed on, but...
Ooh.
Whatever was happening was happening later
because Lisa's Chinese was open for lunch.

By hall change Sherisse could see
freshman year would be straight.
Her's would be easier than Tucker's, at least
... still no sign of her best friend's face.
Then...
Police. Social worker. A crew of Principals pushing.
This school was too wild! Fights, kids lost,
now something really bad happening.

Tucker thought and thought about it
all the commotion she left.
Maybe what she did was stupid;
at least she'd have a rep.
UGH! That stupid song! Why
Ms. Younge's favorite DJ
can't see fit to play what everybody else plays
in the middle of the goshdurn day!
Tucker got up, got her stuff, and
got ready to meet Sherisse as planned.

Lisa's never made Tucker sick before
but, for real? Her stomach danced!
G-Walk, C-Walk, Mono
Heal toe, Nina pop, in toe.
Out the doorway, across the parking lot
to Jennings Station Road.
Right back in the school building,
just as grown, and still bold.

"Sherisse, I'm so glad to see you."
                              "Tucker, What did you do?"
"Went to Lisa's. Got me some rice."
                              "Where Mine? Ooh, you ain't right.
                              "Lisa's ain't even open."
"Uh, Mug? I just came from there."
                              "You smell like Chinese food."
"Your locker stuff is right here."
                              "Tucker, are they looking for you?"
"Yeah."
                              "Why you being so bad?
                              You're going to hell in a hand
                              basket, girl.
                              Did somebody make you mad?"
"Yeah, but I was in trouble already."
                              "why?"
"I hid in the bathroom to see—"
                              "what?"
"So they wouldn't think I was trying to be —"
                              "What? Why? What?"
"So I wouldn't get caught skipping, but they caught me."
                              "Tucker, you did skip!
                              Don't act like a jerk!"
"You sound like, Mr. Thomas."
                              "Tell the truth.
                              That'll work."

"Tell on myself?"

> "To get out of this mess?
> Yes!
> You got enough problems, babygurl,
> Don't add no bad rep.
> Just admit you did the wrong thing,
> for whatever reason."

And before Tucker could protest
Sherisse took off like track season!
Tucker was a speeding hug
as Sherisse pulled her and ran
looking for the principal's face, and
calling for the man.
When the girls finally found him,
they were both stunned.
He was quieter than silent lunch,
And ready to hook Tucker up, Son!
He pointed towards his office.
Tucker turned and sighed,
but Sherisse was so proud of them,
she nearly stood there and cried.

But then she shook it off,
reached in Tucker's bag and smiled
at her husband Tracy McGrady.
He'd be in her locker for a while.

Diverging
April Choi

Tapping her fingers on the armrest, she looked down at the girl who knelt before her. Her eldest and heir to the estate. She gave a little inward shudder as she looked at her daughter. So much like her father, down to his legendary stubbornness and temper. Pushing the thought out of her mind, she left the past behind and concentrated on the matter at hand.

"But I don't understand," she said bleakly.

"This is what you've trained for all your life, you were born and bred to the position. A decade of hard work gone for nothing. Why give it up now?"

Sighing in frustration, a willowy young girl with raven locks and dusky skin replied,

"Mother, I've told you time and time before. Being a Rogue no longer holds any appeal for me. Too much bloodshed and worry. For once, I want to live the way I want to and make my own choices instead of being held accountable for the entire state of Assyria!"

The lady looked down at her hands, beautifully expressive, pale slender hands. Hands that have killed more than once. Hands that have followed the tradition of her people. Gaining resolve from the thought of the responsibility they had inherited, and the honor of the family name, she shut her ears to her eldest child's plea. Rising from the ornately carved oak chair, she said,

"The family of Melaeri is a proud and distinguished one. We have watched over Assyria over many generations, it is due to us that she is safe. Blood is shed in the struggle, that is true. But we have always worked for the common good. We harm none who do not seek to do us harm. Do you seek to stray from such a tradition now? Risking all you could have, as heir to the estate. You may go your way, but know that if you do, you are no daughter of mine."

The girl looked at her mother pleadingly, asking for the chance to seek her own path but to no avail. Tears spilled down her face as she murmured,

"Father would have let me."

"Your father never did understand the bigger issues that were at stake. Like father, like daughter. Very well. Since you refuse to see sense, know that you are banned from the Melaeri clan forever."

The woman gave her daughter a look of contempt and uttered the words of the traditional evocation to remove her from the family line. After she was done, the Lady of the Alvaenis left without a second glance. Slamming the door behind her, her richly embroidered brocade gown trailing the floor, she left behind a weeping girl, desolate in her grief but resolute to leave the path of her family.

As if the thousand-year old castle understood, the halls were silent, leaving her alone to grieve.

For it had seen it all before.

My Mother's Prayer
Natalie E. Illum

My mother has one wish for me,
one daily mantra like *Good Morning,*
she calls to me over long distances.
Don't Fall. Try not to fall down.

OK. I promise. As though language mitigates
condition, as though a lack of balance
was semantics. So I put down the phone.

Inside my head is a trip wire,
a stuttering endgame,
a wild gesturing
of genetics and alchemy. The equation of movement
sounds like static. A spastic afterthought of normalcy
encased in blue. I move forward through mud.

I go down and pick up the metaphor for pain
I call the bruising Persimmon. I hold lightning
in the synapses. I cushion the need for gravity

My body harbors titanium like war rations. My body
fucks the ground more than it should. I am a prostitute,
needing asphalt over flesh. My bones are gravel and concrete.

Falling is like flying and the impact is not
death. I expect an easy shattering except
I get up. I haul muscle and torn
flesh into an approximation
of walking, a simulation of standing.
A promise I broke to my mother,

who swears every time I crash and [audible gasp],
cold sweat threatens to break into my own flesh.
Every time I grow bruises like purple and yellow crocuses
dying on my skin. She knows I have fallen and prays for me.

Hair Inspection

Dahlma Llanos Figueroa

Miss Bacon, our gym teacher, made the announcement at the end of class that we would not have to change into our green gym suits the following day. We let out a collective "yeah!" and were excited about the news until she finished her little speech. The following morning she would check our scalps for lice. We were to wash our hair and have it squeaky clean for the inspection.

All the girls were still celebrating their anticipated freedom from the dreaded uniform. But slowly, the black girls went quiet as the news sunk in. We marched silently out of the gym, but all hell broke loose when we hit the locker room.

"Ain't that some shit?"

"Is she crazy? On a Wednesday night?"

"*Lice,* what she trying to say?"

"Ain't nobody got no coodies around here!"

Miss Bacon had short shiny black hair that swung around her head every time she moved. She was of the 'I-wash-my-hair-every-morning' school of beauty. In fact, she often walked into first period class with still-wet hair plastered across her forehead.

This woman had no idea what it took for most black women to do their hair in those pre-Afro days. My hair was pressed with a hot comb because my mother didn't want me putting those strong chemicals in it to relax the natural curl. So, 'just wash your hair tonight' translated into hours of grooming. Washing, air drying (no money for a hairdryer back then), pressing and curling—not the kind of thing you asked your mother to do for you on a weekday night after a long day of work. So I knew what the answer would be.

I was doing my homework that evening when Mom came home from work. In one motion, she dropped her bags on the kitchen table and looked in the pot to see what I had made for dinner.

"*Bendicion, Mami.*"

"Good bless you, *M'ija.* Smells good. I'm starving too."

She kissed my forehead and headed for her favorite chair. She let her weight down slowly and began removing her white shoes and stockings. I brought in her soft slippers and sat down by her. She massaged her wrinkled toes to get the cold out and the comfort in. I could see the weariness in her face as she arched her back and settled into the cushions.

"I've been waiting for this all day," she let out a sigh of relief.

"How was school, *Mamita?*" Even in her weariness, I could hear the honeysweet when she called me that. She reached down again to massage her swollen feet and was still rubbing her instep when I broke the news.

"Mom, can you do my hair tonight?"

"*Como que* do your...? Tonight? What's gotten into you? I just got home. It's *Wednesday.* You know better than..."

"I know, I know, but Miss Bacon is doing hair inspection tomorrow and she says we *have* to wash our hair tonight."

She looked at me like I had grown another head. I braced myself.

"I don't care what she's going to do. Has she lost her mind? You have homework to do and I just got home from work. We don't have time and I certainly don't have the energy for all that. No way. Not tonight!"

I tried to explain but her hand whipped up, palm out, in a stop motion. I knew to shut up.

"I'm not doing your hair tonight and that's that. She can check another day. The day she comes home from working a sixteen-hour shift, on her feet almost the whole time, that's the day when she can tell me when and what to do with your hair."

"But Mom..."

"We're not discussing this anymore, *Nena.* I'll press your hair over the weekend. We'll curl it and style it and make it *real pretty.* But, she'll have to wait til Monday to do her inspection. And that's final."

The next day, attendance was way down in the gym. A number of girls stayed home or were very late for school. I noticed most of the absentees were black girls and I kicked myself for not having thought of the same solution to the problem. But I knew I didn't have the guts to cut out. My mom would kill me if she ever found out.

Miss Bacon stood in front of the room behind a wooden chair, a little table and a trash can beside her. She wore surgical gloves and had a box of Popsicle sticks nearby.

The girls who had come to class stood in fifteen rows, in their assigned places facing her. I stood near the back and looked around. Those rows reminded me of prison movies when the inmates are taken out to the yard for supervised exercise. I had never noticed that before. I stood near the back of the room trying to blend into the wall.

As she called each girl up, you were supposed to sit on the chair, with your back to her as she parted your hair with the sticks. The white girls and the Hispanic girls with straight hair did fine. She smiled at each and moved on to the next. But as each black girl sat in front of her, Miss Bacon made a face. Some girls had chosen styles with neat parts that didn't require separating the hair into sections for inspection. But for the rest, it took a little more effort to part hair that had been freshly oiled and curled. I knew it had taken hours of work. But Miss Bacon was not pleased.

Finally, it was my turn and I sat down face burning. I could feel the stick on my scalp. I knew she would find two weeks worth of normal scalp secretions: dandruff, oil and perspiration. I imagined the look on her face and couldn't wait to get it over with. The sooner I got up, the better.

I felt the first tug all the way down the back of my head to my neck.

"WHAT'S WRONG WITH YOU PEOPLE?" The words bounced off the tiled walls and seemed to reverberate all around me.

She punctuated each word with another tug at my hair. "Didn't I tell you yesterday to wash your nappy head?" She was talking directly to me.

Her words fell like acid over my head and shoulders and sank into me.

"Yes, but I..." My words came out small and finally just disappeared into the charged air.

I could feel all the girls' eyes of on me. The black girls had a look of recognition when they saw the shame on my face. It wasn't my hair but the public humiliation that shamed me. I tried to control the tears of anger that pushed up against my eyes and were threatening to gush out. I closed my eyes but tears of frustration burned my lids. In my mind's eye, I saw myself getting up on the chair and slapping that woman until her face broke open and everyone could see her ugliness oozing out. Time stretched out in the silence of the gym. The black girls fumed but held their tongues. In the back, a group of white girls laughed out loud pointing at me as they whispered. The black girls in the front turned to stare them down. I closed my eyes to them all, knowing the girls in the back would be taken care of later.

Miss Bacon's barrage continued.

I tried again. "But my mother works and..."

"Aren't you old enough to wash your own hair? Can't you manage even that?"

"Yes, but..." The words choked me.

"Just get away from me," she said as she pushed my head away from her.

She flung the stick in the basket, making a great show of disgust as she snapped off her gloves.

"I don't care what happens to any of you. Class dismissed!"

I sat in the chair, on fire, ears, throat, eyes burning. I sat with my dignity in pieces on the floor around me. Girls walked all about me picking up their books and clothing. Then they were all gone and I was the last person left in the world. I just couldn't move. My mouth was straw dry. Time was gone.

I must have been sitting there for a long time because the light in the windows had changed when I finally felt two arms and then four wrapping around my shoulders. I looked into the familiar faces of my friends Marjorie and Dawn. I didn't know when they had come into the gym. I never knew how they had heard about the incident. But they kneeled on either side of me and held me—tight. Their sweaters absorbed all the misery that flowed from my eyes. They sat on the hardwood floor and rocked me. In soothing me, they tried to heal their own unspoken injuries. Neither of them said a single word the whole time. They didn't need to.

a letter to God, while thinking about my hair
j.scales

dear God,
i am sitting here/ dwelling inside my head/ wondering — too
much — if i should grow dreds.../ i want to change my head/
it itches/ it is growing out/ like maybe how it shd be.../
natural...not like the sinful nature/ but/ natural/ meaning
like eve/ like woman/ like eve probably didn't have a comb
eva!/ like natural/ like a tree or a plant/ growing closer
to the sun/ everyday/ like natural/ like a flower blossoming
taller/ sprouting leaves off its sides/ natural like river
flowing & cannot be stopped natural/ like rain that
nourishes & makes things grow
    natural/ like this here
ladybug on the window
      trapped inside its
       foreign unnatural surroundings
NATURAL/ like the little sparrow
last week/ who crashed upside
the clear glass, not realizing the glass
was there
    natural — like the way you fall &
      get back up
    natural — like tears
        like blood & sweat mixed together
        cried & prayed out for a world
        that would not listen & would not
        CHANGE
    natural — like 40 days & nights of fasting
    natural — like "take nothing with you but your tunic
     & sandals"

natural — like the dreds
         He musta had,
   cuz any body doin
             that much healin
             & that much preachin
             & that much lovin
             & that much teachin
   woulda had no time
   to be worry'n
   about his
   "do"

Anticipating Mourning
Wendy Altschuler

I stood at the end of the dusty dirt road as I meditatively waited for the bus. I enjoyed this time of solitude, of peace, as it was really the only time I was completely alone with myself, with my thoughts. While looking up to the sky with my arms stretched out, I let the crisp Montana air fill my lungs and just at that moment the sky cracked open and pissed rain the size of grapes. My hands smoothed over my slimly satin skin and slowly worked their way up to my face. I felt beautiful. Then, as if I were punched in the throat by the fist of a lover, the school bus arrived.

While focusing on my feet and glancing up just long enough to find a vacant seat, I accidentally made eye contact with Jason Corban. He was starring at me with these fierce hazel eyes and a grinding tight lipped jaw. I could feel my pulse beating in my chest as he stood up and made his way over to my seat.

"Wendy, hellllllllllllloooo, you're looking mighty nice today in your Salvation Army clothes. Did you even wash them or is the sweat of some rich girl still soaked in the fabric?"

Jason buried his face into the sleeve of my rootbeer brown sweater while using his body weight to slide me over to the window.

"Yep, rich girl."

I sat paralyzed and unable to move with my hands tightly clutching my back pack and my eyes focused on my knees. Jason wrapped his hand around my shoulder and squeezed so hard that I winced in pain.

"I bet I could make you cry without even touching you," he whispered in my ear with a throaty breath.

It was at that moment, I wished my sister Jan was on the bus. I wished she wasn't at home, pregnant at fourteen. Jan was tough. She had to have a root canal one year after she got her front tooth punched out during a fight that she caused. I considered what she would have done if she were in this situation. I imagined that she would spit snot in Jason's face and scream for the bus driver to pull the fucking bus over!

She didn't subscribe to the social norms that many people did at her age. She didn't care how people perceived her and she would just as soon kick you in the crotch rather than try to argue or see your side of the story.

As I sat imprisoned on the bus, I thought about when Jan and I took Brandy, our St. Bernard, for a walk in the woods a few winters ago. After about thirty minutes we stumbled upon a dead deer that had decayed just enough for its filthy fur and skin to be stretched so thin that its insides were visible. Jan was fascinated by the massive creature that so many of the men in our lives would have dreamed of killing. She took her walking stick and snapped it over her knee in one quick motion. As if she had methodically planned this "chance finding" she lifted the sharp stick over her head and plunged it into the deer's stomach! Like a rubber band, the taught thin skin of the deer snapped open revealing its' blue and red organs. I watched mute and horrified as Jan excitedly tore into each organ with the stick and rapidly gave bloody parts of the deer to our dog with her naked child hands. As we walked back to the house Jan giggled and said "Look at Brandy, she's wearing red lipstick".

Jan was not someone to mess with. She wouldn't feel bad about breaking your nose and making you bleed; she would feel triumphant. I, on the other hand, was sensitive enough for the both of us. I knew in the depth of my soul that Jason could make me cry with only his words and this phenomenon made me feel like my family was right in thinking I was weak. The bus finally reached the school and I was free of Jason's nasty grip. I made it to my home room class and sat down in my assigned seat. Today we were going to learn about the elite British royalty in literature.

I didn't excel in school. I always thought that I was stupid and unable to grasp what was being taught. During English, Mr. Darbow pulled me out of class to have a discussion with me about my "academic career."

"Wendy, have you ever thought about being in remedial English?"

"Um, no Mr. Darbow," I said as I could feel my face getting hot and my eyes swelling with tears.

"Well, you're really behind," he snorted while taking short sniffs.

"Do you smoke" he exclaimed with menacing and accusing eyes.

As I nervously bit my lower lip, I explained with defeat, "Ah, no, my parents and my sister do".

"Isn't your sister pregnant" he said while looking down his nose.

"Yeah."

"Well, should I sign you up or not?"

"Um, no, I'll try harder Mr. Darbow", I said with the last bit of pride and dignity I could muster.

As I re-entered the class room, nearly everyone was starring at me wondering why he had pulled me out of class. Embarrassed, I just awkwardly smiled and buried my nose in the text full of stories that didn't relate to me.

After returning home that day I spent nearly all evening in my room reading, which was the best escape. I usually gravitated towards romantic novels about women who were enamored by men who expressed heroics with confidence or books about traveling to exciting destinations that I believed I would never see. The book I was reading that evening was about hikers in Canada who had a dangerous encounter with a fierce grizzly bear. I remember this because this was also the same evening that I thought my mother had killed herself.

I was about half way through my book when I left my room to get a glass of water and some cheese to munch on for dinner. My mother, as usual, was sitting in the dark at the kitchen table starring off into space as she smoked her cigarette and drank her Budweiser out of the can. Like the round red and white bobber on a fish line, my mother's head was nodding up and down while she leaned over her skinny crossed legs. I got a glass from the dish rack as she focused her attention on me and I tried to ignore her.

"You don't love me do you?" she coughed breaking the silence.

"Of course I love you mom," I said impatiently while trying not to add a log to the flame.

"Sit down".

"I'm in the middle of a book, why don't you just go to bed".

"My mother never loved me" she slurred unhappily as she uncrossed her legs and tried to stand up.

She grasped the counter and violently swayed back and forth like she was being bucked off a horse.

"Let me help you to bed."

She threw her tiny body onto me as I tried to hold her up long enough to put her into bed. I could feel the anger bubbling inside of me for being forced to be in this maternal role night after night. Why couldn't she just pull herself together and function like a normal adult? How could she be so selfish to get wasted nearly every evening?

After putting her into bed I took a deep frustrated breath and retreated into my bedroom. About an hour later I heard the door slam and I assumed it was my father returning from the graveyard shift at Wal-Mart. I turned the light off and tried to sleep. Jan came plowing into my room minutes later.

"Did you hear that?"

"Hear what?"

"The door slam; mom is gone".

"What! No, dad is home."

"No he's not Wendy, mom is outside."

"So what, let her go outside. We live in the middle of nowhere, what is she going to do? Dad will be home soon and he can deal with her this time."

Jan and I froze as we heard an earth shattering pop noise coming from outside.

"That was dad's gun! Mom shot herself," Jan screamed in a hysterical shrill voice.

Not knowing what to do I entered shut down mode. With my arms securely wrapped around my legs I began to rock back and forth while sobbing spastically. My mother was dead.

"I'm going out there!"

"No, stay here Jan! Wait til Dad gets home!" I screamed through burning tears. Jan ran outside and I sat in my dark room thinking about what I would say to my father when he returned home after working two jobs only to find his wife and oldest daughter dead in his front yard. Would he blame me? I immediately felt guilty for being so impatient with my mother. I should have let her hug me and sob on my shoulder while she told me about her hateful mother and the uncle and step father that repeatedly raped her.

My eyes glazed over as I starred at the bright red coils of the little gray space heater that warmed my room. Like an immobilized idiot, I just sat there waiting to hear another pop. I didn't even think to call the police or a friend for help. I just sat there, waiting, anticipating mourning.

It was 4:00 am when my father came into my room. He had found my mother and my sister outside. My pregnant teenage sister was holding the hand gun that he had loaded and stored in his closet for protection against intruders.

"Everything is ok. Your mom got a little drunk and she was just shooting beer cans outside. Go to bed, you have school in the morning."

I thanked God for sparing the lives of my mother and sister as my father shuffled his tired body out of my room. In a couple of hours I would wake up, get ready for school, and stand alone by the side of the road as I waited for the bus in solitude.

Like Water For Soap

Charneice N. Fox

I wonder how Lil' Kim cries at night
mismatched socks
sweat pants
questioning her worth through materialistic things
what's her motivation to get out of bed
each day after a lonely night of tears
when she and I share the same space
in abstract time, as women
ugly truths and souls needing showers.
I wonder how she cries?
Is it softly so as not to wake up herself?
Or is it loud uncontrollable tears,
does she guard her affections?
Boxed into fake breasts, begets and a Benz
Longing for the construction man to come over
Lie beside her, without lust in his heart
blowing the whistle when the shift is over
helping her to rebuild from the inside
it's time to take a shower
she grabs the bar of soap
she removes the wigs and MAC
she is fresh, new, naked.

What God does she serve?
Selling prostitution over inflated beats.
tongue kissing the masses
misusing the power of mass communication
to mask her pain.
Hands dirty, but she is fresh daily
like a new bar of soap.
I wonder if she cries as I do?
Heart hung heavy
soul wrenching
like water cries

when her voice goes gasping for air
cause it hurts
heaving over
Alone.
No cameras to smile for, no TV
Reality.
Make up stained tears now on white sheets.
Lonely. Naked. Dirty.

Does she know that
women bragging about who they slept with
is shameful to ears?
mouths sing along cause it's catchy
and spirits transfer — cause it's catchy.
No need for women's liberation
cause she and I are Hard Core
But water knows truth
no matter how many times you dress up
Even bars of soap get dirty
You gotta cleanse the soap dish.

I wonder if she cries
when a teenage girl looks up to her
decides she wants to be that
never knowing that sweat pants
and tears at night exist naturally
in the façade, in reality
even bars of soap need to be cleansed
after washing dirty hands.
I wonder how Lil' Kim cries at night.
Wakes up
Dresses herself everyday in lies
washing hands clean with dirty soap
as teen age girls listen
as I listen
and buy MAC and lust after Prada
tempting men with a façade.

There was a time when I got caught up
Believed that I was empowered by controlling dick
1996 — first album released — 19 years old
She had me convinced that a woman could be Hard Core
Capable of having a hard on, like men
Lyrics hard on ourselves
Dirty hands snapping
Trying to be fresh
like a new bar of soap.

Reality is, we cry
Midnight songs in correct harmony
with women everywhere,
our greatest show nightly
in sweat pants and mismatched socks
for an audience of one, ready to pose
for the cover of normal.
Cause even bars of soap need to be cleansed
after washing dirty hands.

"Starfucker" or For All My Friends Who Bought the Bootleg
C. Sala Hewitt

In the beauty shop getting my hair locked
My neighbor runs off at the mouth:
"my husband works for the precinct, and we watched the original."
I smack a loud smirk through the suck of my teeth
and find bigger truths in that brag and conceit.
Watch:

An anonymous envelope arrives in a mailbox
addressed to the family's oldest girl. It passes
through a few hands until it lands on her pillow.

She sits, perched in silly banter with friends. One,
with long micro braids flips her hair to her back
n cracks, "if he was your boyfriend, he wasn't
LAST night!" while everyone breaks up in laughs.

Except for the girl whose room their in. instead
She smacks a loud smirk through the suck of her teach
finding bigger truths in that brag and conceit.

Bored, she opens the envelope left for her on the bed.
It reads, "Nice performance. I heard you got a record
deal, trick. Check it — I'll let you hold my ice at the next
album release party if you suck my dick." signed,
"Whose Your Daddy, Bitch? Deeeez NUTTTZZZZZ."
with a post script that lists an illicit web address.

Girl folds the note and shoves it in the back of her
chest'a drawer. There, it will wait for the others.
micro braided girl asks, "what's wrong witchu?"
And everyone silences at the drawer slamming shut.
No answer. She continues, "any ways. You going
rollerskatin' wit us tonight? Malik an'em gon' be dere."
Girl says no, and promptly calls her friend a ho.

Tonight she's putting on her D&G sweater and tightest girbauds
Tonight she's getting picked up in a phat ride, paid to put on a show.
Tonight she's living in a fantasy — somebody elses nasty world.
Tonight going all alone — somebody thinks she's a nasty girl.

Her friends leave, and nervousness sets in. The letter,
tell tale throbs in her chest. When the door bell rings
she runs to the bathroom to vomit.

This is not on videotape —
    Her tears are not on tape. Her regurgitated meal of greens and
pork chops is not on tape. Her   desperate crush on 16-yr old Malik,
her vain attempts to impress him are not on tape. Her fright at the
first sight of blood three months before that hasn't returned in proper
menstrual time and her additional dread of its lateness is not on
tape. How she does her hair just like her older cousin —the one who
really does have a record deal, the one she admires most, wants to be
just like — aint on the tape.

Return to the beauty shop
my locks and my neighbor
Pontificating on the size of an R&B singers penis
The proof of which she sold to the local bootlegger.
"he bought it for a thousand dollars cash but he'll
Make more than that selling copies on the street."

Sho nuff, in walks a lanky man dragging a heavy luggage bag,
"Tapes ladies! I got tapes! Its P. Kiddy weekend special today!"
It's local bootlegger dave peddlin thrice removed copies
from my neighbor's husband's precinct if you believe what she say.

One head perks up from a heat nap under the dryer
and flashes him a 20, so she can testify to the act authentically.

I cant take it anymore, I feeling nauseous and something
tell tale is pounding in me. I want to chastise, but I'm too
young to be these people's mama. I want to serve them

subpoenas and make them testify in court.

> You are witness to a criminal case! (I want to say)
> That is my sister on that tape! That is my mother's daughter
> As a matter of fact, that's me, porn star un-consenting, illicitly

> It is my body: my tits, my ass... here — Do you really want to
see?

A ballad plays in the background
A raspy voiced man hums over the beat
I ask the gatekeeper to the CD's,
Can you play something different,
I mean choose your music mindfully?
A nod and flips to the radio, so I recede.

But the same song erupts from the speakers
brazenly. How can they air this music so blatantly?
And I realize, I cannot harbor this girl. She is not
even safe with me.

I can not close her ears to radio waves, or bind
her eyes from magazines that try to erase her pain
and evaporate her self esteem. She is not even
safe as me.

In the cities, a different club commemorates her
humiliation on every night of the week. Heads
nod and booties bounce celebrating another
song that wounds her being. She is not
safe from you or me.

Because if we'd switch places
And she were I and I were she,
We together still be raw
still unsaved, in a beauty shop
just down the block, on any given

Saturday, head locked and raped.

**In commemoration of the public release of one famous entertainer's molest-capades. Look behind the silence. Speak out against all domestic and sexual abuse & violence. And put your music money where your mouth is.*

Bootyshaker

Patricia Corbett

hey little girl in the those
come fuck me boots
weave so long
tracks showing from the roots

does your mother know
that you
shake that ass fast
or is she clubbing beside you
red Alize in her glass

bootyshaker

Sugar Daddy
By Kelly Warren

Fuck it. Sometimes your parents are right. It kills me to admit it. My fingers are shaking just tapping it out on the keyboard, but sometimes they actually do know best. I can't tell you how many times my Dad warned me about dirty old men. He made me take karate lessons for 10 years so I could fend them off, if the need ever arose. He even felt it necessary to warn me about the notorious 'sugar daddy'. As if, Dad.

He was the first to introduce me to the idea of 'Sugar Daddies', and I must admit, I found the concept to be quite alluring. In theory, that is. Alliterated phrases such as, "Lady of leisure" and "Dripping in diamonds" were dancing through my head, although "Feral old fucker" is probably closer to the truth. Unfortunately, the images of Marilyn Monroe and a dashing older man, soon fade into a disturbing visual of the mutilated breasts of Anna Nicole Smith being forced into the face of a ninety something, wheelchair bound, geriatric gent. When you actually put a little bit of 'real' thought into the issue, it quickly becomes very unappealing. Who would have thought that I, would one day, have the 'sugar daddy' window of opportunity opened up to me? It is not something I have ever seriously considered as a life path. In fact, I had written the idea off as one of my Dad's paranoid myths that only happened in America.

But, once again, the Gold Coast rose to the occasion, and proved to me that despite our relative distance from the rest of the world, we are still able to create every day dramas that are worthy of a one hour slot on the Jerry Springer show. So, as the buildings rise higher the morals fall even lower.

I had never imagined myself to be the kind of girl a wealthy older gent would be interested in. I spent the best part of my youth refusing to wear a bra and being chastised for the 'wombats' that were growing under my armpits. I was angry, swore like a truck driver and was often mistaken for a lesbian. I rebelled against the dominant male paradigm; but I also enjoyed collecting stamps and doing jig-saw puzzles. Perhaps the old chap saw through my feminist exterior and was attracted to the latter two, more demure qualities of my personality.

One night after I had just finished a furious piece of cuss filled performance poetry at a local nightclub, I was introduced to an older gent, under the guise that he was interested in providing funding to have some of my works published. He propositioned me with a dinner invitation to discuss the project. My daddy had warned me about situations like this. So, I had a quick chat with the lass who introduced us, about my concerns of potential perversion. She vouched for his character and insisted that I would have a great time. 'Oh, he's just a harmless old fellow with a bit of money to throw around.'

The man in question must have been pushing 75. He looked much like any other older man, with grey hair, saggy skin and watery blue eyes. He was not much taller than me, and I just clear 5 foot, so he wasn't exactly a man of looming stature who could overpower me. I doubted that he would even be able to catch me if I started running, so I was happy in the knowledge that I would probably be safe.

Physically, at least.

Being an old school chap, he insisted on picking me up. Being a home schooled gal, I insisted that we meet in a public place. I didn't want him knowing where I live. And so, we decided to meet in beautiful downtown Southport. He ushered me into his Rolls Royce and chauffeured me into the bright lights of Surfers Paradise, or Surface Parasites as it was known among my circle of equally angry feminist friends.

We had a pleasant enough dinner in a fancy pants Chinese restaurant. It was one of those exclusive dining establishments with extended ceilings and surly wait staff. Perhaps the wait staff were scowling because I was the fourth sucker he had bought in this week. It was yet another warning that I didn't heed.

We must have looked ridiculous. I certainly felt a little absurd. The conversation was kept fairly informal. Towards the end of the meal was when things started to go slightly askew. Out of the blue he opened his wallet and placed $300 on the table and pushed it toward me.

"What's that for?"
"For having dinner with me," he said.
"I can't accept that."
"Yes you can, humour an old man."
"No really. I can't accept that."

I needed the money, you always need money, rego was due and I wanted to buy some pot. But it was just a little weird to be handed $300 dollars at the end of a meal. It made me feel like a hooker. I am not one of those chicks who lack self respect. This is not what I signed up for. Woo, woo, woo, went the warning sirens. I have a tendency to not listen to my instincts.

He told me I should take it and put it toward the costs of publishing my works.
"Well if you put it like that, it is like a sponsorship for my creativity. Why not?"
I took the money.

I shouldn't have taken the money.

Preoccupied with the anticipation of how stoned I could get with my new found fortune, I foolishly agreed to drive with him to see his penthouse suite. I must admit, I was a little curious to see what the abode of a man who can afford to throw away $300 to a relative stranger would be like.

Curiosity killed the cat.

On the drive to his apartment was when things took a turn toward creepy town. He started telling me stories of how his now deceased wife had a special relationship with her miniature poodle. According

to gramps, grandma used to sit commando on the couch and call the dog over to pleasure her private parts while he watched.
Fuckin' gross man.

I mean even if it is true, why the fuck was he telling me. It certainly wasn't going to make me like him any more. It was around that time that it dawned on me that I was expected to earn my $300.

Then the propositions started to come.

"Let me lick you," he insisted.
Gross! No fuckin' way. "Um no, I'll be right thanks."
"We don't need to have sex, just let me lick you."
He was not coming near me with his creepy old man tongue.
"No, no I am all good in the licking department, thanks."

"I like to pleasure women, many young women have let me lick them."

Even if I was into older men, after hearing stories of bestiality Biddy I was grossed out just breathing the same air as him. There had been far too many nasty visuals for one night. I felt like throwing up, but he was probably into that too. I desperately needed a shower to try and wash away the bad man.

"Would you mind stopping the car and letting me out, I think I'll just catch a cab back to Southport, it shouldn't cost any more than $300 dollars... Good night."

In the taxi on the way back to my car, there was only one sentence that kept running through my mind. 'I should have listened to my Dad.'

In A Maxi Taxi • On The Way Home From School

Lauren K. Alleyne

The man who sits next to me is angry
I refuse to respond to his queries:
Psst. Aye gyul. Sexy, Yuh have a boyfriend?

I smirk, a study in girlish disdain
so he slides closer, his face a mere inch
away: I don't flinch; he says *listen, bitch.*

My heart pounds beneath my scornful protests
'cause no one seems to notice my distress,
my ineffective rebukes; I call out,

no one turns. For half the ride home he taunts
now what? And I don't know the right answer
so he keeps on; I keep learning. Later,

the driver swears, *Looked like a lover's tiff,*
contrite; promises he'll get me home, safe.

One-And-A-Half

Jessica Del Balzo

Last week I tried to break up with Elliot again. That makes six attempts so far this school year. And it's only October.

"I just need to be on my own right now," I said. "I have a lot of shit to take care of."

"What, like college stuff? You know you'll get in, Allie."

"No, not college stuff. Just trust me, okay? I've got a bunch of things to sort out in my head and you just need a lot more than I can give you right now."

He'd been so whiny lately, about how I never seem to want to see him, and how he doesn't understand that because he always wants to see me. Sometimes he'd even start crying about it, bringing up the fact that he's adopted and unwanted, and I never knew what to do then. Made me feel so damn guilty I kept losing the nerve to flat-out ask him if he even noticed I'm vacant half the time.

"It takes two," I countered, "not one-and-a-half." It was sharp on my tongue, but I wanted to make him understand. The first period bell rang and students began to crowd the hallway. My eyes caught on the rush of colors and fabrics.

"You're so silly," he said, smiling. Then he whispered, "I acknowledge that, but I won't accept it." He kissed my shoulder.

"Jesus, Elliot, you're impossible." I turned and headed off to Calculus, making a point not to look back at him. I already knew he was still wearing that dumb grin on his face. He had no idea at all. Not a fucking clue. Sure, it was partially my fault for not telling him what was really going on, but it wasn't like I hadn't ever tried.

We'd been going out since June, about a month after Jake and I had broken up. I had thought it was going to be a casual sort of thing, but Elliot had something else in mind entirely. I never should have said I loved him back because now it felt like it was expected of me to say it all the time, or risk him getting all pouty and sad. It felt like when you push the button on a stopwatch and you're just not ready to take off running, but hey, the clock's ticking. Are you going to just stand there? What are you waiting for, a postcard?

As I walked into the classroom where I had Calc from 7:53 a.m.

until 8:48, the mix of cold air (some asshole had the windows open again) and stale fluorescent lighting hit me the wrong way. The room seemed to get sucked through a straw. I could feel the air pressure gnawing at me as I tried to make my way to my seat as nonchalantly as possible. This had been happening long enough for me to know it was just me imagining things, but I still didn't understand it.

I'd been normal enough all summer, but once September hit and we started school again, things just got really weird. It started with my legs hurting a little. I thought maybe it was because Elliot and I had started having sex (a sort of "might as well" thing on my part, and something a lot more meaningful to him) and, well, of course that would take some getting used to, physically. It wasn't like I'd ever really been with anybody else before. Well, not regularly. Anyway, then it was more than my legs. Simply walking to and from class began to wear me out in a way it really shouldn't have.

I still don't know what to do about that. If I get tired, I just ignore it and keep walking. You can't just stop in the middle of a crowd of people. One thing that really gets me is when Elliot calls me in the middle of the night saying he just wants to hear my voice, dialing over and over until I finally pick up. But what difference does it make? No matter how much sleep I get, I always feel and look completely drained.

Sometimes I just want to run outside and scream, draw a circle somewhere and stand in it. Stop believing in gravity and live on the ceiling a while. It feels like the bottom's fallen out of everything. I just want somewhere safe to go, and as much as I hate to admit it, sometimes Elliot is the closest thing. Even if he drives me crazy, at least I know that when I start to feel like I'm being pulled out of myself he's there to hold me in place.

I'm scared. I feel so cold all the time. My back is all twisted up too, and I get dizzy a lot. I'll be walking down the hall at school and everything will flip over for a split-second. Or I keep thinking I've died because I'll start to feel lightheaded, and if I happen to be in an empty room, I have no proof that I'm alive, really, if there's no one around to see me. I've woken up in the middle of the night and started calling random phone numbers off of shampoo bottles and such, just to make sure. Sometimes I'll be really "up" and laughing so much I can't speak in full sentences, and then a short while later I'll be falling asleep.

I wonder if it has to do with the fact that I didn't see Jake at all during the summer because he was off at his grandparents' in the country, but now that we're in school I see him around a lot, and it's been bringing some of it back. Right after we broke up I was still pretty hazy on what had gone on between us. I knew something was really fucked up, I could feel it, but it was buried somewhere in my head and it didn't start to come to me until September. When it did, it started coming in pieces, and it continues to. Throws me off balance. But then again, if I were balanced or had been balanced at all I wouldn't be with Elliot. Just all that stuff that happened with Jake last spring really spun me around and into this really weird place. All of May I was so quiet and it never seemed to stop raining. When I came out on the other side (or so I thought) and the rain let up, Elliot had been there, holding out a hand for me to grab. What else was I going to do? There wasn't anybody else around who seemed to give a shit.

I still have no idea what to make of any of it- what happened exactly and who to blame, if it's even worth figuring out. It happens to lots of girls. Apparently you've got a better chance, statistically, of going through this than you do of being born left-handed. You trust the wrong guy, drink and smoke things you shouldn't, not stop to think you're too small to push him off of you until there's nothing you can do about it. It's like math, really, a perfect little equation.

Deep down, I know it wasn't my fault, really, that as much as I cared about Jake, he was still an asshole. I knew it too, but I loved him and he said he loved me back, so I'd forgive him when he would get weird and then I let it slide when he tried to get me to stop wearing makeup and hanging out with my friends. I just wanted to keep him happy so he wouldn't yell at me about being a shitty girlfriend all the time. He had a way of making me feel so guilty when I should have gotten angry. Fucking masterful. Where can I learn that one?

Oddly, Elliot's really good at it too, but in a different way. While Jake would scream and curse and throw things, Elliot gets whiny and starts to whimper so I feel bad for making him cry. Makes it impossible for me to do anything about it except give him what he wants or needs, as the case may be.

Sex with Elliot is frequent, if nothing else, but it is plenty of other things. Like confusing, for one. On some level, it's satisfying (he's a lot more generous than I am in many respects), but often I just lose it in the middle. It's like I fall out of the moment and get stranded somewhere else entirely. Sometimes I'll even think he's Jake. I won't be able to see anything that's really going on. I'll start thinking I'm lying in the back of Jake's car again, everything happening in slow-motion. April lightning flashing on the other side of the windows and that horrible tilting smile that used to creep across his face when we were alone. There have even been times I've started kicking and screaming, not realizing. More often than not, I'll just go numb. It will only dawn on me that I've blanked out because all of a sudden Elliot will be shaking me to, saying my name over and over.

"Allie? Are you with me? Allie, Allie..."

Either way, I always end up crying and then feeling terrible for ruining things. I hope he doesn't think it's his fault. I doubt he does though. What does he have to do with it? Maybe the worst part of it is that he actually thinks he was my first. I almost wish that were true sometimes.

• • •

The following Friday was Halloween. I went over to Elliot's early in the evening, hoping we'd catch word of some parties that might be going on. I'd had a really rough day (seeing tons of people running around the school in costumes had been even more of a sensory overload than usual), and I was just in the mood to get drunk and then go to bed.

I was feeling pretty edgy and probably shouldn't have had sex with Elliot at all. I actually tried not to. I kept trying to tell him no, that I was too emotional, even though I was feeling more detached than anything else. Guys just seem to respond more quickly to the word "emotional." Then I played the "I'm just not that into it" card, but he just wasn't having that. Elliot seems to know how to get me to change my mind. He's so damn persuasive. Barely gives me a choice. I kind of hate that.

Still, I was finally able to relax a little and actually enjoy myself, though closing my eyes. That was probably a mistake. At first I saw this peaceful harbor scene (kind of ridiculous) from high up above. It was autumn and there were all these sailboats and ducks and it was so calm. Then the image faded into an explosion of sunflowers, bright yellow and screaming and alive, but all of a sudden they burst into flames, and I was falling through an elevator shaft with nothing beneath my feet, trapped by walls on all sides.

"Allie? Allie..."

I opened my eyes and found myself half-wrapped in Elliot's Star Wars blanket, facing the wall. He was lightly tracing the top seven or twelve notches in my spine, like he was feeling for clues. Not again. I started mumbling something about how I was going to leave because I was just feeling way too weird to stay. I needed to go somewhere else, maybe drive or walk around for a while. I told him I'd come back. Just let me go, please. He started to get mad, and I realized that the only way I could keep getting away with this would be to tell him the whole truth.

"Sometimes I just get this, this need to run away. I, I don't know what I'm afraid of, but it's just that I've been having these flashbacks, and...God, I hate talking about this to you. It's not fair."

"No, no, it's okay. I just want you to be okay."

I was starting to cry. I hate that. He was holding me as I curled into myself, trying to make myself as small as possible, almost to the point of being able to rest comfortably in someone's palm. Crying just makes it impossible for me to talk. And worse, it reminds me of how Jake could twist things around so I'd feel bad for upsetting him so much he'd be mean to me. I don't like feeling like I'm doing that to someone else. I was starting to feel like I usually do when I cry in front of Elliot, thinking in zigzags and deciding that maybe I did deserve what Jake had done to me. I must have deserved it if I'd been naive enough to trust him.

Here I was, just another of your one-in-three-or-four girls, another numb idiot blinking awake in the middle of moments in dark rooms that would never feel totally private. There would always be that shadow over my shoulders, taunting and ambiguous like a consistently flashing clock, twelve o'clock (a.m. or p.m.?) forever. I was afraid I'd always have that fog over my eyes, and I only had myself to blame. I should have known better. And here I was, subjecting Elliot to it. He didn't need to put up with my shit; he had enough of his own to deal with. That's what I had been trying to tell him.

I swallowed and tried again. This time, the words managed to escape my mouth. Elliot's eyes went wide like moth wings.

"He raped you?" he seemed to shriek. Unconsciously, I covered my ears, and then started sobbing all over again.

"D- don't s-say it like that," I stammered. Where were my clothes? I had to get out of there. I pushed myself to sitting.

"Hey, hey, where are you going?"

"I told you, I just need to go somewhere, be by myself. I don't want to talk about this anymore." I was about to step one foot on the carpet when Elliot wrapped his arms around me to keep me from leaving.

"Yes you do."

"No, I really don't," I said. "Please, just let me go for a bit,"

"Allie —"

Then the phone rang. It was Dan. Party at Sara Carlson's. Thank God. Oddly, I calmed down right away, probably out of sheer relief at not having to stay in Elliot's room any longer. I didn't really know Sara that well, but according to Dan, there would be alcohol, and the mood I was in, that was enough for me. Sometimes I wish I had a regular group of female friends to hang out with, so I wouldn't always be available to see Elliot, but pathetically, I don't. They all ditched me when I was going out with Jake. They got tired of me spending so much time with him, and then when I tried to bring him along, he'd be such an asshole they finally asked me not to. They wanted me to choose either them or Jake, and I think I made the wrong choice. There are still one or two girls I talk to on occasion, but I there's nobody I'd feel comfortable ringing up just to say "hi."

Elliot and I rarely seem to go out anywhere unless Dan is along. Dan and I have become sort of "friends by association." Once in a while we hang out without Elliot, but he doesn't know about it. He wouldn't understand. He would think it "means something," and maybe it does or will, but I'm sure as hell not up to admitting that to myself. I like pretending to believe in the possibility of platonic relationships.

By the time Dan picked us up, it was nearing eleven. When we got to Sara's there was virtually no alcohol left. I tried not to seem disappointed. It wasn't that big of a deal. Even just going to a party was still better than staying at Elliot's. There were plenty of people at Sara's, some of which I knew. It was kind of fun to watch, all the fucks I go to school with stumbling around slurring obscenities and wide-mouthed revelations. It soon got old, though, being one of the few sober individuals. Elliot and I settled onto a couch in the living room, both of us quiet. Then he draped his arm heavily over my shoulders and started whispering drippy syllables into the hollow of my neck. Maybe he was trying to make me feel better, but I only felt smothered and trapped, short of breath. A familiar tingling started in the front of my forehead.

As Elliot leaned in to kiss me, I stood up. "I'll be right back. I'm just going to go find the bathroom," I said.

"Upstairs," Sara said, passing by. Okay then.

I really needed a few minutes to regroup. I was still feeling wobbly from the conversation Elliot and I had had a couple hours earlier. As I climbed the stairs, the carpeting was grass beneath my feet. The pictures on the walls were flexing, preparing to pounce on me as I passed. All those eyes. My arms felt hot under my sweater sleeves. My cheeks burned, and the tingling had moved into my ears, making it seem as if all the electricity in the house was rushing towards me. My vision narrowed and filled with black dots. I stepped one foot gratefully onto the landing, and then the other. I ran for the second door on the left. Some cold water on my face and I'd be fine. I practically fell against the door as I turned the handle, pushing my way in.

I saw her before I saw him, even though he was on top. No idea how his bare, thrusting ass took longer to register with me than her tangled cranberry-colored hair, which was crushed against the cool white-and-pink tile, but it did. She was moaning his name like she was trying to remember how to ask for water in a foreign language.

I didn't know what to do first, react or leave. So I did neither. I just stood there, framed in the doorway with my mouth hanging open, my vision painfully clear. Then came a rush of darkness, buzzing in my head. Jake. And what was her name anyway? How long had they known each other? Was this the first time they'd...did she even...Well she sure sounded like she wanted it.

That night in his car (the first of either two or three times, I still didn't know for sure), had Jake thought I wanted it? I've heard it's really hard to tell, that if a guy's horny enough, yes and no sound awfully similar. Even Elliot can be like that, only it's more like he hears me say I don't feel like it, but he thinks that surely I must not be aware of my own carnal desires, and therefore need to be coaxed, however quietly. He knows it's hard to say no to someone who lavishes you with attention.

It horrified me to realize that even now, I preferred Jake to Elliot. Sure, Elliot was sensitive and seemed to understand my body, but with Jake, it had actually felt like there was someone else on the other end of the line. It was exciting and raw and charged when we so much as kissed. I used to see roads when I kissed Jake, or sometimes I'd get a picture of the two of us on a windy beach in the middle of the night with the sky gone purple and syrupy with pink stars. It was dizzying and almost too much sometimes, but your body gets used to things, levels. It's like once you've had a taste of something that intense, it's hard to find anything that compares.

Jesus, Jake. Did the two of them see me standing in the doorway at all? Just as I thought this to myself, the girl tapped Jake's shoulder and he stopped (just for a second), turning his head. He smiled. He fucking smiled at me. I wanted to either throw up or pass out. I was shivering and breaking into a cold sweat now, even though just minutes before I'd been hot. But no, throwing up would be a bad deal. I couldn't even get over them to the toilet — I'd have to do it in the bathtub. Maybe that's where they should have been.

Jake was fucking someone else, and he was smiling at me.

"Oh my God, I am so sorry," I breathed sharply as I darted out backwards, slamming the door.

I made it about halfway down the stairs before I just stopped. I sat down and wrapped my arms around my legs like I was trying to fold myself up, but I must have been pressing too hard. I sunk my head down; it was too heavy with stale tears to hold up anymore. But now, when the only thing I wanted to do was cry, I couldn't. Of course. And I was stupid enough to be surprised.

Already, I could feel the image of Jake and that girl slipping into the back of my mind. I wanted to grab onto it, let myself at least cry over it while it was still going on, not wait for it to burst into the room weeks from now, dripping cold water over everything. But it was no use. Black splashes were drowning the memory already. I pressed into myself tighter to try and trap it between my chest and my thighs, but it was no use. I uncoiled and sat with my elbows on my knees, staring straight ahead.

I couldn't go downstairs and face Elliot yet. My mind felt so clear and cold and blank now, it seemed to be floating, anchorless. I was afraid to try to use my voice. What if it didn't work? Was it connected to anything? I didn't even know that I could coax my legs to stand. I noticed there wasn't any sound. The lights seemed too bright and still. What time was it? Was it any specific time? Shit, where was everybody? I breathed in several times, each breath shallower than the last. Calm down. I let my eyes fixate on the banister until it seemed that the angle was off. Then I looked up above it, to a picture of Sara and her three sisters, staring until it blurred into the flowery wallpaper. Were any of them left-handed?

I looked straight ahead once again, trying to breathe deeply. Oxygen, that's what I needed. In a few minutes, I'd stand up and go back downstairs and tell Elliot I'd just gotten a phone call from my mom or something and needed to go home. He'd probably ask why and make a big deal about it, tell me not to listen to her, and I'd come up with something on the spot. I often used that excuse, even though my mom would have laughed if she knew how strict Elliot thought she was. But the important thing was that then Elliot would take me home and I could go to my room and close the door. Maybe then I could make some sense of everything.

I closed my eyes as I drew in more air, trying to send light to the dark areas in my head, some warmth to the cold ones. I imagined electricity coursing through me, swirling in my elbows, knees, down my spine, across my shoulders, spreading to my arms and wrists, my palms and fingers. When I started to feel it in my calves and ankles, the room sprang back into my sight. Oh no. Now I was totally charged, awake. I glanced into my lap, and as I did so, a stringy pair of girl's underwear, silky and red and telling sank down. What?

I looked up and Jake was standing over me smiling that same

cruel smile I hated to be able to recognize. Fuck. Why him?

"Yours?" I said, and threw the underwear at him, but they just dropped at his feet.

"Hey, Allie, what's the matter?" His voice was soft. God, why did he have to say my name like that?

"Are you kidding me?"

He sighed and sat down, put the underwear in his pocket.

"I just bought a hip flask," he informed me, sitting down and brandishing the thing to take a swig. He held it out to me.

"Of course you did." I took a sip and handed it back. For a moment we were silent, but then I said, "Sorry to interrupt earlier." Why was I so calm all of a sudden? All that deep breathing shit? Maybe it was better this way, though. I hadn't talked to Jake since right after the breakup, and being civil with him seemed like more of a mature way to handle this.

"Oh don't be sorry. You always did apologize too much."

"I know. I'm sorry, I just can't help it. Ah shit. There I go again. It's just that...Jake, I'm so fucked up right now."

"And let me guess, it's all my fault, right?" He took one more sip and returned the flask to his pocket.

"Well —"

"Hey, hey, I thought we agreed not to talk about this," he said.

"Yeah, well, that was before I started remembering stuff."

"Stuff, huh?"

"You know."

He cupped my chin in his hand and turned me to face him, but so gently. "Listen, Allie, stuff happens, but that's all that everything is. It's just stuff."

Just stuff. That was all it was to him. I dug my nails into my palms, squeezing as hard as I could. I started to get so dizzy I had to look down and close my eyes for a second, but when I opened them again, I realized I was crying.

"Just stuff?" I pleaded. "Are you fucking kidding me, Jake? Don't you remember anything?"

"Okay, so I'm a bad person. What do you want me to do about it? That's just who I am. You knew how fucked up I was, but I have to give you credit for trying. And anyway, it's all in the past. Just stuff

that happened. You'll get over it. I know you.
I loved you, Allie, remember? I loved knowing you."

I nodded as his fingertips began tracing the underside of my left wrist.

"It's been so long since I've held your hand," he said, taking one and then the other.

"Just stuff," I whimpered. I sounded like one of those fucking broken-record morons. Tears were dripping down my cheeks but I couldn't wipe them away because Jake had both my hands. "But — "

"Shh," he said, letting go of my right hand and putting two fingers to my lips. "I just need you to be quiet for now. Just trust me. You're going to be all right one day, and then none of this will matter."

I felt like I was looking at myself through a telescope the wrong way as I kept nodding along, staring at his palms closed around my fists. "But — "

"I promise." He patted my head and walked back upstairs.

Death in My Own Home
Danielle Ramona Thomas

Pale and shrinking
On the family room sofa,
We watched you die
Day after day
Your friends
And co-workers dropped by
Waved to you and went
In the kitchen
And queried on your condition
With mama
While I only four years old
 Poked my small head
Around the corner
Of the family room entrance
To look at you
You; your once pleasant smile
Was gone
Lost in the
Mysterious clouds
Of a coming death

Summer of Shards
Katharine Walker

Nothing forces you to grow up like death. One minute a person is there and suddenly they are nowhere to be found. Sure, people will feed you a line about how they are in your heart or watching you from above, but the reality is they are gone. Watching my father die was like shoving a knife in my heart a little more each day. And the irony is I I use to hate the man. I blamed him for all the problems in my life, and when life was tough I would send hate mail just to make myself feel better.

I was a wild kid growing up. I liked to live life fast and hard and never once did I stop to think about what I was doing to those who loved me. With ever bottle of alcohol I drank and every pill I swallowed I fell deeper into this shell of a being, and all the while I kept hating my father more and more. Hating him for leaving me and finding happiness someplace else. Hating him for having another daughter. But most of all, hating him because there wasn't a day that didn't go by that I couldn't forget him. No matter how much I drank or how many guys I kissed could I ever get him out of my head. I even tried calling him a few times, but when I heard his voice I would freeze. Wouldn't say anything until he hung up and even then I just sat there listening to the dial tone for hours. Replaying all the conversations we had ever had or at least all I could remember. And if that wasn't enough I would make them up, telling myself the things I had always wanted to hear. I was on a path to nowhere and I had no way of getting off until one day I got my call. More of a letter really, enclosed with it was a plane ticket. A letter saying my father had cancer and a ticket asking me to go spend a summer, his last summer, getting to know him.

You think for a girl who spent so much time and energy trying to love her father wouldn't have much choice. She would have packed her bags and hopped on that plane immediately. But stubbornness has always been my downfall, and in this case my mental undoing. I deliberated for half the summer trying to decide if this is what I wanted or not. My poor mother drove me to the airport six different times and finally as we sat in the car watching another plane fly off without me, she looked me straight in the face and said, "You got two choices here honey, you can go be with your father, or you can spend the rest of your life wishing you had." And at the moment I realized the fool I had been. Saw myself, the real me, for the first time. Here I was thinking that I was teaching him a lesson by not going, but I was being hurt too. And when a dying man asks you to do something as simple as spending his last hours on this earth with him, you go. No questions asked. Mistakes are made and people get hurt but life goes on. You can either spend your whole life angry and blaming other or you can pick up the pieces and build something different.

So that is what I did. I picked up the shattered shards of my relationship with my father and built something beautiful that summer. It wasn't perfect and it most certainly wasn't what I spent my life imagining, but it was ours. My father's and mine. And that made it beautiful. No questions asked.

reunion
asmara ruth

woman-child sits in a psychological corner
of conflicting emotions,
facing a man she should know,
but does not,
not knowing what to say, to do.
a voice comes from outside of
the magic circle of silence,
"so what do you think of her hair?"
the almost-disgusted reply comes,
"she looks like a confused african girl."
woman-child reels defensively,
denying her confusion verbally,
lamenting it in her private mind.
she does not understand what
reason there is
for this belated, now unwelcome reunion.
as a child, she would have acknowledged him
for what he should have been,
but too many years
have widened the chasm between them
and now as she strikes out,
yearning for her independence,
she has no desire
to build the bridge that
would allow her to meet her father
on the other side of the abyss.

Love & Basketball
Lea Robinson

It's Saturday night at last. I've been waiting all week...and at last it is here. Tonight *Cat People* will premier on HBO. It's coming on pretty late but late enough to render my parents and siblings asleep. I head upstairs yawning and acting the part.

My sister is the first to go, my brothers are out next. However, I can still hear my parents downstairs talking; laughing and watching television...damn Saturday Night Live. In the meantime, I'm hanging on by a thread. My eyes are getting heavy and I can barely keep my head up. I confirm that my sister is asleep and move with stealth to my sock drawer. I creak the top drawer open with great care assuring no noise. I remove the piece of paper that's been folded 7 times (because that was my favorite number, that and 11, but the paper wouldn't fold that many times) and hidden in a tube sock. I know that the only thing that will keep me awake is a thought of her. Of whom you may ask? Nastasia Kinski of course. I had scanned through pages of the TV Guide and found a stunning photo of her...in full color and shiny paper, a small treasure indeed.

I remember removing it earlier in the week and making an executive decision that my folks would not miss the shinny advertisement for the small crystal unicorn (that was being offered at this amazing price only through this one time offer of $29.99 with a mail in rebate) complete on a crystal log. The area surrounding the unicorn's hoof placement on the log was magnified to showcase the true detail which had gone into this collectors' item. Removing this photo was a calculated risk for many reasons.

One, I could've ripped the photo while quietly trying to remove it...that would have been the end of the world. Two, one of my siblings could have spotted my actions and blackmailed me for the remainder of the summer. And three, my folks could have caught me, leading to an investigation and conversation after conversation about me in the wee hours of the night, like most parents do when the children are suspected of drugs, sexual promiscuity or perhaps HOMOSEXUALITY. How would I explain this to my parents if I had been discovered? They'd like to believe that I was feverously tearing out the spread on Kenny Walker (University of Kentucky's star basketball player) or the Wildcat basketball schedule for the upcoming season. Ah, luck be a lady, the pages of the glossy divider in the center of the guide weren't numbered and it was already Saturday meaning that if my parents hadn't noticed it by now, I was home free. As if you couldn't tell, Nastasia Kinski was my first true crush. I worshiped and adored her. I was in Junior High School and totally on the edge that very fine line that separates the cool and the cool.

I loved The Police and was determined that the song "King of Pain" was written for me...ah, pre-teen angst. I had seen Nastashia Kinski on an interview or maybe a preview for the movie *Cat People* and was immediately smitten. And I knew that especially on rainy nights, she was out there somewhere looking for and longing for me. One day we would meet at last and marry. I revealed this to my mother because I thought it was worthy information and she simply said "okay, dear." That was as good a time as any to test the water.

So, finally it's Saturday night and the movie comes on in 45 minutes. I close my eyes and imagine the many images of her on the screen. I try to imagine what the movie is about and who the love interest will be. I begin to create the perfect love interest for Nastasia Kinski (me of course) I imagine picking her up in my convertible Miata (like the one Crockett drives in *Miami Vice*) perhaps I am Sonny Crockett on *Miami Vice*. He's sexy and smooth, I imagine picking her up and taking her to dinner...as I close my eyes, I can see the sunlight shining on the palm trees, and the ocean to my right as I drive to her house. I can see the sun glistening on the surface of the water, I can see the sunlight...coming through...the...window? NOOOOOOOO!!!! I roll over and survey my bedroom. It's Sunday morning and I slept through the premier of *Cat People*. Not only did I sleep through the night, but I can't find my picture of Nastasia Kinski and my dad is calling for us to get ready for our Sunday morning ritual...bible school and Church.

For me Sundays meant no sneakers, gym shorts and t-shirts until late afternoon, if I was lucky, I'd still pick up some court time before the rush of the evening ballers. Sunday morning always started with the decoy of breakfast as my mother suggested the outfits we should wear. I was the only one who needed parental supervision. I'd emerge from my room wearing off-white, knee length dress with lace, black paten leather pumps and a hat. Not just any hat, it was a Kentucky Derby Easter hat...crafted flowers and all. In retrospect, I'm sure I was the finest drag queen ever to grace the steps of Broadway Baptist Church. We would pile into the family car and head to East Broadway for the early sermon. The hardest part was walking from the far away parking space to the church. My heart would pound with the fear of seeing Pam. Pam was older than me and she lived in Spruce Court (the bourgeoisie part of the neighborhood) and I had a crush on her too. I was afraid of her seeing me because I was convinced that she thought I was a boy. If I even saw a car, slightly resembling the car driven by Pam, I would've thrown myself into the bushes in my Sunday clothes to avoid the risk of her eyes falling upon me in this state. On our journey to the doors of the church, we would walk pass the preacher's sons; I would challenge the youngest to a game of one-on-one, while the oldest challenged my sister to a similar game, yet a slightly different arena. At this point in the morning the anxiety gripped both me and my sister as we approached the orifice of dread. The space just before the steps to the church was always occupied by "the pack."

"The Pack" consisted of about five elderly women, they were also known as "snitches with switches" a name given to them in honor of their selfless, courageous roles of informant to all parents within the neighborhood. They had even been known to grab a switch and raise the village. They stood strategically planted just before the entrance of the church, eyeballing and surveying everyone as they passed. Their looks of amazement never really changed or lost their potency, each Sunday morning when we passed. They would gasp and cover their mouths, "She makes a cute girl you know," I'd hear as I passed. I'd sit in church and endure the curious looks from the boys, the angry looks from the elders, and the encouraging glances towards the baptism chamber from the preacher. After church, I inched my way to the exit, being careful to avoid the Reverend and his flock of groupies.

Some days I would need to quickly dash into the ladies room if he managed to close the distance between me and the door. I knew that the ladies room was a safe space even though I didn't like being in there. I'd allow a few moments to pass and I'd peek out, the coast is clear. Up the steps I would bound in dress pumps and all. I'd burst through the doors to the sidewalk and sure freedom. I'd lay down a cross-over move to avoid the Preachers' sons on the steps. "The Pack" would be hovering near the sidewalk; a spin move got me pass them without as much as a blink. I saw the car and went coast to coast.

At home, I take my Sunday clothes off, replace them with *my* Sunday clothes and head to the park to play with the guys. Later that night, I realized that I was going to become something amazing someday.

That summer, I also began to realize that it was okay to be a boy, a girl or both. I didn't find my picture of Nastasia Kinski until later that summer. It was simply laying in the middle of the room on the floor one afternoon. I'm not sure how it got there or who put it there. I guess I wasn't the only one who came to some realizations that summer, and that was simply okay.

I gave YOU back to GOD
Thembi Duncan

My blood flows, a phantom in your silent veins
I imagine your eyeless sockets unable to weep for the life that
escaped you
the beauty of language, spoken & seen
the planting of the butterfly gardens of youth
the fights, the triumphs
the vision, the anger, the pain

of life

I could not allow you to be born
into such a place as this
to a child mother
to a father profoundly sick & confused
trapped inside a skin that would bring a lifetime of struggle
absent even the simplest considerations

or so I convinced myself

your hopes and dreams rested bittersweet on my tongue
and I closed my eyes
tight
and swallowed your future
as you were ripped unceremoniously from the comfort of my young
womb
your unformed, sacred flesh became waste
you went to eternal rest upon a bed of cold metal
I lay a shroud of regret upon your tiny, shapeless remains

This cold world did not deserve your divine light
        you remain unnamed
my beloved little could-have-been

I will grieve until I am joined with you
again

The Struggle of a Latina Girl

Janet Vega

She struggled all her life
no one listened, no one cared,
one day he walked into her life
he spoke gentle loving words
soon she fell in love.
three months later she was pregnant
out the door he went
a baby was on the way,
no one to turn to, nowhere to go
she felt so alone.

she walked through those doors
down the hall
into the room,
she thought *this is for the best.*
Few pains and minutes later it was all over,
no more worries she thought.
A year passed
more alone than ever she regretted
what she did in that cold room.
She felt so much pain
the only way out
to take her life
like the life she took from her child.
All because her parents
were too ashamed
to have
a single
pregnant
Latina
as their daughter.

Blue Skies
Siobhan Leftwich

It's the bluest sky I've ever seen. It stretches from north to south and east to west. I stick my head out the window and count the cactus growing alongside the highway. They seem to dance for miles. The land is brown and flat and hungry looking. Me and Ethel lean out so far that we have to hold onto the rusting handles so we won't fall out the car. We mimic Mitch's tobacco spitting technique, and laugh when the gobs return like boomerangs. Spit happens.

"What are you girls doing back there?" The voice is thin and spacey, because Elinor's been smoking joints all day. We're all in a daze, but me and Ethel have the windows open so the air's not so thick back here. Baby Jed is sleeping in Elinor's arms. I'm reading a book, I think it's John Bellairs. And Ethel is reading Beverly Cleary. We're real small, but we're all scrunched up because we're sitting on top of boxes and boxes of clothes and books and pots and pans from the Goodwill. Everything our parents could pack in the car. If I read and read and read, I won't have to think about it. And the sky is real big here. It seems to sop up the pain. It's the West, where new things can happen. It's the final frontier. But it may not be big enough for the Wesleys.

Two weeks ago, we all piled into the car and hit the road. The cops evicted us because Mitch hadn't paid the rent in years. As Elinor says, we lost everything. Everything. We lived on Keystone Farm, in the Keystone State. Me and Ethel roamed those woods and swam in the lake and played fairies in a clearing. We took our Big-N bikes out in the morning and rode for miles and miles. Up the mountain and down into the valley, jumping into the Delaware for a nice, cool swim. I carried lots of pennies, because we always stopped at Mr. Riley's store for treats. Mitch and Elinor never missed us. Just one time. I got us up and out too early, on the road before they were awake. When we got home, they weren't there. I knew we were in trouble. But the whole day had been great. Swimming and candy and biking. Past the abandoned stone houses, whizzing on the flat highway after pumping up the dusty dirt roads, stopping to speak to Mr. Joe and Miss Maggie, who owned the cows we bought our onion-tasting milk from. A great day. But all spoiled when Mitch and Elinor pulled into the driveway. Elinor had the door open, even before the car stopped, and ran toward me, her hand raised. "Troublemaker, troublemaker, troublemaker," she shrilled.

She's quiet today. She's stoned. I turn to Chapter 10.
In Santa Fe, we stop. Mitch has a friend I remember from back when. He used to sell plastics, like his father, but after meeting Mitch, who picks a mean guitar, he decided to open a music shop. A late 1960s, bourgeois dream, says Elinor. Mitch picks but Murray profits. "Do you remember the girls?" Mitch asks Murray, who is tall and lean and has curly brown hair and a big nose. He doesn't look like a nice person. And he ignores me. I'm 12 and chubby and brown from the sun and me and my frizzy hair are buoyed by the electricity in the air. Something about nuclear plants in Albuquerque. Or that's what Elinor says. Her black, wavy hair's sticking up, too. Murray pats Ethel on the head. "Ethel Jane," he smiles. I've gone invisible again. We shift gears and head toward the music shop. It's called Freight Train. Me and Ethel lag behind. Small Mitch and Elinor walk with tall Murray, who smiles at our pretty mother, who is in heavy flirtation mode. Mitch is too busy talking to notice. We pass the Palace of the Governors and the Indian women selling turquoise. I stare. A woman stares back, bored, and then smiles. With their hair piled high, and in their colorful clothes, the women look like the pictures in the National Geographics Mitch reads in the bathroom. Elinor's lectured me about Reservations and how terrible life is for the natives out here. She fancies herself a kindred spirit. So, I'm in the know.

The next day, we're shacked up at Murray's. Me and Ethel share a piece of the floor in the living room. It doesn't pay to complain, because it'll make Elinor freak out. Maybe have an asthma attack. The strategy is to remain quiet. And invisible. I'm doing a good job of that, so far. People out here just stare, but don't say nothing. I know why. So, I hide behind Harriet the Spy, reading it for the millionth time. The book is so worn that the spine is broken and the pages are getting crunchy. I'm sitting in the shade in the yard, away. Ethel is nearby, doing chin-ups on Murray's daughter's monkey bars. Up and down, up and down, up and down. Her face is red and her hair sticks to her forehead. Mitch pulls up in the old Chevy, powder blue with push button transmission. Elinor is in the house, asleep. There's an air of doom and depression. Of bad moons rising.

That night, I wake up to shouts and screams. It seems Murray's fancy shower is on fire, and it's Mitch's fault. He was smoking Murray's weed and fell asleep and the wood went up like kindling. The fire department comes and puts it out, but the jacuzzi is destroyed. Mitch and Elinor always cause a disaster. It's up to me to try to stop them from ruining everything. But I've been asleep on the job. Maybe it's the crisp air, the bright, bright light. Whatever it is, I missed the signs. The next morning, we pile in the car. Murray gives Mitch some money and tells him about an abandoned adobe near Española. "Thanks, man," says Mitch. "Sorry about this." He's working his good-old-boy, aw shucks number. Murray slaps him five. "Don't worry about it, man," he says, grimacing in the fierce sunlight. "It's good to see you. And at least you didn't burn the place down. Call me if you need any more help." I pick up my book and am on Chapter 12 before we even pull out of Murray's circular driveway.

The highway up to Española, on this clear, cold morning, is almost bare. Prairie dogs skip across the asphalt, moving from hole to hole. Maybe they're visiting their neighbors on the other side of the road. The fumes from the car are making me nauseous. And I wonder where Mitch is taking us. Little Jed is wailing in the front seat, because he needs his diaper changed. It smells. Ethel is leaning out the Chevy, her towhead gleaming like a ghost in the sunlight. I keep my head in the book, trying to block out the tension in the car. If I look in my mother's direction, she might snap and turn on me. She'll have that crazy, witch look and she'll say something like, "It's all your fault." The car slows now, something about going down a dirt road and hanging right at the third intersection. Around us, gas stations and fast food restaurants start popping up. Lots of low riders whiz by, mufflers roaring. The boys behind the wheel are brown or tanned and have slicked back hair. They wear flannel shirts and walk around in high heeled, black shoes made out of plastic. An Indian boy leans out of his red low rider, driving south, and mouths "nigger." I turn the page of my book and it's the end of the chapter.

Well, we have a house. Adobe brick, two rooms. No stove, no running water. An outhouse. We'll get a hot plate. We'll eat canned soup and subsidized school lunches. I haven't been to school since the third grade and I'm excited. I'll get out of the house. Maybe I'll make friends. We meet a girl named Patsy, who lives down the road. She's my age, but she's built like a Mack truck and drives her father's car up and down the road, up and down, raising the red dust as we stand by the side of the road, mesmerized. There's talk of Mitch taking a job, but he don't want to. Goes down to Social Services to see what he can see. I stay home. I feel like Pigpen in Charlie Brown. Raising dirt and dust everywhere I go.

But the sky is surely blue. It's clear as a bell. Clean as a whistle. And it goes on forever. At sunset it turns red and it looks like a painting. You can see for miles across the desert, too. At night we hear the teenaged boys —they're Castilian up this way, they ain't wetbacks —playing Eagles songs. Lying eyes and pretty women. In the morning we drive all the way back to Santa Fe, seems like hours. It's school-shopping time and Ethel slips into size 6x dresses, even though she's 9 years old. I'm all breasts and behind and I can't find anything to fit me. My mother is disgusted and angry and murmurs, "I can't believe this is my daughter." I want to say something smart, but don't want to start a scene. Behind a book, I'm invisible. But in the glare of J.C. Penney, in a brown bathing suit that's too small for my boobs, I'm a great, big black boogie woman. I pick out an extra large, red flannel shirt and put the bathing suit away. I'll swim some other time, some other year.

On the big yellow bus to John F. Kennedy Jr. High, nobody wants to sit with me. The Castilian and Indian kids stare and whisper. Ethel's on another bus, being called "gringa," but everyone likes a gringa better than a nigger. My face is burning and I feel my body floating away. We bump, bump, bump down the gutted road, stopping at the Indian reservation to pick up more kids, stopping along the side of the road to pick up Spanish girls with winged hair, Tough Skin jeans, flared Levis. The Indian boys have high cheekbones and wide, flat faces and jet black hair. I look at myself in the bus driver's mirror. I'm brown like them, lighter, but my nose and mouth are flatter and fuller. I wear my hair in two braids, pinned atop my head. And I have on three shirts, one over the other, trying to disguise my big breasts and big behind. I'm out the window, floating alongside the bus. Every time we pass a church, the kids make the sign of the cross. I wonder why. We move through miles of desert, fast-food trash and old soda cans decorating the landscape. Soon, we pull into the junior high. The sun is so hot, the asphalt looks like its sweating. I walk to the guidance counselor's office and he's nice. Tall and brown, with salt-and-pepper hair. Mr. Montoya has a poster of black, brown, and yellow children on his wall, with the year: 1976. He smiles at me and looks me in the eye. "Aisling Wesley, he says, "you tell me if you need anything at all."

My locker. I've never had one before. I'm not sure how to use it. An Indian boy comes up, looks me in the face, and runs back to his three friends, huddled nearby. He comes back, grinning. "You're a nigger, ain't you?" he says. I turn away. Numb, numb, numb to my first class. People stare and snicker. Some girls push the boys and tell them to be nice. I think about the farm, and think about how I miss being outside all day. Just me and Ethel and the trees and the breeze. Hard to sit still and pay attention. Elinor and Jed and Mitch can't be left alone. But lots of classes and desks and kids and teachers who stare. At lunchtime I sit alone and try to stop shaking. I look up at the clock and play with my food for an hour. More classes, and kids, and snickers, and stares. And gym class where we have to change into blue suits. Mine is the largest and the girls laugh. Then the bus takes me home and the buzzing of the busy bee kids doesn't stop until I get off. I run along the side of the road, slipping in the silt. Elinor is waiting for me. "The kids don't like me," I say, out of breath. She looks me up and down and walks away. "It's because you're too goddamned fat," she says.

Back at the adobe, chaos. Screaming and crying, I know people can hear it. I've been riding around and around the yard on my bike, barefoot. I fall off the bike and get a foot full of cactus. Then I run inside and pick up Jed, who's crawling on the cement floor. He's trying to avoid the dishes crashing around him. I take him outside, to the car, put him in his car seat, and open my book. Ethel climbs in beside me. She never cries. Just reads or sits quietly. Best not to make noise. Could get you hurt.

The next day, we pack up the car. We're heading for West Virginia now. Mitch's mamaw says we have a place to stay. Mitch has packed the last box and is braiding his long ponytail, Willie Nelson style. He's trying to be cheerful, singing "Froggie Went 'a Courting" until Elinor tells him to shut the fuck up. They light up a joint, Elinor puts Jed on her breast, and soon they're quiet. I lean back in my seat and close my eyes. I know what I'll do. I'll count all the prairie dogs until we leave this state. Then I'll look for things to tick off in Texas. Ethel snuggles against me and falls asleep. She's hot and sticky and smells like sweat. My mother looks at me in the rear mirror and sneers. "Think you're her mother, do you," she says. I pick up my book. Chapter 15. Then I look out the window. Blue skies. The bluest skies I've ever seen.

beautiful meets sweet
alexis pauline gumbs

when wasn't she here?

i woke up one morning
after dreaming myself
baked brown sugared fresh and edible

not just to the eyes of slow passing strangers
not just to the weirdly held hellos of the boys on the block
but really fragrant hot and craved
by
my
self

and I swallowed three brown to brighter helpings of myself
feeling strangely empty
dry breathless dizzy
felt
weightless anxious thirsty
and suddenly

the ground was lemons
and it was all I could do to
breathe
and stand
and breathe
and
fall
into a full body drink
through every pore
as it were lemonade
or the sun in my eyes
and sweet coating my skin
my mouth filling with the taste
of almost enough to save me from myself
when we dreamt each other awake.

Circles

Jennifer Patricia A. Carino

Today is the *Flores de Mayo*°.
I had forgotten
completely, until I heard
the whine of a marching band; still
out of key, like the same
Santacruzan°° from
my mother's childhood.
When she was *Reyna Elena**
and her own mother
made offerings
of flowers and money.
Blossoms on the canopy
above still, beyond,
were patches of sky.
A blanket for the
fragrant air.

Still the steady beat
of drum. The trumpets play
like voices of long forgotten
lovers. Trapped. Yes,
they echo in the pavement.
I hear them in the scratch
of heels on concrete,
in the drones
outside my bedroom window.
The street below is warmed
by a sudden downpour.
Drops hit with a hiss.
Murmur of heat and cold.
It fades into the hems
of long dresses. They brush
the earth and muffle
its sighs.

Another sigh
is more audible. In my bed
she shifts in a dream.
I mistake it
for a sign of waking.
Oblivious to my fingers
smoothing out the wrinkles
of bedspread and dreamsong,
she slips deep once more.
I long to sleep the way
she does: without fear.

One of the young *Reynas***
laughs as her crown slips
to the ground. It is only
a circlet of steel.
It hardly makes a clink
meeting the stone.
When it tumbles,
I feel as if a window
has been broken, its shards
flying out in all directions.
I duck to keep from getting cut,
and grin sheepishly
as I look back out the window.
There was no glass. Only
the hope for a sharper sound
maybe. A singular passionate
arrival.

Turning to look back in,
I know that I have my own circle
to attend to. I'd like to
give her gifts. Wreaths
of flowers, or a ring to wear
on her finger. I have nothing
of the sort at the moment,

so I lie beside her warmth and
whisper my history in her
ear, and she pulls me into her sleep.
So I know that for
now at least, my circle
is safe, and that the flowers
can wait.

° *Flores de Mayo: Literally, the flowers of May. A Roman Catholic flower festival celebrated in the Philippines annually, in honor of the Virgin Mary.*

°° *Santacruzan is a religious-historical "beauty pageant" held in many cities, towns and even small villages throughout the Philippines during the month of May.*

* *Reyna Elena: One of the most colorful May-time festivals in the Philippines which depicts the finding of the Holy Cross by Queen Helena, mother of Constantine the Great.*

** *Reynas: Queens.*

sweet meets beautiful

alexis pauline gumbs

i woke up one morning and she was in my bed
with her hand on my stomach
her mouth pressed against my wrist
breathing a slow everything
I tried to stay still
but I sank in
I stared at her
Blurry twisted softer
than my pillow warmer
than the sun on her shoulder

and I looked for a hole in my ceiling
looked for strange clothes on my floor
looked for a time machine, or at least a clock
but
found nothing but her hair
and her cradling sametime cradled shape

my bed seemed bigger
my wall safer
than ever

right then I vowed to pretend that she had always been here
pretend that I had enough nothing for both of us
pretend that half of the shirts in the dresser were hers
that she was as safe with me as she was in her
purple camisole open palm cool sunlight
dream
and we woke up.

The Seven Of Us
Katrese Watts

If she hits me one more time, just one more time, I swear I'll just curl up and die right here on this kitchen floor. My arms were numb, and my legs felt like spaghetti from the pounding that they were taking. Gramma had been beating me with a pair of nunchucks for over ten minutes and now there was no feeling in my left arm. Maybe I was going to be an invalid or crippled for life. I was praying she would be satisfied with the swelling and redness in my limbs. I was wrong.

"You kids have bad blood, aint never gonna be anything." My grandmother yelled as she took one more swing at my arm. Every action in my body was telling her that I had given up. I give up. But she kept swinging. She finally grew tired and walked away. I thanked God for his mercy as I lay there on that cold kitchen floor trying to muster up the strength to get up. Finally, I forced my legs to move, then walk. I needed them to carry me away, as far away as possible. I only made it to the cold damp basement. The place my siblings and I shared. The place that was called our "room". There was no love, no heat, no children in that room. Just four sisters ripped away from the one person who really loved them!

My mother had seven kids. She had six girls and one boy. Donnell was the oldest. Then there was me (Katrese), Latrell, Tawanna, Latrisha, Joannna, and Justina — in that order. We were taken from her when my aunt called DYFS on her for something or other. I never found out what that "something or other" was. As a result of that one act: one of her girls was put up for adoption (we have not found her yet) and her youngest daughter was put in a separate foster home than the rest of us. That left the five of us to be everything for each other.

I dragged myself to my bed and lay limp. Tawanna came over.

"What happened to you?" I didn't answer her. I knew that she was not asking me a question. She knew what happened to me. Tawanna had heard the beating. She was just looking for me to speak and to show signs of life. She came around the side of the bed where she could look into my eyes.

"Are you ok?" I looked at her and I knew that I had to live so that she would live. I had to protect her. I knew that if I died she would follow me so I smiled and said "I'm ok". Her eyes started to tear. "I hate them, I hate them!" She was the feisty one and I was the emotional one. I could not understand for the life of me why the very people who were suppose to love and protect us seemed like the ones we needed protection from the most. Although we knew our grandmother had only taken us in for the money from DYFS, we still hoped that she would treat us better than this.

I looked at my baby sister and I wanted to hug her and tell her not to hate them. I wanted to tell her that it wasn't nice to hate anybody because that is what my mother taught me. I wanted so much to have those words leave my mouth and reach her but I couldn't do it. I couldn't say it. I needed her strength. I needed her to hate what I was feeling that very moment. We sat in silence and Tawanna rubbed my back.

Later that night I woke up to:
"God, please kill me, God please let me die. Why don't you kill me?" I turned over and even though it was dark I could make out my little sister's silhouette. The same sister who had been giving me strength was praying to God to end her life.
"Tawanna what are you talking about?" I questioned her, hoping she would see that the prayer was a foolish one. I wanted her to change her prayer. She looked over at me, her hands still folded, still on her knees and replied. "Why would God do this to us?" I didn't answer her. I couldn't, because I had asked myself the same question almost every night. Instead I forced a smile on my face and I told her every thing would get better. She got off her knees and back onto her cot. I watched her little body tremble in the dampness, and I prayed to God to please let her live.

As I watched Tawanna I wondered if maybe my mother prayed the same prayer when her family was ripped away from her. Maybe her prayers were answered. When my mother didn't get her children back she started using crack cocaine as a way of coping. She didn't die physically, but spiritually she was dead. On the days that we would visit her if she had been using she was not herself. She wasn't smiling or dancing to music like she usually would. Her inner light seemed to be snubbed out. But if we caught her on a sober day she would tell us stories and make us laugh. She would forget her problems and hug us, and make us feel loved. Those visits always ended too quickly. I know this is not what she had planned for her life. Our life. I could often see the disappointment in her eyes. In her younger days she had dreamed of being a model and becoming a registered nurse. But those dreams were also dead. All she was left with was a four bedroom house with renters in the rooms instead of her children. Instead we woke up every morning in a place that was slowly breaking our spirits and robbing us of the will to live. 10 Allen Street.

In the morning I had to get all my sisters ready for school. I had to make sure their hair was done, their clothes ironed, and make sure everybody was off to school on time. I was the oldest sister by only a couple of years, but it seemed like more. We were glad to leave 10 Allen St. We were happy to go to school. When we got to the living room our brother was standing on the steps. Some mornings it seemed like he had been waiting there all night. I use to think he stood there so he could count all of his sisters in the morning. I think he needed to feel we were all living before he could go to school. He would never have piece of mind but he never left that house until he saw all four of his sisters were accounted for. He spoke to each one of us. He was our father figure and our hero. I watched him and I knew his burden was too heavy to be a teenager. I smiled at him. "Hey Donnell." I wanted him to smile. I knew he wouldn't, but I wanted him to. He told me everything would be all right. It was like he could see through me and he needed me to know that he knows what I know and that I know that he knows! One of my male cousins came running down the stairs. He was another positive role model. It seems sad that our role models were our peers but that is how it was at 10 Allen Street. "Hey T," he said. He looked over at my brother and they left for school. My sisters and I grabbed our book bags and headed for elementary school. We walked down a steep hill in our dollar store sneakers and this was one of the greatest experiences in the world to us back then! We were free until the school bell rang at the end of the day. The only freedom we had between the abuse.

"Get your black ass up! Latrisha peed the bed. Did you know Latrisha peed the bed?" I was wiping the cold out of my eye and trying to focus.

"What," I managed to get out of my mouth. My grandmother was hovering over me in the darkness.

"Get your ass up, your sister peed the bed. I'm going to beat your ass. I told you that every time she pees the bed I was going to beat your ass. Get your lazy ass up!" She grabbed me out of the bed and I could feel the leather belt rip into my skin. She beat me until the welts on my body were red and swollen. She kept hitting me until she thought I had enough. "Now change these sheets and get your sister cleaned up." I did as she told me to do and I made sure my sister was quietly asleep before I cried. I cried silently, I covered my mouth and closed my eyes and I cried from the inside out. I woke up the next morning excited about going to school. I made sure my bruises were not showing, that my sisters were dressed and we headed to school. Down that steep hill in our dollar store sneakers. We were free again. But even inside this bubble of freedom, we sometimes created our own violence.

"Loppy cut it out," I yelled at my sister. She was only a year and some months younger than me, but sometimes she seemed like the oldest. She had one of our female cousins jacked up on the fence at the park. "Let her go." I tried to get her to stop terrorizing our cousin. "No I'm gonna kill her, I'm gonna kill her." She spoke those words with force and seriousness. My cousins' eyes were wide and afraid. I knew I could have just grabbed my sister off of her, but something inside me needed to see my sister get her "relief". Tina had always gotten her way. She had all the pretty clothes. She would tell on us and we would be beat from one side of the house to the other. I let my sister hit her once and then I grabbed her. I knew that if I didn't stop it that we would be beat fiercely for it later. My cousin was shaking and crying. I walked with her home and I prayed for my sister because I knew she was going to pay dearly for fighting the beloved Tina.

That night Loppy stared wild-eyed at me and ranted. You would have never known that she was just beaten with a switch and that she was bleeding on parts of her body.

"I'm not scared of Gramma, I hate that bitch!" I listened to her and I didn't stop her because everything inside me knew that she needed to get that out of her. I knew she had to get all the hate and hostility out before it ate her up inside like it was doing me. She finally grew tired and fell asleep. I didn't sleep well at all that night. I was hoping that Latrisha didn't pee the bed.

• • •

"Renee put a curse on you!" Latrell yelled. I looked up and laughed but inside I was trembling. My fathers ex had been working her roots again and this time she chose to put them on me. A lot of southern women practice this ritual. I looked at my sister.

"I don't believe in roots, I believe in God."

She looked at me, "Well you better." That night I read Psalms 37 and told myself "no weapon that is formed against me shall prosper."

I was a teenager by that time and I was beginning to look like my mother. I had her shape and some of her features. I began to resemble her Dominican father and my dad. My hair was down my back until my grandmother decided to have it all cut off. My other sisters were growing into their own beauty and they were blossoming into women. Tawanna had grown into a tall slender long-legged creature. Latrell's caramel-colored skin and thick hair made her look like a Spanish looking black girl. Latrisha had the smoothest clearest prettiest skin I had ever seen. I looked at each one of my sisters in amazement. My brother, my uncle, and cousin had to keep a lot of men up off of us. Truth be told we just needed to mention their names and no guy in his right mind would try to talk to us.

I wonder who protected my mother from the jealous women in her life. The one's who threatened her with curses. She was envied and hated by most women. Maybe it was because she was built like a brick house and had long wavy hair down her back. Maybe it was because she was a redbone with a Dominican father. Men loved her. They called her Cherry. One of my father's girlfriends called herself putting roots on my mother. She somehow got a picture of Cherry and used it in some satanic ritual. Her name was Renee. My mother never believed that roots worked, but I bet she would sometime wonder.

"You know that we are going to have Oreo cookie babies, Katrese, you know you are my baby."

I was in high school and my high school crush was sitting in the seat in front of me leaning on my desk and looking me right in the eyes. His name was Sam and he was Italian. I smiled at him. I could tell that he was serious. The teacher came into the class and he turned towards the front, but then he decided that he didn't like the fact that he couldn't see me from that position and he changed his seat so he was sitting next to me. I was blushing and all the other girls were looking at me and turning their lips up. I guess it was strange to them to see a white guy talking to the only black girl in the class. We never cared. Sam and I flirted in that class every day from beginning to end. I covered his books and checked his homework assignments. For his part, he gave me massages and talked sweet. He and I never officially became boyfriend and girlfriend, but we sure enjoyed each others company.

Sam died in our junior year. Part of me wondered were Renee's roots working.

The Speaking Lesson
Jackie Warren-Moore

I come from a long line of women who are speakers. Women who planted their feet firmly on Mother Earth and spoke out. Women who have spoken out to praise and sustain what was right in their world. Women who balled their fist, prepared for battle and screamed out against injustice.

I was destined to be a speaker, my history, my family, my own sense of placement in the world would not let me shirk the job. My Grandmother, Louise Lee, an Ancestor I never had the opportunity to meet, set the tone. From all accounts she was a big, bold woman with strong opinions. Grandma Louise was prohibited by her family from marrying my Grandfather, Harry Lee, back in 1915 because he was "too dark." But she planted her feet, covered every inch she stood on and made her own decision. My Mother, Leta Mae Lee was born from that decision.

If any doubt remained regarding my destiny, the events of a 1970s summer evening dispelled it. My Mother and I were driving through a well known strip of bars and restaurants on Syracuse University Campus, in Syracuse, NY. We saw a crowd gathered. At the center of the crowd lay a young African American man. His body lay in the road with his neck on the curb like a pillow. A young White man stood with his foot pressed down on the young mans neck. Three or four other White men urged the one to "Break his neck."

My Mother's reaction was immediate. She slammed on the brakes, threw the car into park and said simply: "Come on". She got out of the car and opened the trunk, reached in and pulled out two tire irons. She handed one to me. She raised hers to her shoulder and quickly stepped into the crowd. I held my tire iron tightly and followed.

My Mother demanded that the young White man back off and release the Black man. The crowd was silent. The White man looked at the two of us. Perhaps he was surprised to see two tire iron wielding women. Or perhaps they were surprised to hear someone voice an objection to what they were about to do. Whatever they thought, the White man removed his foot. The Black man, My Mother and I moved slowly back to the car. As we drove away from the still staring crowd, my Mother laughed and said: "That was a close one."

After asking his name and where he lived, she began to talk to the young man about the ways Black people had to survive in those trying times as she drove him home. I sat in the back seat shaking. It was then that I knew that I could not make my mark in the world the same way that was second nature to my Mother. I admired my Mother for her guts and strength and wisdom. I wanted to imitate the way she served the community. But I realized that my weapon of choice is words. I have been writing every since.

To shut my mouth and sit silently by as some would have me do, is to suffer many deaths. I choose life, and must therefore speak. As Audre' Lorde, noted Poet/Sister and Ancestor has said: "Your silence will not save you".Even Helen Keller, another woman who might have been silenced tells us: "Life is either a daring adventure, or nothing at all".

So I speak. I speak about what I see, what I feel and do as an African American Woman in today's world. I try to make connections. The connections between two listening hearts that honest words of communications are capable of making. I believe poetry cuts through all the societal 'BS' that keeps human beings apart.

My Mother used to tell me: "There are no new feelings under the sun." Beneath the skin, class and lies that separate us, we are all the same. It is only open hearts, open hands and communication that will connect and save us all. So I speak, to try to pass on the courage and art of speaking to my daughters, my grandson, and anyone else who will listen.

American History 0110
Rasheedah Phillips

I trotted into the classroom at my usual, hurried pace, and glanced up quickly at the clock above the entry door before sliding into my regular seat directly next to the exit door. "Early", I sighed out loud to myself, trying to catch my breath after having jogged from Trinity Hall to Smith Building. It was almost inevitable, given the distance between the two buildings, that I would be at least five minutes late to class everyday. However, fate, as it would have it, placed me in class about five minutes early today.

Doc Tuttlevich from Philosophy of the Mind had scooted us out early today to hustle to a conference, and, with the winter season well on its way, it was too cold to sit on the benches placed directly outside the entrance to Smith Building. However, due to my reluctance to be in that particular class, I must admit that I did not really care about being late. It was not that I lacked the enthusiasm to be present in the class and learn the material; it was the atmosphere that made my routine lateness negligible. There was a list of personal wrongs that I felt had been committed against me in my American History class — which I sardonically termed "Whitey's History". Well, maybe not 'against me personally', but the damn class just left a bad taste in my mouth. The first in this series of bad tastes was the professor, good 'ole Dr. Bane, PhD both in American Studies and Political Science, and a probable slave owner in his past life.

The way he treated the subject matter, from an obviously white supremacist perspective, was infuriating and disheartening, and the way he ran his class was tyrannical. He gave the class ten minutes in the beginning (the ten minutes you could usually find me absent from) to speak on the previous night's reading, and would lecture for the rest of the 80-minute class without stopping for questions. Any questions you had were a personal matter to be explored when he wanted to make office time. So if one were so inclined to dispute Dr. Bane on the meaning of so-called facts such as 'Blacks are four and a half times more likely than Whites to be on welfare', one would not be given the chance, even if one could come up with a separate set of facts that could either illuminate or prove this statement wrong. He did not know the meaning of promoting an intellectual environment where students were not force-fed information, nor was he familiar with the phrase "Question everything." And this pissed me off to the highest level of pisstivity, so I strolled in late every morning between 11:50 and 11:51 and took my seat near the back of the lecture hall, right near the exit door. I skipped out on the comments section of the class for two reasons: I knew that not a damn thing that I said would throw even an inkling of awareness on the part of the races and cultures of people, my race specifically, that Bane's "facts and statistics" liked to demean so much, and that, in my attempt to raise the consciousness of the mostly upper class, Caucasian crowd around me that called themselves my classmates, I would become frustrated and start showing off what may be construed as my "Black-girl attitude". Unfortunately, I could not afford to drop the class; it counted toward those stupid CORE classes that Ramen University imposed on your education.

Now, don't get me wrong. I am not some elitist asshole on a Black power-consciousness trip that sought to educate the masses of mentally enslaved human beings who had been brainwashed by the white man. Or maybe I am, but I wouldn't exactly put it in those terms. I just knew my shit. When having to choose between this class and others to satisfy my CORE, such as 18th Century Geology and Macrolevel Principles of Economics, Bane's class sounded the least boring. Besides, I thought it would be an excellent supplement to my African-American Studies and Women's Studies majors, for I have always believed that, in order to defeat the enemy, one must know him completely and thoroughly. And my enemy was not the white man himself — more so patriarchal, oppressive, hegemonic America itself, with the dominance of upper class society creating disproportionate opportunities (i.e. white privilege) for their kind — usually manifesting into racial conflicts. So this class was an 80 minute waste of my time, for I, as gung-ho Black consciousness as I was, did not believe, or did not want to believe, that the majority of America saw minorities as Bane's statistics portrayed them through his portrait of American History. And though I know that Bane did not pull the data out of his ass, I do know that he chose this particular curriculum for a reason, which, in my opinion, was to give the negative portrayal. The most biased part about it, however, was how these same statistics often highlighted the disadvantages of being black, but never emphasized the benefits that whites receive from those same disadvantages.

Speaking of the asshole, he sauntered behind several other students who were filing in during the last minute or so before the class started. Some people, who may have had borderline racial prejudices, if they were not racist already, actually enjoyed his ludicrous banter. They would openly nod their head in agreement as he would state how the 14th Amendment was invalid based on several reasons, or how Christopher Columbus had sought to civilize Native Americans after "discovering" the Americas. Drones, they were. Everyone found a seat and waited for Bane to open discussion. With eighteen seconds left, the arrogant bastard actually sat there and waited for the clock to read 11:40 exactly before approaching the podium.

"Good morning, class. Glad to see that we could all make it on time this morning." Dr. Bane muttered in his depressingly flat voice, Clear Eye guy, Ben Stein style. I couldn't help but get defensive at the statement, for I felt that he noticed me specifically, being that I was early today and not disturbing the class by walking in late, and, given that I was one of the few minority faces that decorated the room. Then again, he could have said that every morning when he started class, for all I knew.

"This morning's discussion will be on a more contemporary topic of sorts, following the reading that you had for Monday regarding ghettoes and slums created in New York City by Italian and Jewish immigrants in the early 20th century. As you may or may not be able to tell, just from walking three blocks outside of your scenic, serene campus, ghettoes are, in this day and age, a problem most prevalent in the black community."

"In recent news, you have heard of the creation of a board game called Ghettopoly, a spin-off of the Milton-Bradley game Monopoly which depicts life in the ghettos with blacks. It has game pieces that include a pimp, a prostitute, a machine gun, and a marijuana leaf. Instead of putting up hotels, you are putting up crack houses. My question to the class, before espousing my own opinion, is, how realistic is this game? I mean, why are these people so outraged at something that, in many respects, seemingly depicts their lifestyle, their very quality of life? Is the creator of this game pulling this out of nowhere, people? You have ten minutes.", he said to us. And this is the reason why I did not step foot in this classroom before discussion time. The fact that he could sit up there- white privileged as he was- and talk in such a demeaning tone on a social problem that he had never experienced, only read about, boiled my blood. I raised my hand in the air to advocate my own damn opinion, but Bane passed over me several times.

Asinine statements from "Well, isn't that how they really act?" to "The game is for entertainment purposes, why are people so touchy?" were called out by the white kids who had only heard about ghettos from the rap music that they listened to, from the black cultural customs that they adopted and exploited, who thought that they have some sort of special insider knowledge since they brought *50 Cent's* latest album. The ignorance was appalling. And he kept calling on these uninformed fuckers. Finally, I could not take it anymore, Bane was purposely ignoring me and I had to get out what I was going to say before I peed on myself.

"How dare you people!" I yelled out from my seat at the very top of the auditorium. "This game, it, it perpetuates horrible, negative stereotypes! It makes a mockery of our culture! Not only that, but you would condone a man profiting off of actual, real-life economic problems? Where is your sense of decency, humanity, fuckin "all men created equal under God"? Oh, I get it! Why don't we go back to minstrel shows while we are at it to keep you entertained? That's all we are here for anyway. Keep the Massa happy, so that you can then consume our culture, replicate whatever exaggerated behaviors and images you garner from rap music and videos, and then continue to reinforce the stereotypes, then go home to your 3-car garage and 10-bedroom mansions!" and with that, I did a little jig. The other students looked at me with shock, but Bane just stood there, staring, stone faced as always. I continued; I wanted to outrage them. "How would you all like it if I came up with a game, we'll call it, say, Middleclasswhitefolk opoly, where there are cocktails and lines of powder cocaine for icons and the goal is to build up as many dirty, underhanded corporations you can without getting busted for white collar crime. You are given cards such as 'Spend one day in jail for insider trading'. You see the potential for absurdity, right? Right?" I said, out of breath at this point, damn near pleading with the offspring of the American Privilege club that I was addressing. They stood there, all pale skinned and wide-eyed, but not one person backed me up. Not even the other black kid in the front row. All of the passion, the heart, the soul I had just put into trying to educate these people, open their eyes, was just — worthless. Fucking worthless. But if they did not get any revelations from my romantic speech, I certainly got one. I recognized what I did not want to believe — this was micro-America, represented right here in History 0110. History equaled propaganda in this classroom, and blacks would never get fair treatment, nor would we ever see an accurate record of the Black American experience in here. I could either deal with it, or leave, but it would not change their perceived facts. Bane made this face as if I had offended him by calling out, and closed the rest of the discussion.

All that I could do, in that moment, with no acknowledgement, after not even being so much as scolded for interrupting the class, was put my proud head down and close my ears to the rest of the period.

"Eboni!" Dr. Bane called to me as I began my mad dash out of the door to get to the Zion Building on time for my Black Woman class for some real enlightening discussion. I stopped for a moment and walked to the podium where he stood rustling papers. "I'd like to see you back in class on time on our next meeting date. You add an interesting perspective to the discussion. However, I would advise you to stop giving up so easily. So far, few of my students this semester know the meaning of 'question everything', and you could possibly set a good example for the notion that. No one can make you feel inferior without your permission." He spoke in his monotonous tone, without so much as glancing at me. I moved to walk away.

"One more thing. Learn to learn first, then you shall teach." I only nodded, then began retracing my steps to the exit, surprised, not even knowing that he had known my name. Perhaps, unlike I thought, there was a thing or two that I could learn, and even teach, by the end of semester. Eye opening could work both ways, if I allowed it.

Flags
Jane Jiang

The tinted window was halfway open in the back seat as the girl leaned back into the smooth gray leather upholstery. Her eyes were half-closed to shut out the offensive brightness of the September sun; a faint murmur of mixed Chinese and English drowsed back to her ears.

Somewhere outside in the busy street a flag snapped. The girl stirred, remembering that she had to remind her parents to buy two of those, one for each car. They were Americans, and a flag would be a fine symbol of an appropriate patriotism, especially fitting in light of recent events. Some clichés you could just never have enough of.

The traffic god was congested (hay fever, the girl had proclaimed, smiling whimsically), and the erratic flow of cars passed her window brought a dirty white minivan into view. The girl absently noted the mud spattered on the car; it reminded her of dried and dusty mustard. It was undecorated except for the American flag sticking out of the back — an ungainly tail — and a window sticker featuring a waving Stars and Stripes with the slogan "United We Stand" emblazoned across the top. She was tiring of the minivan's plainness when it ebbed back into the line of traffic behind the frame of window. A sporty little coupe appeared; she lost herself in the procession of cars tha passed her window, content for the moment to be quiet and attentive to the little details she noticed.

A light breeze brought back a whiff of conversation, which the girl tried to ignore. Her parents were talking of it again, as if talking would somehow solve the mystery and ease the pain of the loss. Well, let them talk, she thought, but she was going to try to sleep. She was still too haunted by the images from the news stations to think about New York, which she had visited only half a year ago, with any sort of equanimity. It had come as such a shock...

She registered the shouting first, and dismissed it as one would an annoying fly. Her fellow Seattleites, she thought, were becoming more obnoxious by the day. That was before she comprehended the words.

"Hey! Hey you! If you're going to talk, talk English —" the girl sat up straight and glanced out the window; the words were too

256

pointed to ignore — "or go back to where you came from!" The voice came from the fat, balding man with a squashed and sunburned face driving the white minivan, which had crept back up to her mother's car.

The numbness came first, tearing all sensation away and whiting out the other thoughts in her mind. From some great distance away, she heard her father's infuriated voice reply. "Yeah? And where are you from?"

The statement was rather garbled with indignation, and certainly not a good example of his near-flawless English. But it served to rally her thoughts, and then all the voices in her head broke free from the suffocation of dumbness to clamor and rant, outraged and scared and shocked beyond compare. Then, mercifully, the lights changed, and the dirty white minivan was swept back and away for the last time as her mother's new burgundy Mercedes charged to the front, eager to be rid of that man, that place.

A flash of red, white and blue waving in the wind — a flag — caught her eye as they surged forward, and the oddity of the window sticker finally hit her groping mind.

She would reflect on the incident later and muse that a silence fell on the street then, in those seconds before her father replied. And perhaps, if she were feeling especially inventive, she would add that a few others spoke back to the Dirty White Minivan as well, condemning him as a paranoid, uneducated racist.

But nobody did. It was strange, being on a busy street plugged with cars of all shapes and sizes, and having a private conversation — if what had transpired could be so termed — with the man driving the car in the next lane. The world kept on spinning, but for a split second, it seemed as if that part containing the two cars and their passengers had stopped. They had been transported, the girl was sure, because this sort of thing did not happen in real life.

But the car had passed in the end, and they had returned to the familiar world. And since the Chinese idiom dictated that the great man did not begrudge the small man's faults, the girl and her parents, being good Chinese Americans, felt an obligation to let go of their anger.

In time, the memory began to fade. The spatters of mud were no longer the color of dried and dusty mustard, content now to be a nondescript gray. And as "squashed and sunburned" was relegated to the annals of memories better lost, the man's face began to blur into a shapeless white patch. The hot indignation and the rankled jabbering of the girl's thoughts were quickly lost, and in too soon a period of time the event seemed something from ages past, small and unimportant against the great trials of the day.

But a few things remained with the girl. The first was a heightened awareness, a consciousness of being different from others which showed up always in the most unexpected of times. It was a feeling that would never quite go away to leave her with the quiet peace she had enjoyed before that fateful day. There was also a prevailing sense of oddity concerning the flag: not exactly irreverence for it, but she never could look at it quite the same way again. Before, a buoyant pride surfaced when the Old Glory flapped and waved in the breeze, but now, she felt something akin to pity for those who wore their supposed patriotism proudly on their sleeve. And somehow, she knew that she would never be able to shake that image of a cheap plastic flag snapping mockingly at her disbelieving face.

A Ghetto Girl's Story
Brittney Ball

I was a girl in the ghetto
growing up grown.
From age five
I've been on my own.
Nobody by my side
No mother to teach
No one to provide
So I turned to the streets

At age 10
I knew how to please a man
Using my mouth
Vagina
And sometimes the hands
I used what I had
To get what I needed
Transported drugs
Stripped
even sold weed
I slept with dudes
old enough to be my father
I would do anything
to get the all-mighty dollar

At age 12
When I first got knocked-up
I should've turned my 23 year old baby father in
and got him locked up.
You see he was mad
and didn't know how to express his anger
So he held me down and gave me an abortion
with the tip of a coat hanger

At age 13
My confidence was as low as it could get
I felt my life wasn't worth living
I felt lower than worm shit!

By age 14
I went in for stomach pains
and was diagnosed with AIDS
and this is when the regret
disgust, humiliation, and fear came

By age 15
I was dead in a grave
and this is the story
Of my life
A life
No girl should pave

There Are No Victims Here
Tricia Snell

I am alone.
I live on a street.
Just skin and bone,
No socks on my feet.
I am alone.

It is cold.
I am afraid.
But I must be bold,
And not parade.
For it is cold.

I have no dreams.
For sleep cannot be.
Because fear it seems,
Is always in me.
I have no dreams.

I have no home.
I have no friend.
Except for this poem,
Which has nothing to lend.
I have no home.

I wrote this poem when I was in high school. At the time, I thought I was writing about someone else, some character I was only imagining. Looking back, I don't know how I didn't know that it was clearly me. Maybe it was the living on the street without socks that threw me. I took things so literally in those days.

This is where my story begins, or atleast where I choose to invite you in. For if there is one thing I have learned over the years, it's that in order to truly convey the significance of any major life event, you must always back track a little first to set the scene. So I will start with the major life event before the major life event...my parents' divorce.

Everyone knows that there is no such thing as a clean divorce, that two people choosing to separate everything they have created together can never be a simple process. But this divorce was by far one of the messiest I have heard of yet. I'll save you all the terrible details of my parents' marriage and summarize with a few crystal clear examples.

I could only have been four or five at the time, making my brother six or seven. Due to the many years between my present me and the me then, the whole thing is rather foggy. All I remember is that they'd had another fight. My dad finally walked away from my mom, only to find my brother and I. He pulled us into the little bathroom, where my brother and I had to stand shoulder to shoulder to fit between the narrow walls. "I'm leaving," he said, "and I don't know if I will ever be back."

But he did come back, and so did the fights. We came to expect it. We could practically time it. For instance, we always knew the car ride to grandma's would call for a four-hour screaming match, ending with outright ignoring the rest of the weekend, followed by an inhumanly quiet four-hour ride home. That's the way it always was, for as long as I can remember. I still can't figure out which was worse-the car ride there or the car ride back.

One particularly cold fall day, however, the pattern changed. This time the screaming escalated. My mom began repeating, "pull over the car, pull over the car so I can get out." We were on a rural highway in the middle of nowhere, farms as far as the eye could see. I assume that is why my dad ignored her, not believing her threat to leave. His non-response only fueled her anger, and eventually she grabbed the wheel. The next several moments are a blur. I see the jagged memory of her running from the car, my dad running after her. Then he was forcing her in the car. Did he pull her to the car, or carry her? I cannot remember, I can only remember that she did not come at will. Roughly, he pushes her onto the floor of the minivan, squeezing her legs up against her chest. She is balling, but she does not fight back. She lays there, crying so hard there is no sound. What did my brother and I do? This I cannot remember either. Some things our memories spare us.

These are but moments, moments in a life of fighting. But there were good times too, just enough to make me go on caring about the fights. So now we return to my high school years, and the divorce. I was 16 when it happened. Finally. Finally. After all the years of threats, I never thought they would actually do it. Well, neither did my mom I guess. And she sank into the biggest depression of her life, which nearly ended her life. Three times.

So this is where the story starts. Remember this is only the major life event before the major life event. And as I said before, I tell it here only because in real life there are no true beginnings, just as there are no true ends. No, real life goes on spinning, and we can never fully grasp the meaning of any one particular event without understanding the life that has lead into it. Put another way, I tell you because our society functions so heavily on labels, and this is where my labels start — depressive mother, insecure attachment disorder, caretaker, co-dependent, alone...

I am in Colorado now. I have moved across the country to set my roots far, far away from the place I no longer call home. I work in a bar & grille as a cocktail waitress. It's great money and even better booze. I've met many people here, quickly. We party together. Most nights I don't get off work until three a.m., but we still party. We watch the sun come up together through a drunken haze. It's glorious, or so I think.

Here enters Jake. Jake is the mysterious and sulky cook who works the night shift with me. Though as the kitchen closes long before the bar does, he only works for half my shift. The other half he spends drinking and smoking at the bar. And it is during my trips back and forth through my section that we exchange small interludes of romance. He is so deep. Deeper than anyone I have ever met before. And he shares with me so openly. About who he is, about his dreams and hopes for the future.

I become intrigued with him, enthralled in his mysticism.

Then it happens. I get invited by another friend from the bar to go hear him play. As I watch him on stage and hear his heart and soul pour into his songs, I realize — I want him. I need him. And so I pursue him. Within days he invites me to his house after work, and this time we watch the sun rise alone, though still through a haze. He wants me too, I can feel it. But he doesn't make a move, doesn't even hint at anything more than friendship. This throws me into a tailspin. I have never been here before, never wanted a man who didn't already want me, "I will have him," I think, and soon.

Soon comes quick enough, and before I know it we are moving in together. We are inseparable and share to the world, and our place of employment, that we are together. "Why no reservations this time?" I think. Normally I am so cautious, wouldn't dream of telling anyone at work until much, much later. But "this is it," I think. He is the one.

The one to change it all that is. It doesn't begin as they always portray it — one terrible fight, and then bam! No, it comes in small doses. A push here, a shove there. I never thought he would take it that far. Of course, that's what kept me there. That's what hardly anyone understands. You don't stay in an abusive relationship, you're not in one. People spend so much time trying to figure that one out. "What is it about her that she would stay?" Always asking the wrong questions. We are so good at that.

No, I was not in an abusive relationship. I was not that girl. — victim — Never that girl. — victim — Not even after I called the cops on him, and they took pictures. — victim — Not that girl. — victim — Never that girl. But I thought I'd call the number they give me anyway, just to see what they had to say of course. I will never forget what she had to say, that cold, over trained and yet truly uneducated woman on the other end of the phone. Straight from my high school psych text. "It's a cycle. He'll never change. It will only get worse," she says, before I even tell her what happened. "How stereotypical can you be?" I want to say. "You know nothing of us, nothing of him, and especially nothing of me." But nothing comes out, and so ends my cry for help. — victim —

Will she ever know that she is the reason I stayed for round two? Will she ever know that by spewing lines straight off a paper and failing to connect with the real me, the real situation, she caused my defenses to rise? Will she ever understand that making someone defensive makes them have to believe their own lies, no matter how much they don't want to? No, she thinks she did what she was supposed to. Text book case, plain and simple.

But of course, it was not her fault. I cannot blame her anymore than I can blame him. That's just it. I play a role in this too. That's the part they always leave out. Because, well, then who would be the victim? And who would be the mean, terrible shadow of a man? The truth is never that simple though. These are just the lies we tell ourselves so we can sleep at night. Yep, throw him away. He's a "perpetrator" and get her some counseling, she's a "victim." We love our labels, oh, how we love our labels. What would we do without them? Think.

Yes, without our perfect little labels, we would have to actually wonder about him and her. And if we took one minute to see, to truly see, we would understand that it isn't all about the man having some evil gene that he just happened to be born with. And it isn't all about her not having the will to leave. It is about two people trying to find their way through a lonesome, confusing world. Trying to make sense of their past and carve out a future. The crash and bang of all of those pulls, of the clash of dreams, and the smack of reality, gets to be an awful burden on two young kids just trying to make the rent.

No, it isn't about him being terrible, or me being weak. I was strong, I am strong. I could leave at any moment. But I didn't. "Why?," you ask. There you go again, asking the wrong question. See, as I said before. I was never in an abusive relationship. I was only in love. In love with a man who drank too much, who enjoyed the haze of a nice buzz rather than the sting of reality. See, he never hurt me sober. And how can you be in an abusive relationship, if only one of you remembers? How can you say, "I'm leaving." if every morning is a new day, a new chance at a different outcome.

Hope. Hope is all we have in this world. Hope is what keeps us alive. And hope is what kept me from leaving. But that gets left out of the picture when you start framing the question in negatives. No, the truth is more complicated than we are prepared to hear. Nobody wants to hear that the reason people don't leave is because of the very beauty inside of us. No one wants to know that it's a positive decision. That it is a will to life, to survive, and to be happy.

No one wants to hear that because that blurs all the lines. For who shall be "perp." and who shall be "victim," when there is will and hope. We lose the comfort of our labels if we really open our eyes to see. And nobody wants that. Especially not some woman on her way to a psych. degree, working the late shift on the other end of the victim hotline. She doesn't want to hear that we can't be put into a box, that we have our own unique story, and our own unique path. That he wasn't born the beater, and I the victim. That cycles can be broken, that love doesn't fit between the lines of her pre-written sermon.

Ask a woman to explain why she stays, and you ask her to remember all the reasons she is there. Ask her to envision herself happy, ten years from now. Picture everything to the blade of grass next to the mailbox, and then ask her if she sees him there. Now that's a better question. For every woman in this situation knows, deep down in her heart, that he is not part of her future happiness. And given the space, at the right moment in time, she can see that perfectly clear.

But how often does that happen? How often are you free from the questioning, the loving concern that forces the defenses? Even when those voices are quiet, how often are we free from our own voice? The voice that constantly questions, that seeks to explain, that justifies our now. Oh, that voice rarely quiets, and its constant chatter blurs our vision. Many women stay in relationships they know they are not happy in. This is no different. We all want to buy into the fantasy of happy ever after. And in this myth we strangle ourselves.

See, there is no happy ending to this tale, though there is happiness.

As most of us who have been around for awhile come to understand, there is no one end point. Life never wraps up into a happy little bundle that concludes for all eternity. Rather it goes on, and new sorrows form. But with those sorrows come joy. For we cannot truly experience one without the other. And thus, this tale does end with happiness, as it began with sadness.

My happiness came the minute I struck back. No, I didn't hit him. I could never do that. But I did something far, far worse. I smashed his guitar. That's right, I smashed it to pieces. Now some people would say that's an act of violence, and how could an act of violence be the happiness of this story? But this is the moment I broke free.

I'll never know why I grabbed the guitar. I only know it meant more to him than anything in this world, more to him than I ever could. No, I'll never know why I grabbed it, but I'll always remember how it felt. It felt good. It felt good right down to the core. I hadn't felt that good in, how long? How long had it been since I felt free?

Now, don't think me terrible. I didn't want to break his heart, anymore than he wanted to break mine. I only wanted to show him... needed to show him, what he was taking from me. He was taking my passion, my belief in love, my hopes, my dreams, my soul and smashing them slowly right before my very eyes. I just needed to give him a taste of what that felt like, what torture felt like — not through the smashing itself, but through the watching. And the knowing that the person you hold dearest is the cause of the smashing. That's what I needed him to understand.

And he did, oh...how he did. He cried like I've never seen a man cry in my life, whaling, stomping, delirious in his pain. He cried so hard he didn't see me packing, didn't see the sudden calm that flooded me as I picked up the pieces of my life to carry on, without him. By the time he did, he finally got it. He finally knew deep down to his very core how he had made me feel all this time, and he knew it was over, saw it was over all over my face. "I'm sorry," he said as I walked past him. "I never meant to hurt you." "I know," I said. "...but you did."

And so concludes our little tale. You may leave this story and think but how could it end like that? Some people will look at me and see that evil gene. Heck in some states, I believe I could be thrown in jail for what I did, believed to be a villain, a "perp." But I believe this was my shining moment. In that moment, I was a hero.

It was the hardest thing I ever had to do. But I believe he will never hurt another woman, not physically. And I will never let another man hurt me that way. Because in that moment I made visual to both of us what we had become. I shattered the hope that kept us together, and left no possibility of a reconciliation. I walked a way that day, not a victim of my past. Not a silent observer, handing over the reigns. Not a woman with labels, conditioned to accept fighting and violence as just another characteristic of love. No, I left that day knowing I was just as responsible as he was and, therefore knowing I had complete control never to let it happen again.

Earning My Stature

Nora K. Yates

After the treacherous storm
the grass has sprouted
into blocked view
where just yesterday
it only shaved the bottoms of the signs

my exposed vertebrae
that I earn with every storm
have just gained "une autre amie" [another friend]
she is her, built on a foundation of truth
that the others have never seen

I sprouted with those storms
I grew firmer and stronger, able to stand
with only fingertips for my balance
and yet it is so easy just to fall
into the waiting nets that are ready to envelop.

I wish I could stack them all now.
The ones already there, dry from the brittle wind
and cold from the lack of warmth
I wish they all could be together
because then the forming skin of maturity could be their sheath.

I saw a woman yesterday
with her vertebrae slowly falling out of place
and she was fumbling for a height
she knew she had earned

but nature's forces had decided
those vertebrae were not well won
and shook her spine until they all splintered to the ground
reflecting all she had lost in the puddles covering her feet

And the witnesses just stood
women cringing and holding their backs
knowing that it could happen to them at anytime

men craned their necks like voyeurs at a terrible accident
tilting their heads
posing unanswerable questions

Of course, they were served their spine on a silver platter
Intact, nearly indestructible
there was no struggle for its very origination

some have had it shaken
some have had it punctured
but there is no complete destruction waiting around the next corner

I know a man with such a corrupted back
It swivels automatically at every "pretty lady" walking by
And as her spine cowers from his view and his corruption
he is harmless from his refrigerator home,
cackling at her shaky stance

You see, although corrupted, his vertebrae remain intact
and he laughs at that woman
whose hard-won battles slipped from her careful column into
disarray
because he has never been
attacked at seven
in a game of guns and Cops
his teammate claiming he was "hiding" him
while his hands grabbed at whatever strength he had

pinned during puberty
to a cold bedpost
in a friendly game of Truth or Dare
by an older boy who was his only way out of rural isolation

because he isn't surveyed everyday by random judges
for the proper weight, height, color, function
in a game of constant reduction
in every interaction, every conversation, with every person he meets

That woman has, and she has finally lost her grip
I wish I could loan her my newly acquired
it is surely the strongest, having withstood a recent brutal storm

I have had many a crumble
and know her panic
at losing the stature she thought she had

those grasses, which grew overnight with ambition
are bound to be cut
bound to be reduced
after being overly nourished

and yet they will continue to grow
despite the high priced destruction
I will see them again

sprouting overnight
after a long rain or torrential but quick storm
they are not decimated, only stunted

I know they will remain, endure
but who will tell her
her exposed strength that so easily crumbled
and the scrutiny and treachery she dwells in
is all she has in her reflection.

May Anti-capitalist Riots, London

Kimberly Jane Simms

That's the McDonald's I did not smash
I did not throw a chair through glass
I did not crush the register with a rock
I did not fling the burgers to dogs

that's the cement I did not shatter
I did not plant flowers in the black dirt
I did not make mud statues against the wall
I did not create a guerrilla garden

that's the bank door I did not brick up
that's the graffiti I did not dab
that's the plastic mask I did not wear
that's the bridge I did not blockade

that's the window where I watched it happen
saw the carnival costumes, heard the chanting
that's the office where I was typing letters
that was the riot — I did not join

Fat Like Me

Lilli Lewis

Being fat like me
Is like being in a constant state of pregnancy
Pregnant with love
Pregnant with joy
Pregnant with creativity
And most of all,
Pregnant with the knowledge that God,
She always blesses the beauty within.

Being fat like me
Means I'm more likely to be free
Free to read between the lines
Free to see behind the eyes
Free to say what I want
Do what I feel
And BE
WHO
I
AM

Because sometimes I'm cute
Sometimes I'm cuter
But most of the time
My sex is not for sale.

You wanna get with me?
Connect with me.
Come correct with me
Lord knows I'm too big to dismiss
But I bet you can't wrap your mind around this:
My love is just too large to sum up in a kiss...

Because being fat like me
Disallows a false ID
It's plain to see

That I am
Living
Life
Large.

Living in a spirit as wide as the ocean
Living in a constant state of devotion
To the warrior in me
The warrior that is proud to be
FAT LIKE ME.

The warrior who's embrace is as warm
As her bow is taught
The woman who sees she will
And does what she ought.
A whisperer who's screams come in song
And I'll be damned if she don't sing
All night long!!!

This warrior quakes mountains,
She spills over rivers
And when she makes love
She shapes lips into quivers.

So why does my jiggle offend so many?
Why, when this body implies nothing but plenty?
Plenty of kindness
Plenty of time
Plenty of loveliness, rhythm and rhyme,
Plenty of graciousness,
Plenty of care
Plenty of reasons to love what is there
Plenty of miracles,
Plenty of fruit,
Plenty of ways to love at the root,
Plenty of wishes
Plenty of woes,
Plenty of patience to find out how it goes.

I admit
I am more woman than most people can take
And many like me
Hide behind
Not beside
Taking pride in the fact
That they don't wanna be "like that."
Well I don't know what "that" is
But it's none of my biz
'cause I'm sure being fat "like that"
Ain't worth what it's cracked up to be.

Being fat like me
Is like living poetry
A walking metaphor for the roundness of things
The circles in life,
The cycles of strife
That become new lessons
The new learning that begets the new yearning.
A yearning that's born into passion
And fashions itself
A new kind of child
Makes itself a glorious
New kind of wild.

So the next time you see
Someone fat like me
Make sure you greet that fertile ground.
Make sure you bless the beauteous bounty
Make sure you savor the flavor
Of every bone
Wrapped layer upon layer
Of succulent splendour.
It is the sweetest meat,
I can guarantee,
That is of course,
If it's fat like me.

Good People Sometimes Don't Look That Way from the Outside, But They Can Always Spot Each Other

Yael Flusberg

I'm 13. It's dusk and the four of us — Rob, Tommy, Danny and me — are down on all fours on Laurel Hill Boulevard, palms in pavement, scrounging for stray black beauties in the shadows of the Brooklyn-Queens Expressway as it winds its way from Astoria and Jackson Heights to this elevated stretch in Woodside. From here, it'll hit Maspeth and Brooklyn beyond that, meandering its way to neighborhoods like ours, blue-collared and multihued, places with names like Greenpoint and Williamsburgh, Fort Greene and Red Hook, Bay Ridge and the Verrazano Bridge. Like us, the BQE is a master at adapting, wedging itself in between apartment buildings and warehouses, churches and gas towers, factories and baseball diamonds.

Moments before, Danny, a high school junior with a slight lisp and full 'fro, reached into the chest pocket of his olive drab military jacket wanting to show us what the neighborhood junkies were willing to pay "good money" for. Triumph quickly transforms to panic in the pre-Ziploc era. The baggie comes out breech, spewing a trajectory of the fast life on the sidewalk and in the street and we follow suit. More than anything, we understand the value of things lost.

Danny was half Italian, half Puerto Rican. His baby brother went to Aviation High, wanted to be a plane mechanic. The money was good, he shrugged when I asked why. Danny's friends were old enough to crush on, none as sharp as him, but infinitely more alluring than the eighth-grade boys at the impoverished and immigrant-laden orthodox yeshiva where I spent long days, a world away from my neighborhood friends. I couldn't imagine my classmates having hiding places.

Danny held hugs long enough to let you close your eyes, inhale the scent of his day: ivory soap, U.S. history class, the musty clubhouse on Dead Man's Hill where we once found a hen and her chicks camped out in an old engine. I liked how he talked, like there was no rush to get to the point. There was no point, only time that didn't move fast enough, making us older, getting us out.

Like a younger sister I tagged along with, exploring the soft underbelly of our neighborhood, gently extending the borders of what I could call my own. There were places he would not take me, would never so much as let me take a toke. Instead, we'd take long walks-catch movies-sit on top of benches because we didn't need such wide spaces to hold ourselves firm.

It's March 31st. A frigid wind whips off the headstones at the Calvary Cemetery and into the underpass of the Brooklyn-Queens expressway. I cross quickly, shoulders rounded, hands thrust in pockets, wishing the school bus would pick me up in front of my building so I could wait in the lobby on cold days. On warm days, too, I hate that corner before the bus comes. It delivers me middle-aged men who circle the block in their used Cadillacs, honking as they approach, wanting me to catch them masturbating as they watch me waiting.

It's here, on my way to the corner of my waiting, in this passage where there is a constant rumbling overhead where my mother once scolded me for something I had or hadn't done, index finger pointing toward my chest. Just then, a pigeon had skillfully steered its shit; it landed on her outstretched fingertip. We looked at the wad in disgust, foreheads-nose-lips crinkling up small, then released our fight in laughter.

Between cackles, she gets out "In Hungary, they say if a bird cacas on you, it's good luck."

"Who made that up?" I go, always the wise-ass, "The dry cleaners' union?"

It's here, that morning, I see the ambulance blocking the pedestrian path. Two emergency care personnel have just hoisted someone up. I'm attracted and repelled at the same time. I want to ask what-happened-who's-in-there-can-I-help but repelled wins out and I arc around the ambulance's front end.

Later at school, I'm summoned out of Algebra. Last and most-hated class of the day.

"Your mother's in Rabbi Abramson's office"

Always the wise-ass, I proclaim: "saved from a moment of mathematical humiliation!" My classmates' laughter propels me out towards the door, away from the florescent overhead lights of my days.

Exuberantly, I race down the hallway that smells of decades-old grime despite the copious amounts of disinfectant mopped on its checkered linoleum floors daily, to the dim stairwell that leads to the principal's office on the second floor. There, I find my mother, my father's three sisters and Rabbi Abramson, whose oldest daughter Aviva has been in my class since first grade and who has a special way of calling for her father when she wants 50 cents to buy a Sunkist from the soda machine: "Dee-ah-deeeeeee."

In college, I will be imitating that voice for my roommate, and suddenly realize how close her pronunciation of "daddy" was to "deity."

I kiss them all hello, and wonder aloud what special surprise I'm in for. My aunts do not live so close that they drop by. All visits are planned. I learn it was my father the ambulance came for. On the way to mail a letter to the editor — he sends these all the time to the New York Daily News where he works as a printer about everything from apartheid to the economy — on the way to the mailbox, his heart stopped. It was best for me to stay in school while they dealt with the arrangements, I'm told.

I do not go home that night. I'm sent to a friend's. While my father's body is being gently washed and wrapped in a burial shroud, I am in a dreamless valium-induced sleep.

I do not cry until the next day — April Fools — at the funeral parlor when my entire class and most of the 7th grade walks in.

My mother will not cry until a few weeks later, when she opens a condolence card signed by all the guys on his shift.

A week later I come home from sitting shiva at my aunt's in Carnarsie. I go straight to the clubhouse on Dead Man's Hill. There's no need for questions. Burying my father has made me older. My friends look like they are afraid that I might start talking. I squeeze onto the sofa next to Danny, who rolls a fresh joint and passes it to me. I do not need to say anything.

That first time, there was no high, only a headache.

I think: My father had never gotten beyond polite greetings with Danny.

I think: If my father could have seen Danny as more than an imminent threat to my childhood, he would've liked his sense of humor, the way Danny could engage in debate without arguing.

I think: My father had blind spots the size of his failed heart.

A few weeks later, Danny comes for the first time to visit me at home. We sit with my mother at the round dining room table drinking coffee. She asks about his family. He asks about The War, the one she was in when she was his age and survived, the one that sometimes make her nerves break down. They share one cigarette, then another. She tells him stories about Over There, about the selection at the train ramp, about the time she contracted scarlet fever and was accidentally released from the infirmary, instead of being sent to the showers with the others.

The hour grows late. Danny apologizes and says he has to leave. She invites him to come back for supper whenever he wants. She'll make him goulash they way her mother used to make for her.

That night, the two of us sit at the table listening to the whirring of cars on the expressway below. She says goodnight, starts to head toward her room, then turns to me and says softly:

"I like Danny. He's good people."

Black Gurl

Seshat Y. Walker

we were vaseline queens
hotcomb survivors
pressing our nappy crowns
into christy doll regalness

we were double dutch champions
turning tricks for quarters and funnelcake
while sucking the artificial color
off apple now a laters with cherry kool aid lips

or stomping out ghetto rhythms
in scuffed buster browns
ashy legs covered by white knee hi's
magenta legwarmers we can only wear to ballet practice

in one summer we changed identities
losing our innocence in bathroom stalls
penning the moment inside our heartcovered girlfriend
whose mouth remained shut
with a tiny silver key we hid in our tiger beat magazine
under our kiss pillow

we traded pads for applicators
a cup to b
undershirts long gone
'dem mosquito bites
swelled to oranges'
grandmom would say

we picked our fate off switch trees
rubbed our stinging smacked faces
the result of sucked teeth and rolled eyes

at times we were daddy's princess

and mommy's last nerve

never thought we'd stop asking
mother may i
skip sunday school
jump up and down on my bed
wrap my head in a towel
put on your best going out dress
parade down my runway aka the sidewalk

we'd swore we'd never
tell our children
if you keep making that face,
it'll freeze that way

but we do

its all as natural as twisting a wild strand
or withstanding a black leather belt

we accepted it
we're black gurls
made of honey, brown sugar and rice
and everything stereotyped

For My Mother
Whitney A. Jones

Where is she, who am I?
Who to claim me,
Not try to tame me or chain me.
Who to find me,
Not lease me not sign me.
Who to hear me,
To help me see things more clearly
Who to know me,
Not shape me, not mold me but show me...
Where she is and who am I?
Is she hiding?
Leaving me here crying?
Does she hear me?
Will she come to rescue me?
Do I need to be rescued?
I feel alone, with a house but no home
Show me where she is and who am I...
Does she even care?
That into the open arms of death I stare that I seek comfort deep
within the pain that I could drown in my tears that fall like rain that
this cold worlds driving me insane
Does she want me back?
She gave me away just like that no strings attached she cut me too
much slack
Tell me where she is and who am I?
I haven't found myself, though there are things I regret I don't
wanna forget because those memories keep me in check
Let's me know that I might want her but don't need her
But where is she who am I?
I might lie here forever and dread the days I live till I am dead
and forever it will be unsaid that I love her in spite of the truth she
threw me away like a gone baby tooth might be forgotten might be
replaced and if I ever see her face I might evermore be displaced

Where is she who am I?
"Mama, you leave your daughter here alone, do you miss me, I miss you" Is the message I send to her... she's the missing piece of my puzzle she should be my conscience in times of trouble.
She's that void I long to fill. When I get knocked down she should be my band-aid to help me heal.
She should've been the first to see me walk the first one to listen the first one to hear me talk. She should've held me in her arms late at night, dry my tears, and take away the fright. She should've been here to catch me her fallen angel but instead she threw me into this web of the world for which now I am entangled.
The cold world smothers me my words are choked and strangled
Where is she who am I?

Daddy's Nursery Rhyme

Lisa Joyner

My daddy sure was fine
skin three shades darker than a glass of red wine
Head was bald; made sure with a daily shave
when around others it was a beautiful smile he gave

Teeth shined bright inside his dark chocolate skin
many women wanted to be closer than kin
His height was about 6 foot 4
body looked like he could knock down any door
I recall him being in such good shape
didn't gain weight 'til his years were close to 10x8

Had a young wife
of that he made sure
married my momma,
he was 45 she was just 24
& she gave offspring to the number 4
3 girls, 1 boy, plus the 2 that she had
outside looking in you could tell he was so glad

Now notice I said, around others he shined bright,
but its his family that saw the true light
Meanest person I ever did meet
when he was not around it was always a treat

Don't get me wrong, Daddy was a Christian,
a church going man
knocked down church doors, gave neighbors a hand
Respected by others, they said he spoke his mind,
not realizing that he just was not kind

Example, for Christmas we got every toy in the book
right after Christmas it was those very toys he took
The Grinch is what we called him 'cause he stole our joy

spent all that money for us to play with not one toy
Now daddy loved his children of that I don't doubt
but when they began to come into their own
he threw them out
Out of the house never to return
I'm tired of you not listening
one day you will learn

The ages varied from 15 on up
no longer allowed to drink from daddy's cup
Momma fought to keep me around
she finally got backbone, her other girls she let down

Living with him our wars never ended
because at the age of 14 my virginity rescinded
Often called by him a jezebel and a slut
words that felt like a kick in the gut

He never molested but he raped with his words
dumb, stupid, bum, things that out of a daddy's mouth
should never be heard

When he got angry he'd really lash out
a brook, a stick, anything he could grab he'd sling about
At times he beat beyond abuse
spare not the rod or spoil the child was always his excuse

I can recall him pinning me down to punch me in the mouth
hurting so bad, his knee in my crotch
Timmy was the one we felt sorry for
he'd beat him with words then knock him to the floor
His son, part crippled, could barely walk
you'd think he's share love, lift him up when he talked

Not my daddy, he was as mean as sin
he used to always say, "If you see a good fight jump in"
As he got older good fights became rare

It's a shame to his children he decided to give his share

If Daddy was alive and knew I was gay
to my momma down laws he would lay
Don't call her; don't see her, she's out of my life
I'm so sick and tired of this girl being trif
Momma would turn and most likely walk away
scared for her baby, but the Bible says a good wife obeys

When he died people did not understand why I had a smile
why I had a grin
You wonder if I loved him
oh yeah to no end
I mean really he was my blood
he was my daddy
he's kin

If I wrote the book many things would have change
20 some years they would have never remained
all the crazy bullshit would have been washed down the drain

So, I write this poem 'cause I'm ready to let go
it's taken 18 plus years for this seed from me to sow
I forgive you daddy
I want you to know
I am tired of being stagnant and am ready to grow

When Everything Seems Wrong
Lacy Sundine

When nobody seems to care
when you feel worthless
And life means nothing
You have no place
You thought you were something
But you looked in the mirror and see nothing
Now you're alone scared and heartbroken
They push you until you're insecure, hurt, and emotional
They wouldn't give you the time or a shoulder to cry on
A person to talk to,
to let everything go
You wish they would get out of your life...
You can run or hide
but you know they'll find you sooner or later
So you gotta face the facts
And step back into reality

Moments

Jennifer Carcamo

There are those moments
When everything looks beautiful
So beautiful that you hear birds chirping
and think it's as beautiful as Beethoven's Symphony
Or so beautiful that you look up at the cloudy sky
and see nothing but heart shaped Clouds hovering above

There are those moments
When everything looks ugly
So ugly that a baby's cry turns into the dreadful screech of the
Bloody Mary
Or so ugly that a bouquet of roses looks like a swamp bush with no
beauty.

There are those moments
When everything doesn't matter
When you can hear your favorite song played on three different
stations as you zoom through the radio tuner and not care that it's
playing
When you find out your favorite movie is on HBO and don't even
consider staying up late enough to watch it.

There are those moments
When everything matters
When you hear a child's yelp come from the monkey bars on the
jungle gym and immediately perk up your ears to listen
for a following cry so you can go help
When you see a plastic water bottle on the other side of the street
and decide to go get it even though it's out of your way because you
remember a documentary you saw on how dolphins kept getting
there mouths stuck in them and dying

There are those moments
When you just wish time would stop

Time would stop just so you could savor the moment
A good-bye hug
A glance at your cute neighbor
A laugh with no cause
Your first kiss
There will always be those moments...
Moments that are beautiful and ugly
Those that matter and don't matter.
Those that you wish you could freeze and stuff in your freezer for
whenever you want to see them again.
We don't remember days or years.
We remember moments.
Moments.

There will always be those moments.
Always.

Rosa's Reality Check
Keturah Kendrick

Rosa does not have her homework.

It is as simple as that.

Or...

Perhaps it is much more complicated than I am willing to admit.

As far as I can tell, it is 11:33. Class began at 11:28 (as usual). I asked students to pull out their homework at 11:29 (as usual). Rosa was talking to Roxanne (as usual). Roxanne already had her homework out (as usual), waving me down to check her's first even as she giggled at Rosa's latest gossipy story that would more than likely be the catalyst for some normally well-adjusted girl crying hysterically on my shoulder by the end of the day.

Perhaps I am blinded to the apparent complexity of the current situation because this is not some new phenomenon. My collecting homework, that is. It has been happening since the second day of school. This is why I am surprised when Rosa seems so surprised.

And Rosa is very surprised. Her perfectly arched eyebrows shoot up. Her freshly applied lipstick sprouts out as if deciding in this moment of crisis to take over the job of Rosa's lips. Or perhaps provide a refreshing distraction to a familiar plea her lips will shortly make.

"Ummmm," Rosa begins.

"You don't have it," I finish her thought, quickly putting a zero by her name on my attendance sheet. For a moment I turn into one of the easily distracted 8th graders I have been given charge of and my mind wanders. I imagine this latest zero joining forces with the three other zeros next to Rosa's name and forming a singing group, their first single being dedicated to Rosa Gonzalez because "we couldn't have done any of this without you!" I wonder how many zeros I will have to put next to Rosa's name before Rosa truly accepts that I will indeed collect, read and grade all of the homework I assign her and her classmates.

"No, wait," I hear her sweet voice summon itself to the appropriate level of manipulation. "I have it today." She looks proudly at me and waits for me to reward her with a thankful smile or maybe a cookie, I suppose. I stare politely at her and wait for her to pull out the homework I know she does not have. She continues to smile sweetly at me.

"See, it's in my locker and I meant to bring it, but since the period is just beginning, I can just run up to..."

"You don't have it."

"No, I do," she continues. "I did it this time. I just forgot it in my locker and if you don't let me go up to get it, I can bring it to you at lunch."

"No, you can't. Either you have it now or you don't. It's good that you did it, though. And when you do get it from your locker, make sure you keep it in your binder. It'll help you study for the test."

"So, I'll get credit for it, right?" She looks naively hopeful. It's a sad, yet heart-warming display of cluelessness. I almost want to pat her on the head and actually reward her with an Oreo.

"Wrong," I say as I finally make Roxanne's morning and check her neatly written, thoroughly answered questions to last night's assigned chapters.

"That's bootie," Rosa sucks her teeth.

"Yeah, it is," I agree. "But the thing is, it's been bootie for quite some time now. If you don't remember the policy on late homework, I am more than happy to remind you. Basically, there is no such thing as late homework. Either you have it or you don't. The policy is genius in its simplicity."

Rosa rolls her eyes. They are very pretty eyes. Green and clear. They really bring out her fair, smooth skin that is covered in a tasteful amount of face powder and mascara.

"The one time I have it, she won't take it," I hear her mumble.

I know what she will mumble next.

"I don't know why she hates me so much. I ain't never did nothing to her."

For some reason I am surprised at what I say.

"Rosa, come see me at lunch today."

Her eyebrows shoot up again, signaling that she is under the erroneous impression that she has gotten away with something.

● ● ●

When Rosa saunters into my room later, wrinkled sheet of paper in hand, I tell her to put it away.

"But, I thought you said..."

"I know what I said. Sit down." I pull out the stool I keep underneath my desk and Rosa cautiously sits on it.

Her eyes shoot down to the floor.

"You're failing my class, Ms. Gonzalez."

The explaining begins immediately.

"I know, I know. But the teachers at this school give a lot of homework and I have other things to do besides study. I don't think it's fair to expect teens to just give up their social life and spend an entire weekend with their head stuck in some book."

"You are failing my class, Rosa."

"I know, I know, but..." The lips move at rapid speed.

"You are failing my class, Ms. Gonzalez."

Rosa seems to get more and more frantic when I do not say more than the five words I have been repeating since she walked into my classroom.

"Why you making such a big deal about this? I have the homework. Here," she throws the half-done, sloppily scribbled assignment on my desk.

I look at it. Then at her. She looks away, flinging her silky hair over her shoulder. Crossing her legs, Rosa flattens out her skirt with the most marvelously manicured hands I have ever seen.

"What do you think is the problem, Rosa?" I wait for the rolled eyes. The heavy, overly exaggerated sigh. The grumbling, "Oh my God!", that serves as the 13 year old girl's warning to the adult that is making her life more difficult than necessary that she is on her way to being really annoyed or worse...really bored.

Rosa sends her warning before I have even gotten the question out.

" Oh my god," she throws up her hands. "Why do you keep bothering me? I'll do my homework from now on, okay? Can I go to lunch now?"

"Why do I have to harass you to get you to do your homework or participate in class or study or make even a minimal effort on projects?"

Another " Oh my god." I've never gotten two consecutive oh-my-gods before. I'm proud; I must be getting better at this teaching thing.

" Rosa, you're smart. You and I both know this. You should be doing better than you are. I'm just curious, what is so hard about completing work you can do and turning it in? You can do the work, can't you?"

Rosa nods her head. A little less defensive. I take this as a cue to continue working from this angle.

"So, is it just that it's a lot of work? We do give you girls a lot."

She looks up at me briefly. Before I can analyze what the look might mean, her eyes have returned to the floor. She sighs. It sounds genuine.

"Is it hard organizing yourself to get the work done? We can help you with that if that's the problem."

" Look, it's not really you or the other teachers," Rosa begins. "Well, it is in a way, but..." I can tell she is searching for the words she will need to get me to fully understand what she doesn't completely understand herself. " It's just that teachers at this school, they are....I don't know, shit. Forget it."

"Yes, you do know. Take your time. Tell me what it is."

"Well, it's just that at my old school. See, I did good there. And sometimes I didn't do the work the teachers wanted me to do. But I did good, ya know?'

I nodded because I did know. I knew exactly how easy it was in a New York City public school to "do good" even though you really didn't do anything at all.

"But, here...it's just...I don't know. When I don't do what the teachers tell me, I get in trouble. I get detention. They call my house and even when I'm nice to them, I still get bad grades." Talking her way through her frustration helps Rosa locate what the real problem is. I see the light pop on in her head.

"It's like, being pretty isn't enough here."

I am not surprised by Rosa's epiphany. I deduced months ago when she smiled her planned, plotting smiles and turned on her sweet voice that she was one of the many pretty girls who learned years ago how to work the system. I sat silently and stared at Rosa not because she openly admitted that she had been unsuccessfully trying to hustle me. I stared at Rosa because I was awed at how very aware she was that she had been hustling teachers and other adults most of her life.

Since she was so forthright with me, I felt it would be patronizing to be any less with her.

" You're right; it's not enough. Pretty is not enough at this school. And contrary to what the men who try to talk to you when you walk down the street will have you believe, it won't be enough after you leave this school either."

Rosa turns uncharacteristically silent.

And so do I.

I am not sure why Rosa is silent. In a perfect world, she is processing what I have just said and truly considering the possibility that her looks are an asset that need to be combined with other more marketable ones — like literacy skills or a set of any type of skills, for that matter.

I know why I have become silent.

I am trying to figure out just how forthright I should be with Rosa.

Should I explain to Rosa that she is a poor Latina in East Harlem whose mother speaks only two words of English? A well-meaning mother who truly believes that all she has to do to save Rosa from the life that awaits poor pretty girls who don't marry pro-ball players is to put her in a good school.

I am silent because I am wondering if it would be inappropriate (or just plain cruel) to tell Rosa that the odds are already stacked against her. That her writing is a step above gibberish and I do not know where to begin in getting her to a point where she is able to write coherent thoughts. That this good school her mother stood in line for hours to enroll Rosa in is still handicapped. It does not have well-salaried alumni who purchase new computers and updated textbooks and other educational tools for the school. It does not have access to the many "secret" supplements that are the true source of the suburban Rosas' academic success. It only has hardworking teachers and even harder working students and parents who cling desperately to the hope that all of our hard work will be enough. Praying that just as he turned water into wine, Jesus will miraculously turn a classist and racist educational system into one that offers not only equal opportunity, but equal access to opportunities as well.

I want to find a non-horrifying way to tell Rosa that the world outside of this cushy bubble that our school has kept her in dislikes her much more than she imagines I do. That it is meaner. It will find much more creative and devious ways to pick at and harass her than I currently do.

But, all I can come up with is, "Being pretty is not sufficient, Rosa. I know it seems like it is, but outside of the six block radius that makes up your life, it is almost useless."

I am not sure she gets it.

I am not sure she even cares.

She looks at her shoes. Then, at mine. Her bright green eyes move to the wall in front of her. They roam around the room, stopping for a split second on my face before darting to the chalkboard.

"Your board is always dirty."

I wonder if this is a rope. I grab it regardless.

"I know. I always say I'm going to clean it, but I look up and it's 5 o'clock and I'm not even done with the work I had planned to do and...well, the board remains dirty."

"I can clean it for you." Her voice lowers. "If you want..."

I point to the closet where a bucket and sponge may or may not be stored and watch Rosa walk across the room. While she searches around the cluttered closet, I pull up her grades on my computer.

By the time she has emerged from the closet, bucket in hand, I am already plotting how I can make the most use of this thin rope thrown to me before it is just as abruptly snatched away.

As she heads to the door, I ask her, " Do you understand the book? The novel we're reading... it can be confusing."

In front of my eyes, Rosa melts into a 13 year old. I notice how much prettier she has become. A look of relief takes over her face as she shakes her head and nervously switches the bucket from left hand to right.

"You're not the only one, you know. It can be a hard book."

"I get most of it, but the words...some of them...the words are hard. Some of them are really hard." I have never heard her "sweet" voice sound so genuine.

Before her age can reveal itself further, Rosa runs to the bathroom to fill up the bucket with water.

I am silent again.

When Rosa comes back, I will need to know what to say.

GirlChild

Michelle Sewell

I woke up this morning with worry on my mind
and as I read my morning paper there it was.
A baby girl — just a few hours old —was left in a desert because one
child is the law of the land and her parents wanted their first born to
be a boy!

As I read the rest of the story my sorrow grew deep because I knew no
one would miss her, there would be no CNN news breaks or search
parties. And the only evidence of her existence, the bloody sheets that
laid witness at her birth, would soon be tossed out with the rest of the
day's trash.

And for some reason - that fact - totally blew my mind.

See, I am a first born girl child.
The daughter of a seventh born girl child
and my mother like her mother made the same promise:
You will always find favor.
But as I think about that abandoned baby girl, swaddled in rags, and a
small portion of food by her side, in case someone finds her.

I can only wonder where is her favor?

But before I pass judgment on this foreign land and its people —
I know I don't have to look any further than the metro section of the
same paper to find an example of how we've betrayed and abandoned
our own baby girls.

But as my day goes on
I find myself obsessing about the complexities of being a girl child.
Mingled with the pink and lace, are the heart stopping moments that
make it unclear if we'll make it to the other side.
As I sit at my desk, my pen poised,
I fantasize about creating a practical guide.

Tucked away for special emergencies
that can only be deciphered by girlchild eyes.

Chapter one.
Baby girl, as you pack your bags for your life travels —
please don't forget your heart song and your north star.
You'll need them both.

The chapter on self esteem would read:
There's no need to live a life of quiet desperation. Dream Big!
Take up as much room as you need.
Girl, take up as much room as you want.

Of course, there would be a chapter on fashion.
The print would be extra large to get this critical point across:
Child, you are more than your size six hipster jeans.
Sure you look cute in them, but you'll need more than that
to cover your ass when the shit starts to hit the fan.

If girlchild falters and can't find her way,
she can search out the chapter on endurance.
There she'll find this message:
There will be ports in the storm.
Drop your anchor sometimes.
Sit long enough to let someone scratch the worry out your head
and bathe you in some scented water.

And before I forget — *drop the title of the super woman. She's like Santa*
Clause — *she doesn't exist.*

Of course when girlchild gets too busy to read the whole book
she can flip to the index and look up a subject as she needs.

> Under relationships:
> *Sex does not equal love*
> Under hunting:
> *You are never prey!*

Under money — which incidentally -by the time you're 34 — can easily be cross referenced with relationships:

If you don't work you don't eat.

But by the time I get to the chapter on super models — I realize this could go on forever.

So

I stop

regroup

and think — what am I really trying to say?

I guess it's simply this:

Beautiful baby girl, you are not disposable.

Your life should not begin and end in the same twenty-four day.

That everything humanly possible should be done

to preserve your life force.

That there is something amazingly unique about a child born a girl.

And I promise

Yes, I promise

you will always find favor.

Male-Identified "Shorties":
Towards a Culturally Specific Understanding of
African American Girls' Self Esteem
Jillian Hernandez

> *Shorty wanna ride with me, ride with me*
> *Let your hair down*
> *You said you wanted a thug don't be scared now*
> *Shorty wanna ride with me, ride with me*
> *You can be my wife but only for tonight*
> *Get your ass on this bike*
> *I'll show you I can ride*

> —*Young Buck "Shorty Wanna Ride"*

The American Association of University Women (AAUW) conducted a study in 1990 of approximately three thousand girls and boys ages 9-15 of diverse backgrounds in order to examine the impact of gender on their self-confidence, academic interests, and career goals. The AAUW results were the impetus for the book Schoolgirls: Young Women, Self-Esteem, and the Confidence Gap by Peggy Orenstein in which she states,

> Among its most intriguing findings, the AAUW survey revealed that, although all girls report consistently lower self-esteem than boys, the severity and the nature of that reduced self-worth vary among ethnic groups. Far more African American girls retain their overall self-esteem during adolescence than white or Latina girls, maintaining a stronger sense of both personal and family importance. They are about twice as likely to be "happy with the way I am" than girls of other groups and report feeling "pretty good at a lot of things" at nearly the rate of white boys. The one exception for African American girls is their feelings about school: black girls are more pessimistic about both their teachers and their schoolwork than other girls. (Orenstien 2000; p. xxi)

The widespread attention the study received perpetuated the myth of African American girls' high self-esteem as related to body image and lower academic self-esteem. Sexual scripts produced by the Hip Hop culture have also contributed to this myth by providing a male-identified model of sexual freedom for young African American women that is limited in its potential for empowerment. This essay will examine the need for culturally specific approaches to researching adolescent African American girls and the colonial paradigms underlying current stereotypes about their self-esteem. The conclusion proposes approaches that could be implemented by psychologists, social scientists and girls advocates to challenge this myth and ensure that the needs of adolescent African American girls are being properly met.

The AAUW survey used an index of statements to measure respondent self-esteem that consisted of; I am happy with the way I am.; I like the way I look.; I like most things about myself. The study found that 22% of white female high school students stated they were "Happy with the way I am." in comparison to 58% of female African American students. Although adolescent African American girls appear to posses higher self-esteem than white girls, it does not translate into higher levels of educational attainment. For example, the National Center for Educational Statistics (NCES) 2004 study, Trends in Educational Equity of Girls and Women: 2004 found that more African American girls drop out of high school than their white counterparts. (Freeman 2004: p.56) The study also reported that 7% of African American girls between the ages of 5-12 repeated at least one grade since starting school in contrast to 4% of white girls. (Freeman 2004: p.40)

It is necessary to analyze the possible flaws in the AAUW survey in regards to cultural specificity that may not have been taken into account. The survey results do not consider the culturally specific ideals of Hip Hop and R&B, which has been a major pop culture phenomenon since the mid-1990s in addition to assuming that white middle-class ideals don't affect minority groups. This disconnect can be linked to Richard L. Allen's discussion of "double consciousness" in his book, The Concept of Self: A Study of Black Identity and Self-Esteem in which he quotes W.E. B. Du Bois' characterization of the condition as, "...this sense of always looking at one's self through the eyes of others, of measuring one's soul by the tape of a world that looks on in amused contempt and pity. One ever feels his two-ness — an American, a Negro — two souls, two thoughts, two unreconciled strivings, two warring ideals in one dark body,..." (Allen 2001: p.29) African American girls, unlike white girls, measure themselves through double consciousness and have the added stress of negotiating two sets of equally unattainable standards. There are culturally specific ideals of womanhood such as Black males expressed propensity for "thick" girls (curvaceous, voluptuous girls), but the survey assumes that African American girls are insulated from the dominant culture's worship of white, thin, blonde females. African American girls attend integrated schools, live in integrated communities and are subject to the same mass media images as white girls. Obese girls or girls perceived by the dominant culture as overweight are still subject to judgment and humiliation in both Black and white peer groups. The myth of African American girls' self-esteem may also be contributing to a health problem. The NCES also reported that 15% of African American female high school students are overweight compared with 5% of white girls. (Freeman 2004: p. 47) Even the desired "thickness" of girls of color has a limit, whose ideal form is manifested in women who appear in Hip Hop music videos. These women often have large breasts, tiny waists, and voluptuous legs, thighs and buttocks.

The dichotomy between the high self-esteem of African American girls in reference to personal importance and lower self-esteem than other groups in their academic abilities appears to have developed from an underlying colonial paradigm. This paradigm is articulated by Dionne P. Stephens and Layli D. Phillips in the paper, "Freaks, Gold Diggers, Divas, and Dykes: The Sociohistorical development of Adolescent African American Women's Sexual Scripts", in which they discuss Sarah Bartmann, the Hottentot Venus, and the pseudo-scientific anatomical findings of the European doctors who examined her, "Drawing on his Darwinist biases and expertise in zoology, Cuvier made interpretations that became the basis of sexual scripts for women of African descent—primitive, wild, sexually uninhibited, and exotic (Fausto-Sterling 1995). Thus, Sarah became the bedrock of African female sexuality, reinforcing the exotic, animal image that separated people of African descent from whites." (Stephens and Phillips 2003: p.7) The link between the high self-esteem of African American girls that has been interpreted by the popular culture as relating to body image and their low academic self-esteem in comparison to white girls, may stem from the stereotype of black women as being more sexual and less cerebral than white girls. The myth of African American girls self-esteem hurts girls of both racial groups as white girls are trying to look like "thick" black girls, black girls are trying to tow the line between both Black and white beauty ideals, and both continue to experience a drop in academic performance during adolescence. Moreover, the fact that these beauty standards are male-defined upholds patriarchal ideals and hinders potential for female empowerment.

The hyper-sexualization of African American females is articulated in popular culture through the sexual content of most contemporary Hip Hop and R&B music. In "Where My Girls At? Black Girls and the Construction of the Sexual", Debbie Weekes summarizes the argument of her essay,

> ...through acknowledging the variety of both celebratory and derogatory imagery embedded within Jamaican ragga and African American hip-hop and R&B, it will suggest that such musical effects on the construction of young female sexual selves enable Black girls to resist where they are placed in hierarchies of femininity. However, it will also be suggested that such resistance may only be temporary, limited to specific representations of Black girlhood...the positions taken up by young women in these sexual discourses are often problematic. Music which congratulates Black women for their sexual prowess creates a false sense of security for young girls exploring their sexual selves... (Weekes 2002: p. 141-2)

Weekes' observations shed light on the challenging nature of addressing the myth of African American girls' self esteem. The construction of Black femininity in Hip Hop allows young girls to explore their (hetero)sexuality without shame, therefore combating the "slut" stigma that is branded upon adolescent girls who are sexually active. However, it undermines the capabilities of young women beyond their sexuality as it is constructed by male desire. The male-identified nature of this female sexual "empowerment" is expressed in the hit 2005 song, "Shorty Wanna Ride" by Hip Hop artist Young Buck.

"Shorty" is slang for a young person, typically a female, and is often used by men to make advances at women; the term's reference to the small stature of females has connotations of subordination and male dominance. The lyric of the song reads, "Shorty wanna ride with me/ ride with me/ You can be my wife/ But only for tonight/ Get your ass on this bike/ I'll show you I can ride". The male rapper offers the female temporary "privileged" status as wife contingent upon her acceptance of his sexual advances. Although some young women recognize the sexist nature of the lyric they dance to it anyhow, stating that they "enjoy the beat" and often separate themselves from the females addressed in the songs. This dynamic further problematizes the nature of the false empowerment offered by chauvinistic sects of Hip Hop as it creates rifts between "good" girls and "dirty" girls.

This dichotomy is fueled by notions of shame that are discussed in bell hook's book, Rock My Soul: Black People and Self Esteem. Good girl/ bad girl distinctions generate stereotypes that cause division among young women and do not challenge the culture that generates them. Her discussion of African American women's self-esteem revolves around skin color,

"In black youth culture white supremacist aesthetics prevail. Yet they are given their most graphic expression in representations of the black female. While black male rappers create antiracist lyrics that project critical consciousness, that consciousness stops when it comes to the black female body. More than any other propagandistic tool, television shows that focus on black youth culture reinscribe white supremacist aesthetics with a vengeance. Dark-skinned females are rarely depicted at all. And even light skinned females get no play unless they have long straight hair."
(hooks 2003: p. 48-9)

The negative effects of adolescent African American female's sexual scripts have played themselves out in my interactions with the at-risk girls I work with through the Women on the Rise! outreach program I created at the Museum of Contemporary Art in North Miami. This gender specific art and art history program aims to expose at-risk, minority teenage girls to contemporary women artists of color in addition to providing them with tools for critical thinking and creative self-expression. The program is conducted on-site at institutions that serve at-risk girls such as the PACE Center for Girls and the Girls Advocacy Project at the Miami-Dade Juvenile Detention Center.

Girl-to-girl bullying is a common occurrence in these facilities. At times I have heard African American girls teasing each other about the "nappiness' of their hair, the "darkness" of their skin, or lack of a "booty". Despite the teasing of their peers, many girls proclaim to have high self-esteem that is usually defined by their attractiveness to the opposite sex. Although positive self and body image are healthy and desirable traits for adolescent girls, there seems to be an undercurrent of concealment that is at play, which is reinforced by Hip Hop culture, in which one's survival depends on repressing weakness and acting "hard". African American youth are reluctant to share their feelings about self-perceived flaws as this might make them vulnerable to attack. bell hooks also links this shame of low self-esteem to colonial paradigms.

> Science and pseudoscience were used as part of the argument for both the colonization of black people via slavery and the continued subordination of black folks from manumission on to the present day. Consequently, it is not surprising that masses of black people view science of the mind as suspect. Psychology has been especially feared because many black folks worry that speaking of our traumas using the language of mental illness will lead to biased interpretation and to the pathologizing of black experience in ways that might support and sustain our continued subordination. (hooks 2003: p.23)

Thus the situation for female African American adolescents becomes more problematic, particularly in regards to the AAUW study. Would young African American girls have told researchers if they weren't "Happy with the way I am."? How could they seek treatment or confront low self-esteem when the culture insists on denying it?

The pressure for African American women to conceal low self-esteem is powerfully portrayed in the essay, "The Black Beauty Myth" by Sirena J. Riley.

> As a black woman, I would love to believe that as a whole we are completely secure with our bodies. But that would completely miss the racism, sexism, and classism that affect

the specific ways in which black women's beauty ideals and experiences of body dissatisfaction are often different from those of white women....To our credit, black women have often been praised for our positive relationships with our bodies...I had read one or two stories in black women's magazines about black women with eating disorders, but it was still treated like a phenomenon that was only newsworthy because of its rarity. (Hernandez and Rehaman; Weekes 2002: p. 364)

Riley's description of the complex nature of African American female body image illustrates the paradigm of double consciousness as defined by Du Bois in addition to the suspicion of psychology described by hooks. Riley discusses her personal struggle with body image and attendance at a series of therapy groups in which she was the only Black woman. This phenomenon may signal a call for a more culturally sensitive approach to treating body image and eating disorders for African American females that combats shame and promotes models of self-esteem that are not based on physical appearance.

The affect of low self-esteem and shame on the life of a young African American girl is the subject of the young adult novel, <u>The Skin I'm In</u> by Sharon G. Flake. The book illustrates the life of Maleeka Madison, a middle school student in a low-income urban neighborhood who lives with her widowed mother. The first-person narrative revolves around the relationship between Maleeka and her new teacher, Miss Saunders, who sparks her self-actualization.

Maleeka is teased by boys in her class about her dark skin and is bullied by a group of girls who exploit her academic skills and poverty by lending her their brand-name clothes in exchange for completion of their homework. John-John, her student peer and the novel's antagonist, constantly harasses her at school by loudly singing a rap song he wrote about her in the hallway, "Maleeka, Maleeka—baboom, boom, boom, we sure wanna keep her, baboom, boom, boom, but she so black, baboom, boom, boom, we just can't see her." (Flake 1998: p. 9) Maleeka tells the reader, "Before I know it, three more boys is pointing at me and singing that song, too. Me, I'm wishing the building will collapse on top of me." (Flake 1998: p. 9) Maleeka begins to dread school as a result of this constant harassment.

The decrease in academic performance and personal self-esteem that are described in the lives of adolescent white, African American, and Latina girls in Schoolgirls are meaningfully comparable to that of Maleeka Madison. However, experiences such as sexual harassment, bullying, and violence can be more traumatic for African American girls due to double consciousness, white colonial beauty standards, and the hypersexualization of African American females.

In conclusion, it is necessary to implement culturally specific approaches to researching the self-esteem of female African American adolescents in order to collect reliable data. This research will make it possible to ensure that this population's needs are being addressed and work toward countering racist and sexist paradigms. Such research should also concentrate on the suspicion of psychology in the African American community.

Programs and advocacy campaigns stemming from this research should challenge the male-identified nature of sexual "empowerment" for girls offered by sexist factions of Hip Hop culture and offer culturally specific alternatives. In addition, girl-to-girl programs should be launched in order to combat bullying such as teasing about body image and violence that is sometimes due to a relationship with a male. The sexist and racist roots of the problem of the "myth" of African American girls' self esteem does not only affect this particular population but has ramifications for the culture as a whole. When this myth is eradicated, boys would learn how to respect women and themselves in turn, as young men of color are also hypersexualized in popular culture. Such reforms would create new models of self-esteem that will be empowering for all youth.

REFERENCES

Allen, Richard L. 2001. The Concept of Self: A Study of Black Identity and Self-Esteem. Detroit: Wayne State University Press.

Flake, Sharon G. 1998. The Skin I'm In. Maine: Throndike Press.

Freeman, C.E. 2004. Trends in Educational Equity of Girls and Women: 2004 (NCES 2005-016). U.S. Department of Education, National Center for Education Statistics. Washington, DC: U.S Government Printing Office.

hooks, bell. 2003. Rock My Soul: Black People and Self Esteem. New York: Atria Books.

Orenstein, Peggy. 1994. Schoolgirls: Young Women, Self-Esteem and the Confidence Gap. New York: Anchor Books.

Riley, Sirena J. 2002. "The Black Beauty Myth" in Colonize This: Young Women of Color on Today's Feminism eds. Daisy Hernandez and Bushra Rehman. California: Seal Press.

Stephens, D.P. and Phillips, L. 2003. "Freaks, Gold Diggers, Divas, and Dykes: The Sociohistorical Development of Adolescent African American Women's Sexual Scripts." Sexuality and Culture, 7, 1, 3-47.

Weekes, Debbie. 2004. "Where My Girls At? Black Girls and the Construction of the Sexual" in All About the Girl: Culture, Power, and Identity ed. Anita Harris. New York: Routledge.

Selected Bibliography

Arnold, Madelyn. A Year of Full Moons. New York, NY: St. Martin's Griffin, 2000

Bethel, Lorraine and Barbara Smith, eds. Conditions: Five — The Black Women's Issue. Brooklyn, NY, 1979

Bordo, Susan. Unbearable Weight: Feminism, Western Culture and the Body. Berkeley, CA: University of California Press, 1993

Brumberg, Joan Jacobs. The Body Project: An Intimate History of American Girls. New York, NY: Random House, 1997

Chesler, Phyllis. Woman's Inhumanity to Woman. New York, NY: Thunder's Mouth Press/Nation Books, 2001

Chevat, Edith, Laurie Piette, and Angie Argabrite, eds. Girls: An Anthology. New York, NY: Global City Press, 1997

Cleage, Pearl. Deals with the Devil and Other Reasons to Riot. New York, NY: Ballantine Books, 1993

Davis, Angela Y. Women, Culture, and Politics. New York, NY: Random House, 1989

Diamant, Anita. The Red Tent. New York, NY: Picador USA, 1997

Edelman, Hope. Motherless Daughters: The Legacy of Loss. New York, NY: Dell Publishing, 1994

Enloe, Cynthia. Bananas, Beaches and Bases: Making Feminist Sense of International Politics. Berkeley, CA: University of California Press, 1989

hooks, bell. Feminism is for Everybody: Passionate Politics. Cambridge, MA: South End Press, 2000

Lamb, Doris, M.D. Psychotherapy with Adolescent Girls. New York, NY: Plenum Press, 1986

Lamphere, Louise and Michelle Zimbalist Rosdaldo, eds. Woman, Culture and Society. Stanford, CA: Stanford University Press, 1974

Moore, Lisa C., ed. Does Your Mama Know: An Anthology of Black Lesbian Coming Out Stories. Austin, TX: Redbone Press, 1997

Perkins, Mitali. Monsoon Summer. New York, NY: Random House, 2004

Wade-Gayles, Gloria. Rooted Against the Wind. Boston, MA: Beacon Press, 1996

Xavier, Cassendre. Making of a Woman/Artist: a book for every black girl and every black woman who has ever wanted to be an artist. Philadelphia, PA: 2005

About The Writers

Eunice Alicea was born in Arecibo, Puerto Rico — the youngest of five. Her family re-located to Yonkers, New York two years later. She attended Hunter College in Manhattan, New York and received a degree in Secondary English Education. It was there she published her first poem, and short story. She later attended Lehman College and received a Master's Degree in Composition Rhetoric. She teaches writing and literature at Lehman College as well as facilitates an after school theatre program for adolescent girls in the South Bronx.

Lauren K. Alleyne hails from the Republic of Trinidad and Tobago. She is a graduate of the MFA program at Cornell University, where she currently teaches Creative Writing and Freshman writing seminars. Her work has appeared in Black Arts Quarterly, The Caribbean Writer, Sexing the Political, and The Hampden-Sydney Review. She is a Cave Canem fellow.

Wendy Altschuler graduated with high honors from DePaul University with a degree in Women's and Gender Studies and Anthropology. She is the first person in her family to graduate from college. Wendy is happily married to a brilliant man who adores her and lives in the suburb of Chicago with her two dogs.

Piper Anderson is a performance poet, musician, author, educator, and activist who has toured her signature brand of hip hop inspired poetry and song nationally since 1999. Her voice has been called "ancient", "inspiring", "pure", "original" and "beyond comparison". She co-authored How to Get Stupid White Men Out Office (Soft Skull Press) and traveled the country providing young people with the tools needed to mobilize their communities to get out the vote in the 2004 presidential election.

Anonymous grew up laughing in the sun, playing in the snow, and dancing in the rain. She never colored inside the lines. Today she is a recovering addict and anorectic. It has been almost a year since she tried to kill herself. Her brother and best friend taught her how to love life. She wants to make a difference. She is 19 years old.

Kesi Augustine lives and writes passionately in New York City, juggling her favorite pastime along with school and other necessities such as sleep (occasionally). She would like to publish longer works of her own in the near future.

Brittney Ball is a 16 year old junior at Thurgood Marshall Academy in Washington, DC. She is driven to write so she can express the pain, stories, lessons, and heartache that she and people like her have experienced. Brittney would like the world to know that girls that grow up in poverty are just as determined to succeed in life as anyone else.

Nana Ekua Brew-Hammond has written copy for Nike and L'Oréal, and articles for the Village Voice and Trace Magazine. The Vassar grad's first screenplay was a Sundance Screenwriters' Lab Finalist. Brew-Hammond is currently at work on her debut novel, Powder Necklace.

Shankea N. Brooks is 17 years old and currently in the foster care system. She has been writing since she was fourteen, when she was placed in the system. It helps to write her feelings down. In the future she would like to publish her own book and make a career as a writer.

Candice Brown originally from Trinidad and Tobago, is currently a junior in high school. She believes there is something in writing which holds an incalculable power. Candice aspires to be professional writer.

Jennifer Carcamo is 15 and a straight A sophomore at HighTechHigh- LA. She is of Hispanic origin and loves to write fiction stories, short stories, and poetry. Jennifer is the Editor in Chief of her school's on-line magazine as well as involved in the school poetry club.

Jennifer Patricia A. Carino is a 24 year old poet, musician, and visual artist who lives and writes in Baguio City, in the northern part of the Philippines with her partner, Might, and their two dogs. Jenny's poems and articles have been published in various Philippine magazines and newspapers including The Philippine Panorama.

Ching-In Chen. Poemsender. A loudmouth organizer hoping for liberation. Sometimes bridge, sometimes islanderdweller. Daughter. Lover. Sister. Karaoke singer. Budding filmmaker. A sunrise. Lover of the thrift store. Keeper of secrets, scraps and misplaced beauty.

April Choi is an aspiring writer and poet who plans to further her study of literature in college. She enjoys reading, writing, singing in the rain and chocolate.

Patricia R. Corbett lives in Maryland with her partner and son. She was raised in Richmond, Virginia where she began her long and tedious pursuit of writing. She has a degree in English from Virginia Union University and teaches high school English. Patricia is the founder of Sisters Rising. She is also published in the Hurston Wright anthology, The Hoot and Hollar of the Owls.

Zoraida Cordova is 18 years old and emigrated from Ecuador when she was seven years old. She lives in New York, where she just graduated from high school. She will attend Marymount Manhattan College in New York City and major in English.

Marie Cornejo is 23 years old and resides in Frederick, Maryland. She has a five year old son who happens to be her hero. Cornejo graduated from Towson University and has her MBA from the University of Phoenix.

Kimberly J. Cosier survived junior high school and went on to become an art teacher. She is currently an assistant professor of art education in the Visual Art Department of the Peck School for the Arts at the University of Wisconsin-Milwaukee. Cosier presently serves as Co-President of the Lesbian, Gay, Bisexual, Trangender/Queer Issues Caucus of the National Art Education Association (NAEA).

Stephanie Croft is 17 years old and lives in England. She is currently in school studying for her A-Levels in Fine Art, Media Studies and English Language and Literature. She has a part time job at Boots which she really enjoys, and is learning to drive which is fun but terrifying. Stephanie really enjoys writing of all kinds and has applied to study English with Creative Writing at University next September. Apart from that she loves music, shopping and socialising; and generally being young and carefree.

Teri Ellen Cross graduated with a MFA in Creative Writing, Poetry from American University in 2004 and a BS in journalism from Ohio University. She is a graduate of Cave Canem- a weeklong poetry workshop for African American poets. She currently holds the position of poetry coordinator for the Folger Shakespeare Library in Washington D.C. She has had poems published in Bum Rush The Page, Cave Canem: Gathering Ground, online at Beltway Quarterly, and in several Cave Canem anthologies.

Cherien Dabis is an Arab American writer and filmmaker with a Masters of Fine Arts in Screenwriting from Columbia University's School of Arts. She has written several award-winning screenplays and have published personal essays and articles in Mizna and Pride Magazine.

Annie Dawid lives with her son, Isaiah, at 9100 feet in the Sangre de Cristo range of Southern Colorado. Her last book is LILY IN THE DESERT: STORIES (Carnegie Mellon University Press, 2001). She has a prize-winning story upcoming in GLIMMER TRAIN STORIES about a NY family's intersection with Sept 11. Her first book is a novel, YORK FERRY, still in print from Cane Hill Press.

Aysha Marie Davis is 14 years old and has been writing poetry since the fifth grade. She comes from an artistic family and her love for poetry was influenced by her aunt and grandmother. Aysha hopes one day to become a well known and published writer.

Jessica Del Balzo is a student at Emerson College in Boston. Her work has been published both online and in print journals. Jessica was a student reader at the 2004 Dodge Poetry Festival in New Jersey.

Tashamee Dorsey lives in Florida with the love of her life and their cat Oreo and dog Gemini. She was raised in Roselle, NJ where she first developed her love of story telling from her mother Barbara, brothers, Anthony and Ely, and father Ely. She has a degree in Theater from Rutgers University and plans to pursue an MFA in directing.

Lauren Dudley is 19 years old and attends the University of Central Florida. After college she plans to work at a treatment center for women with eating disorders.

Thembi Duncan – writer, actor, mother, admirer of all things alive.

Yael Flusberg is a DC-based writer and activist who works as a coach and consultant with social change organizations and leaders, and is a co-founder of Sol & Soul, a nonprofit which nurtures and promotes emerging and seasoned artists of conscience.

.jade foster, 20, is a junior at Sarah Lawrence College in Bronxville, New York. A native Washingtonian she focused on all aspects of writing in high school at Duke Ellington School of the Arts. From a family of mostly women she believes there's more to becoming a woman than the big things, she think it's the little things, the things that you forget that make up a life, and it's her job to write it all down, to remember.

Charneice N. Fox is a writer most of the time, but at least three nights a week you can find her featuring on her red couch watching her kids dance uncontrollably to Green Day and occasionally joining in on her skilled air guitar. Her many hats include poet, artist management for Genesis Poets and Producer and CEO of Straight No Chaser Productions.

Togtokhbayar Ganzorig is an 18 year old poet originally from Mongolia. She grew up in California, Washington D.C. and Mongolia. She is a Liberal Arts major and eventually would like to attend law school. She's had to constantly change her way of life because of her moving so much around the world. Just recently she's settled down with her family in Arlington, VA.

313

Jessica W. Giles is Assistant Professor of Psychology and Human Development at Vanderbilt University. She received her PhD from the University of California at San Diego in 2004. Her scholarly research focuses on the development of social cognition, and she is particularly interested in gender development, violence prevention, and children's involvement in the legal system. Her creative writing deals with themes of femininity, violation, resilience, emotion, and the sexual body.

Alicia M. Greene was born on the small Caribbean island of Antigua but grew up in the state of Maryland. Currently enrolled at American University she is pursing a degree in Spanish with a minor in international studies. Alicia is also interested in song writing, short stories, plays, scripts, singing, dancing, drawing, painting, and ice skating.

alexis pauline gumbs has been a queerly colored black afro-caribbean girl for twenty-three years. She is a PhD student in English at Duke University, studying gender and resistance in the African Diaspora. She is a planning committee and faciliting body member of theInternational Black Youth Summit, and when she creates she is almost a woman.

Amber Hendricks is the daughter of military parents and was born in Kansas City, MO. She has always enjoyed writing poetry and short stories to entertain her family. She attended Mississippi Valley State University where she reigned as Miss MVSU, the campus queen, from 2004-2005. Amber is currently an English graduate student at Northwestern State University of Louisiana. Her dream is to work in administration and ultimately be a college president.

Mary Cate Hennessey is 16 years old and from St. Louis, Missouri. After graduation she plans to move to Montana and eventually go into the field of education. She has always written, and is happy to have the opportunity to share her work in this anthology.

Jillian Hernandez is Curatorial Associate at the Museum of Contemporary Art (MOCA) in North Miami where she developed the innovative art outreach program for at-risk teenage girls, Women on the Rise!.

314

C. Sala Hewitt is a writer, director, and performance artist. As a director she has directed a number of ground breaking threatre productions including "What It Iz! The Spokenwordical" (Blackout Arts Collective, 2006),"Descendants of Freedom" (by Andre Lancaster, 2004), "Lagrimas de Cocodrilo/Crocodile Tear" (by Ingrid Rivera, 2003) and "E to Jamaica Center" (by Justin E. Turner, 2002).

Natalie E. Illum is an activist, writer and federal employee. Natalie is a founding board member of mothertongue, a spoken word and creative writing organization in DC for women and girls (www.mothertongue. org). She has an MFA in Creative Writing from American University and teaches poetry through a variety of local community venues. Having just returned from touring with her Chapbook, Ground Lover, Natalie is almost ready to finish working on a memoir about her disability called Spastic.

Jocelyn James is a nomad from California. She divides her time between writing poems & short stories, designing her anjelkist t-shirt line and earning a living. Jocelyn celebrates artists who reflect a feminist awareness.

Jane Jiang is a high school senior at Lakeside School in Seattle, Washington. She has been writing for as long as she can remember and has won numerous national awards for her poetry and prose.

Whitney A. Jones is a senior in high school.

Lisa Joyner, writer and performance poet, was born and raised in Baltimore, MD. She earned her Bachelor of Arts from Central State Univeristy, Wilberforce, OH. In 2000, she relocated from Atlanta, GA to Washington, DC, where she currently lives. In 2004, she self-published her first book of poetry, Magnolia.

Sheba Karim is 29 years old and recently quit her job as a public interest attorney to pursue an MFA in fiction from the Iowa Writer's Workshop. While dividing her time between New York and Iowa, she is working on a collection of short stories and a young adult novel.

Jennifer Karmin is a poet, artist, and educator, who has published, performed, exhibited, taught, and experimented with language throughout the U.S. and Japan. Currently at home in Chicago, she is a founding member of the public art group Anti Gravity Surprise, curator with the SpareRoom Time-Arts Cooperative, and co-host of the Red Rover Reading Series. Jennifer works as a Poet-in-Residence in the Chicago Public Schools and teaches creative writing to immigrants at Truman College.

Keturah Kendrick is a native of New Orleans the Beautiful. She is an artist and educator who currently resides in New York City. She has done stand up comedy, written and starred in her own one-woman show and her humorous and insightful outlooks on life have appeared in The Louisiana Weekly, Salon.com, and numerous other publications. Keturahk@yahoo.com

Carissa Kiepert is a senior at Port Washington High School with plans of attending culinary school in Chicago. She has been writing short stories since the third grade. She hopes that her story will help other girls to understand that people go through terrible things and still manage to overcome it.

Tanis Kwanette is the pen name for a Louisiana born and raised black lesbian writer. She followed her heart to the Washington, DC area in 1999. A house and five dogs later she calls DC home. Social worker by day, her dream is to write the great American lesbian love novel and have furless babies with Karma, her partner of seven years.

Joy Lee was was born in Taipei, Taiwan and moved to the States with her family when she was just nine years old. She now lives in Westford, Massachusetts. Joy is a junior at Bowdoin College (Class of '07), studying sociology with a minor in chemistry. She loves Jesus, words, community service, and dinners by electric light.

Siobhan Leftwich was born in New York City and raised in the Poconos and upstate New York. Siobhan has written for Black Enterprise, Vibe, Essence, BET.com and a host of smaller publications. She loves to write short stories for the generation of biracial black women who are coming of age and trying to make sense of their place in this mad world.

Raina J. Leon is currently a doctoral student in education at the University of North Carolina-Chapel Hill. Her work has been featured in AntiMuse, Furnace Review, Farmhouse Review, the Poetic Voices without Borders anthology from Gival Press and the upcoming Cave Canem 10th Anniversary Anthology.

Lilli Lewis grew up on a dirt road outside of Athens, Georgia where she mostly enjoyed playing in her father's garden and going on scavenger hunts. Lilli, a self-proclaimed (and celebrated) "FatGirl" is a singer/songwriter/composer based in Atlanta, GA, and is currently in love with the downright revolutionary notion of possibilty.

Dahlma Llanos-Figueroa is a retired high school English teacher and librarian. She has been teaching creative writing to teenagers for 30 years. Her work has appeared in various literary journals and most recently, Chicken Soup for the Latino Soul.

Tess McCray is currently a junior at the University of Missouri - St. Louis and the Pierre Laclede Honors College where she majors in English with a minor in Women's and Gender Studies. She grew up in a very small town in southern Missouri and regretfully has found that the country has gotten into her blood. Tess would ideally love to live in a secluded log cabin on a lake somewhere, while teaching at the college level.

Christine McFarlane, 32, is a First Nations woman of Saulteaux background studying at the University of Toronto. Christine was in the foster care system and a ward of the Children's Aid Society until she was nineteen. She was in and out of the psychiatric system throughout her twenties and it wasn't until 2004 that she finally made steps to stop her self abuse and enter into recovery. Christine is still in recovery for an eating disorder. Christine would like her story to offer hope to others who may have been in similar situations.

Claire B. Mischker is a native of South Carolina and is currently pursuing a Ph.D. at the University of Mississippi. Her poetry has appeared in storySouth, and she is the fiction editor for the 2006 issue of The Yalobusha Review.

Liza Monroy has lived all over the world. Her work has appeared in the New York Times, Village Voice, Time Out New York and has a piece upcoming in a 2006 anthology from Seal Press.

Christina Owens is a child of Southern trailer parks and has since lived in England, Seattle, and Japan. She is currently a graduate student in Cultural Studies at the University of California-Davis. In 2005, she was published in Outside of Ordinary: An Anthology of Women's Travel Stories. Both her dad and her little brother are currently in the South Carolina prison system.

Rasheedah Phillips is 21 years old and resides in Philadelphia, Pennsylvania. She is the proud mother of her seven year old daughter, Iyonna, and a first year student at Temple University James E. Beasley School of Law. Rasheedah is also an advocate and mentor to teenage mothers.

Faye Pompey has been in the custody of the state of Maryland since 2002. Living from pillar to post for the majority of her time in the system, she has decided to make something out of the fact that she was taken from the streets and given something to appreciate. Writing is her therapy.

Tina Pryce is a graduate of Duke Ellington School of the Arts. She has been writing poetry, creative fiction and non-fiction since she was six years old. She has performed her works in various settings such as the Millennium Sound Stage at the Kennedy Center; the Library of Congress; at various coffee houses and events across the city of Washington, DC. Tina graduated number six in her high school class and is currently an honor student at Trinity University, majoring in Journalism or Law.

Roma Raye is a 28 year old stone butch being polished up by a crafty red-headed femme in a little house in Seattle that they share with a cute blonde who wants to be a fairy knight, and an emotional, "no you're not a lap dog" pit bull. Raye is a special education teacher.

Elisabeth Robinson is a 14 year old freshman at Thurgood Marshall Academy and resides in Washington, DC. She writes when life gets "too tremendous." She writes for herself and girls like her.

Lea Robinson a queer-identified, African-American woman, Robinson has observed young women in sports attempting to prove their femininity (or, heterosexuality) through eating disorders, promiscuity and the adoption of homophobic behaviors. Her own struggles with homophobia and racism in sports have encouraged her to come out as a lesbian, and act as an ally to younger college athletes. She is currently the Head Women's Basketball coach at Newbury College near Boston.

Tracey Rose is a writer/filmmaker living in Brooklyn, New York.

asmara ruth was born in a cold town during a cold month. She left at age 20, in search of warmer weather and a place where she fit. She has lived some of everywhere and done some of everything. She now plans to return to her birthplace and spend her thirties building home.

Vanessa Seay is an 8th grader at Newport Mill Middle school. She is bi-racial and has two brothers. She is an avid reader and loves writing about a lot of things. Vanessa and her friends are looking forward to attending high school in the fall.

j. scales is a multi-talented healerartist who enjoys creating poetry and music for herself and others. as a musician &vocalist, she has performed at various venues, including the kennedy center, nuyorican cafe, house of blues in new orleans, and serafemme (queer women of color festival) in west hollywood. she synthesizes her musical production skills to enlighten many, while empowering various marginalized communities. j. gives MUCH thanks to the Creator for the continual development of her many gifts! (www.myspace.com/jscalesonbass)

darlene anita scott is a native of Delaware and currently lives in Richmond, Virginia. Recipient of a 2001-2002 poetry fellowship from the Virginia Commission for the Arts, darlene published a chapbook, moss, and is at work on her first full length collection, Conjugal Visit.

Kimberly Jane Simms is the director of Wits End Poetry, a non-profit poetry organization in Greenville, SC. Her publishing credits include The Asheville Poetry Review, Eclipse, Plains Song Review, The Millennium Sampler of SC Poetry, AIM Magazine, and London's Ape Magazine. She is a first generation American who holds a Masters in British and American Literature from Clemson University and a BA in literature from Furman University.

Ethel Morgan Smith, Associate Professor of English at West Virginia University, is the author of From Whence Cometh My Help: The African American Community at Hollins College. Smith has been published in national and international journals. She has received many awards and fellowships, including a Fulbright to the University of Tubingen in Germany, and a Rockefeller Foundation fellowship in Bellagio, Italy.

Tricia Snell is originally from South Bend, Indiana. She has one brother, one sister, two parents, two stepparents, a stepbrother, and two stepsisters. Currently, she is pursuing her Masters of Social Work at the University of Denver in Denver, Colorado where she lives with her husband and two dogs.

Laura Still lives in Knoxville, Tennessee with her two sons. She is a USTA certified tennis umpire and the assistant poetry editor for New Millennium Writings. She is also a member of the Knoxville Writers Guild.

Amy Sturm was born in a coastal town in England twenty-eight years ago. She has been writing since age twelve and now focuses on an English major at Marshall University in Huntington, West Virginia. In her free time Amy enjoys horseback riding, songwriting, and caring for her three cats.

Lacy Sundine 2nd time in foster care, 2nd time in Day treatment, Domestic violence in family background, 2nd time on probation, and in and out of placement since 6th grade, now in 9th grade.

Sonya Renee Taylor is a performance poet, actress, educator, activist, and 2004 National Poetry Slam Champion. Combining a M.S. in Organizational Management, B.A. in Sociology, and an extensive experience in women's issues, HIV prevention, and working with at-risk youth Sonya Renee has developed an uncanny ability to address contemporary issues with grace and power that is never dogmatic.

Danielle Ramona Thomas is 16 years old and a Literary Media student at Duke Ellington School of the Arts. She has always had a love for literature; writing, reading and analyzing. When Danielle grows up she would like to be a broadcast journalist.

Roxi Trapp-Dukes a native Washingtonian is a 2004 graduate of Howard University, holding a BFA in Theater. Since graduation she was awarded the 2005 Young Artist Grant from the DC Commission Arts and Humanities to produce a series of her written works. The series entitled A Woman's Liberation debuted at the Flashpoint Mead Theater in November of 2005, The Only Black Girl was included in the production. In addition to her writing, Roxi works frequently in production management (theater & film) in DC and New York, and is a working dance choreographer and actress.

Janet Vega is 28 years old, married, and mother to two beautiful boys. She is currently attending Morton College for an Associates in Office Management Technology. Janet became pregnant at 18 and married soon after. Over the years, she and her husband have worked hard to maintain their marriage and keep their family together.

Dinh Vong is a graduate student who lives in Tempe, Arizona. She is a native of Fresno, California, where her family settled after emigrating from Vietnam in 1980. Vong is currently teaching and working towards an MFA in Creative Writing at Arizona State University.

Maikong Vue currently attends Saint Paul public high school. She has dreams of attending college on the east coast and pursing her interest in cinematography, journalism, or fashion. She loves to read and do creative writing pieces. Maikong is also a foreign film junkie, plays badminton and highly competitive.

B. Lois Wadas is a native New Yorker who lives and thrives in NYC. Her work has been published nationally and in Canada. She is also a playwright.

Katharine Walker spends her days going to college and working. During her down time she enjoys reading books of substance, writing, and simply enjoying life. Katharine's greatest inspiration is her mother, who taught her everything she needs to know, and let her grow into the person she is today.

Seshat Y. Walker has been deeply rooted in the Washington, DC art scene as a writer, activist, educator, publicist, and consultant for the past ten years. Her work has appeared in The Hoot and Hollar of the Owls and the upcoming Writerscorp Anthology.

Jackie Warren–Moore is a poet, mother, wife, playwright, ten year former newspaper columnist of The Syracuse Post Standard. She makes her home in Syracuse, New York where she conducts readings and workshops in prisons. Jackie is also a writer-in-residence with the Syracuse School District.

Kelly Warren is Australian and spent two years living in Japan. She is now in the process of writing a comical adventure tale about the experience. Kelly is currently studying Japanese at university at Griffith University on the Gold Coast Australia.

Katrese Watts is a 30 year old single mother of two beautiful girls. She is a full time college student, majoring in paralegal studies, with plans to attend law school after graduation. She loves to write poetry, songs, and stories. Katrese would like to publish a book of poems in the future.

Rachel White, 26, a native of Delaware, is a writer currently living in Washington, DC. Although she has been writing poetry and fiction since she was a child, she only recently started trying to get her work published. She has been published in dividedDCity, a DC publication sponsored by Sol & Soul. For a living she plays with children of all ages.

Latiffany Wright is 24 years old and resides in Chicago, Illinois with her daughter. She is a student in the Masters of Fine Arts program at Chicago State University and plans to write full time after completing her degree.

Nora Yates is a queer rural femme lesbian who grew up in Upstate New York in a lovely town with one stop light and year-round blinking Christmas lights. Professionally, Nora advocates for LGBT communities on a statewide level and works hard to ensure that the underrepresented and often intentionally-quieted identities of the LGBT movement are heard loud and clear.

Jewel Sophia Younge has used several pen names in her career. She has published a short story, "Roots Thing Dirty," a short play, a poems in magazines ranging from English Journal to Rolling Out. New York artist Uraline Hager featured Younge's work in New York and Havana exhibits. Younge also worked on Coquie Hughe's most recent film "Did I Just Look at Her." Younge is a St. Louis playwright who teaches, writes, and resides in Chicago, Illnois. www.at3619.com

Permissions

Grateful acknowledgement to the following individuals who allowed me to include their works in this collection:

Notes:

Notes:

Order Form

To order single copies, send a check or money order for $19.95 per book plus $3 shipping to:

Michelle Sewell
PO Box 93
Hyattsville, MD 20781

Please Include Your:

Name:

Address:

City:

State:

Zip:

Telephone: (   )

Email:

DISTRIBUTED TO THE BOOK TRADE BY:

GirlChild Press
PO Box 93
Hyattsville, MD 20781
www.girlchildpress.com